AF605849

FREEDOM
CHRISTIAN AND MUSLIM PERSPECTIVES

Previously Published Records of Building Bridges Seminars

The Road Ahead: A Christian–Muslim Dialogue, Michael Ipgrave, editor (London: Church House, 2002)

Scriptures in Dialogue: Christians and Muslims Studying the Bible and the Qur'ān Together, Michael Ipgrave, editor (London: Church House, 2004)

Bearing the Word: Prophecy in Biblical and Qur'ānic Perspective, Michael Ipgrave, editor (London: Church House, 2005)

Building a Better Bridge: Muslims, Christians, and the Common Good, Michael Ipgrave, editor (Washington, DC: Georgetown University Press, 2008)

Justice and Rights: Christian and Muslim Perspectives, Michael Ipgrave, editor (Washington, DC: Georgetown University Press, 2009)

Humanity: Texts and Contexts: Christian and Muslim Perspectives, Michael Ipgrave and David Marshall, editors (Washington, DC: Georgetown University Press, 2011)

Communicating the Word: Revelation, Translation, and Interpretation in Christianity and Islam, David Marshall, editor (Washington, DC: Georgetown University Press, 2011)

Science and Religion: Christian and Muslim Perspectives, David Marshall, editor (Washington, DC: Georgetown University Press, 2012)

Tradition and Modernity: Christian and Muslim Perspectives, David Marshall, editor (Washington, DC: Georgetown University Press, 2012)

Prayer: Christian and Muslim Perspectives, David Marshall and Lucinda Mosher, editors (Washington, DC: Georgetown University Press, 2013)

Death, Resurrection, and Human Destiny: Christian and Muslim Perspectives, David Marshall and Lucinda Mosher, editors (Washington, DC: Georgetown University Press, 2014)

The Community of Believers: Christian and Muslim Perspectives, Lucinda Mosher and David Marshall, editors (Washington, DC: Georgetown University Press, 2015)

Sin, Forgiveness, and Reconciliation: Christian and Muslim Perspectives, Lucinda Mosher and David Marshall, editors (Washington, DC: Georgetown University Press, 2016)

God's Creativity and Human Action: Christian and Muslim Perspectives, Lucinda Mosher and David Marshall, editors (Washington, DC: Georgetown University Press, 2017)

Monotheism and Its Complexities: Christian and Muslim Perspectives, Lucinda Mosher and David Marshall, editors (Washington, DC: Georgetown University Press, 2018)

Power—Divine and Human: Christian and Muslim Perspectives, Lucinda Mosher and David Marshall, editors (Washington, DC: Georgetown University Press, 2019)

A World of Inequalities: Christian and Muslim Perspectives, Lucinda Mosher, editor (Georgetown University Press, 2021)

FREEDOM

CHRISTIAN AND MUSLIM PERSPECTIVES

A Record of the Eighteenth Building Bridges Seminar

Hosted by
World Council of Churches
Geneva, Switzerland
June 12–15, 2019

Lucinda Mosher, Editor

Georgetown University Press / Washington DC

Library of Congress Cataloging-in-Publication Data

Names: Building Bridges Seminar (18th : 2019 : Geneva, Switzerland; Bogis-Bossey, Switzerland), author. | Mosher, Lucinda, editor.
Title: Freedom : Christian and Muslim perspectives : a record of the Eighteenth Building Bridges Seminar / Lucinda Mosher, editor
Description: Washington, DC : Georgetown University Press, 2021. | Series: Building Bridges Seminar series | Hosted by World Council of Churches, Geneva, Switzerland, June 12–15, 2019—Title page. | Includes bibliographical references and index.
Identifiers: LCCN 2020053192 | ISBN 9781647121273 (hardcover) | ISBN 9781647121280 (paperback) | ISBN 9781647121297 (ebook)
Subjects: LCSH: Liberty—Religious aspects—Christianity—Congresses. | Liberty—Religious aspects—Islam—Congresses.
Classification: LCC BT810.3 .B85 2019 | DDC 261.7—dc23
LC record available at https://lccn.loc.gov/2020053192

22 21 9 8 7 6 5 4 3 2 First printing

Printed in the United States of America

Cover design by Nathan Putens
Interior design by Paul Hotvedt

Contents

Participants in the Building Bridges Seminar 2019

Muhammad Modassir Ali, Hamad Bin Khalifa University, Qatar
Ahmet Alibašić, University of Sarajevo, Bosnia and Herzegovina
Ovamir Anjum, University of Toledo, USA
Mehdi Azaiez, K. U. Leuven, Belgium; University of Lorraine, France
Maria Clara Bingemer, Pontifical Catholic University of Rio de Janeiro, Brazil
Jonathan Brown, Georgetown University, USA
Jonathan Chaplin, Divinity Faculty, Cambridge, UK
Emmanuel Clapsis, Hellenic College and Holy Cross Greek Orthodox School of Theology, USA
Lejla Demiri, University of Tübingen, Germany
Susan Eastman, Duke University Divinity School, USA
C. Rosalee Velloso Ewell, Redcliffe College, UK
Christopher M. Hays, Biblical Seminary of Colombia, Colombia
Samia Huq, BRAC University, Dhaka, Bangladesh
François Kaboré, SJ, Center for Research and Action for Peace, Ivory Coast
Azza Karam, Religions for Peace International, USA; Vrije Universiteit, The Netherlands
Sivin Kit, The Lutheran World Federation, Switzerland
Ludovic Lado, SJ, Centre for Studies and Training for Development, Chad
Daniel A. Madigan, SJ, Georgetown University, USA
David Marshall, World Council of Churches, Switzerland
Pavle Mijović, University of Sarajevo, Bosnia and Herzegovina
Esther Mombo, St Paul's University, Limuru, Kenya
Lucinda Mosher, Hartford Seminary, USA
Kenan Musić, University of Sarajevo, Bosnia and Herzegovina
Martin Nguyen, Fairfield University, USA
Elizabeth Phillips, University of Cambridge, UK

Peniel Jesudason Rufus Rajkumar, World Council of Churches, Switzerland
Abdullah Saeed, University of Melbourne, Australia
Shirin Shafaie, Centre for Muslim-Christian Studies, Oxford, UK; Visual Academics, UK
Sohaira Siddiqui, Georgetown University in Qatar, Qatar
Muna Tatari, University of Paderborn, Germany

Introduction

Believed to be the longest-running international dialogue of Christian and Muslim scholars, the Building Bridges Seminar was initiated in 2002 by then Archbishop of Canterbury George Carey. It was sustained by Rowan Williams during the ten years of his tenure in that office. It has been stewarded since 2012 by Georgetown University. Annually, the Building Bridges Seminar creates a conversation circle comprising some thirty scholar-believers for the purpose of deep dialogical study of texts—scriptural and otherwise. It has met in the United Kingdom, the United States, Qatar, Bosnia and Herzegovina, Turkey, Italy, and Singapore. The June 2019 convening, upon which this book reports and reflects, was sponsored and organized by Georgetown University and took place in Geneva and Bogis-Bossey, Switzerland, hosted by the World Council of Churches.

Whenever and wherever the Building Bridges Seminar convenes, participation is by invitation only. Christians and Muslims are always nearly equal in number, with each cohort including a significant number of women. Most Christian participants are Anglican or Roman Catholic, but the circle always includes other streams as well—most often Orthodox, Lutheran, Methodist, and Presbyterian. Similarly, most Muslim participants are Sunni, but Shiʿa have always taken part. The collection of texts that participants are expected to read, analyze, and comment upon are chosen and organized to prompt deep discussion of a carefully framed, multilayered theme such as prophethood, prayer, revelation, human destiny, community, forgiveness, power, or (as in 2019) freedom.

As a comparative-theological topic, freedom is far from straightforward. While it has long been identified with modernity and even postmodernity, it is indeed a theme taken up in both the Bible and the Qurʾan. But whereas the New Testament emerged in a region under occupation by the Roman

Empire, the Qur'an was first received in a stateless environment—tribal Arabia—that took political freedom for granted. Hence, the engagement of freedom by Christian and Islamic scriptures is not precisely equivalent. Yet freedom has been an important topic for reflection by both Christians and Muslims, especially in the modern period. With realities such as these in mind, freedom was chosen for study by the eighteenth Building Bridges Seminar. Interrogation of freedom was conceived as a continuation of the Seminar's study of divine and human power in 2017 and a world of inequalities in 2018. As had been the case when grappling with those topics, so also with the theme of freedom came the complex but salutary challenge of engaging in dialogue on an area of concern that, while significant within the Christian and Muslim traditions, has also been the focus of much—often critical of religion—modern discourse and political action; and, to some extent, such discourse and action frames present-day thinking as Muslims and Christians. As one of the planners put it, "What we in the twenty-first century understand as political freedom has to be extracted from concepts of egalitarianism, limited government, accountability, rule of law, and so on." The Bible and the Qur'an may have other concerns.

Indeed, the 2019 seminar studied substantial portions of scripture. That is standard practice for this project. However, planners were keenly aware that, in the medieval and modern periods—and especially with the rise of the modern state—freedom takes on a new meaning. From the Seminar's previous investigation of Christian and Muslim perspectives on the themes of power and inequality, it had become clear that Christians and Muslims are in dialogue not just with each other but also with modern secular perspectives to which we respond in various ways. This given, it seemed essential to provide significant time for dialogical close reading of many sorts of extra-scriptural and modern texts relevant to the Christian and Muslim traditions. Therefore, seminar participants were given resources with which to consider how, historically, Christian and Muslim faith communities have addressed such matters as God's freedom, human freedom to obey God, autonomy versus heteronomy, autonomy versus self-governance, freedom from incapacitating addiction and desire, hermeneutic or discursive freedom vis-á-vis scripture and tradition, religious and political freedom, the relationship between personal conviction and public order, and so on.

Often a convening of the Building Bridges Seminar includes a public session featuring overviews of the topic at hand. In Geneva, the public event was hosted by the World Council of Churches and was held in the Visser 't Hooft Hall in the Ecumenical Centre, home of the WCC. After formal welcoming remarks by Rev. Dr. Olav Fykse Tveit, general secretary of the

WCC, and by Rev. Dr. Daniel A. Madigan, SJ, as chair of the Building Bridges Seminar, the audience heard three papers. Revised versions of these compose part 1 of this volume. In her essay, "Who Gets to Decide What Freedom Is? A Christian Perspective," C. Rosalee Velloso Ewell, of Redcliffe College (UK), keeps this question in view as she asserts that, for Christians, "God is the source of freedom and dignity for all of creation" and love is its expression; yet Christians are far from united in their understanding of this. In "God-Given Freedom: An Islamic Point of View," Tuba Işık explains how the Qur'an's provision of a "new understanding of freedom not only reflects the *Weltanschauung* of pagan Arabs but also sets an alternative interpretative pattern for the human being itself."[1] Azza Karam contributes an essay titled "Freedom in the Contemporary Context: Trends in Intersections of Religion, Development, and Foreign Policy." Now the secretary general of Religions for Peace International, Karam was formerly an officer at the United Nations. As she stresses, she writes not as a theologian but rather as one who is simultaneously a scholar-practitioner of international development and multilateralism and a scholar of lived religion. In her essay, her goal is to encourage appreciation of how freedom "as understood and practiced in . . . the intersections of religion–politics–human rights . . . is being instrumentalized in a neo-colonial context."

As an ongoing dialogue, the goals of the Building Bridges Seminar are to help participants gain better understanding of each other's tradition, to wrestle with theological complexities, and to improve the quality of participants' disagreements. Its structure facilitates this by conducting almost all of its work in closed session; by organizing the participants into four discussion groups (each comprising eight individuals, usually) that remain consistent throughout the meeting; and by opening and closing each day with a robust plenary conversation. Morning and afternoon plenaries feature brief lectures introducing a set of texts selected for their potential to launch a complex interreligious exploration of a theological theme during the ensuing two-and-a-half-hour small-group session dedicated to close reading and discussion. Hour-long evening plenaries are for reflection and synthesis. These many lectures and texts are brought together in this volume for further individual study, incorporation into course syllabi, or for use in new dialogical endeavors.

Three pairs of chapters compose part 2, "Islamic Texts on Freedom." In each case, we have an introductory exegetical essay by a member of the seminar, the primary purpose of which is to introduce the texts provided in its companion chapter. Thus, as the first pair, we have Abdullah Saeed's "Aspects of Human Freedom: Reflections on Selections from the Qur'an and Hadith."

In it he defines freedom as "the ability to choose one course of action, thing, view, or position over another in the midst of various physical, psychological, environmental, political, legal, social, and economic constraints," remarks briefly on God's freedom, then focuses on the spiritual/moral and political/legal aspects of human freedom. In the course of his essay, he mentions each of the texts included in the next chapter, "The Qurʾan and Hadith on Freedom: Selections for Dialogue."

In the second pair, Lejla Demiri's essay, "Freedom as a Theme in Islamic Thought: An Introduction to Selected Premodern Texts," orients readers to selections from the writings of Abū l-Qāsim al-Qushayrī (d. 1072), Khwāja ʿAbdallāh al-Anṣārī (d. 1089), and Abū Ḥāmid al-Ghazālī (d. 1111), which are then provided in the chapter titled "Premodern Islamic Writings on Freedom: Selections for Dialogue."

In the third pair, Martin Nguyen's "Modern Muslim Elucidations and Contentions on Freedom: An Introduction to Texts for Dialogue," introduces four notable twentieth-century Muslim thinkers who have written on freedom and human nature (Muhammad Iqbal, Ali Shariati, Murtaza Mutahhari, and Mahmoud Mohammed Taha) and another four whose focus has been human liberation (Muhammad ʿAbduh, Sayyid Qutb, Abul Alʾa Maududi, and Farid Esack). He then provides contextual information for two collective declarations of consensus made by a significant cohort of Muslim thought and policy leaders on particular aspects of religious freedom: the Cairo Declaration on Human Rights in Islam (1990) and the Marrakesh Declaration on the Rights of Religious Minorities in Predominantly Muslim Majority Communities (2016). In the following chapter, "Islamic Thought in the Modern Period: Texts for Dialogue about Freedom," one finds excerpts from the writings of these eight authors plus the full text of the Cairo Declaration and the Executive Summary of the Marrakesh Declaration.

Four pairs of chapters (maintaining the pattern established in part 2) compose part 3, "Christian Texts on Freedom." Again, with each pair, an explanatory/exegetical essay introduces a set of texts, which are made available as a resource for study in the chapter following. Part 3 begins with Christopher M. Hays's "Freedom in the Hebrew Bible: From Exodus to Ezekiel, by Way of Reba McEntire and Rage against the Machine." Hays points to the varied use of the word *freedom* in popular music as a key to understanding selections from the books of the Pentateuch, Ezekiel, and Psalm 119 having to do with such concepts as liberation, free choice, and responsibility. In the process, he exegetes all texts provided for further study in the companion chapter: "Old Testament Texts for Dialogue on Freedom." In her essay "The Motif of Freedom in New Testament Texts: An Introduction," Susan

Eastman points out some consistent themes in the gospels, Paul's letters, the epistle to the Hebrews, and the letter of James, highlighting assumptions implicit in them in comparison with modernist understandings of freedom. With a focus on themes such as freedom *from* sin and death, *for* human flourishing, *from* bondage and isolation, *for* community and mutual love, she then provides orientational comments (some of them in depth) for interpreting the selected New Testament texts on freedom in the companion chapter "New Testament Texts about Freedom: Selections for Dialogue."

In "Thematic Dimensions of Freedom: Christian Texts from the Classical Period," Jonathan Chaplin considers creation, humanity, salvation, sociality, law, and religion as dimensions of freedom as he provides guidance for close reading of selected passages from the writings of Ambrose, Augustine, Aquinas, Francisco de Vitoria, Martin Luther, John Donne, and John Locke. These excerpts compose the companion chapter titled "Christian Thought on Freedom in the Classical Period: Selected Texts for Dialogue."

In the chapter titled "Freedom in Modern Christian Thought: Introduction to Selected Texts," Peniel Jesudason Rufus Rajkumar provides context for writings by Charles Wesley, Dietrich Bonhoeffer, Karl Barth, Gustavo Gutiérrez, V. Devasahayam, Stanley Hauerwas, and Elisabeth Schüssler Fiorenza—as well as the Vatican II document *Declaration on Religious Freedom* (*Dignitatis humanae*). Most of the items he discusses are excerpted or presented in their entirety in the final chapter of part 3, "Christian Writings from the Modern Period: Selections for Dialogue about Freedom."

Completing the volume is part 4, "Reflections." The hallmark of the Building Bridges Seminar is the opportunity for Christians and Muslims to observe each other grappling with questions important to us and between us—and to offer theological hospitality to each other as we do so. Seminar sessions are not open to the public, nor are they recorded. To compensate, we include here an essay titled "Conversations on the Theme of Freedom: Reflections on the Building Bridges Seminar at le Château de Bossey." In it, rapporteur Lucinda Mosher draws on notes taken during small-group study sessions, reports given during daily wrap-up discussions, and memos sent to her after adjournment in an effort to convey the tone and content of the Seminar's exploration of the theme of freedom.

Throughout this volume an effort has been made to keep diacritics to a minimum. Dates are "CE" unless otherwise indicated. We are grateful to many publishers for permission to use the material excerpted in this volume. Unless otherwise noted, Qur'an quotations are according to Seyyed Hossein Nasr, et al., editors, *The Study Quran: A New Translation and Commentary* (New York: HarperOne, 2015). In most cases, Bible passages are from the

Revised Standard Version of the Bible, copyright 1952 by the Division of Christian Education of the National Council of the Churches of Christ in the USA (used by permission; all rights reserved), or the New Revised Standard Version of the Bible, copyright 1989 by the Division of Christian Education of the National Council of the Churches of Christ in the USA (used by permission; all rights reserved). All are credited as they occur. Deep appreciation is extended to Georgetown University president John J. DeGioia for his ongoing support of the Building Bridges Seminar. As in previous years, David Marshall (the project's academic director) and Daniel Madigan (its chair) were instrumental in setting the 2019 theme, organizing the roster of scholars, and—in careful conversation with those designated as presenters—choosing the texts to be studied. Others playing strategic roles in the success of the 2019 gathering included Lucinda Mosher (Hartford Seminary), the Seminar's rapporteur; Samuel Wagner, who, as Georgetown University's director of dialogue and Catholic identity, serves as the Seminar's coordinator, working closely with the chair and academic director in planning the annual meeting; and Georgetown University's Berkley Center for Religion, Peace and World Affairs—which provides an ongoing base of operations and online presence for the Seminar and has made the publication of this book possible. Finally, gratitude is extended to Al Bertrand and the staff of Georgetown University Press for their patient assistance with this project.

Note

1. Tuba Işık, formerly of the University of Paderborn (Germany), was unable to attend. In her absence, her paper was read by a colleague, Muna Tatari.

Part One

Overviews

Who Gets to Decide What Freedom Is?

A Christian Perspective

C. Rosalee Velloso Ewell

When Christians celebrate the Feast of Pentecost, we remember how God's Spirit came down and inspired Jesus's disciples to speak words of truth and proclamations of freedom and justice in many different languages. We read in the second chapter of Acts that those who had gathered from all over the world for a Jewish festival in Jerusalem were able to understand the disciples' words, each in her or his own tongue. One extraordinary aspect about that story is that the distinctions and differences among all those different people were maintained. It was indeed a proclamation that was meant to unite the people, but such unity maintained their individual integrity. It also created something new: a new type of community, new friendships, and new freedom. Although they lived under Roman domination, those who had gathered in Jerusalem were free to be different from each other. Among other things, it was an affirmation of the goodness of the diversity of God's creation and of the many peoples of this world.

From a Christian perspective, God is the source of freedom and dignity for all of creation—not just for people but for everything. Human beings are free and of immense value not because of what we do or our abilities, not because of nationality or race or gender or anything else. We are free and dignified because we are created in the image of God. Thus, the basis for freedom in Christianity is not the Universal Declaration of Human Rights, although we affirm that; nor is it some form of modern liberal secularism, although things may be learned from it. From a Christian perspective, freedom has its source in the very essence of the Triune God. Love is the expression of this freedom. Not that Christians have been consistent or even understanding of this. Far from it! Our failures, past and present, are ever real, ever in need of prophets and friends who will show us our shortcomings and our failure to live out the freedom divinely given in love.

That said, I want to focus on two critical questions. Who gets to decide what freedom is? And what is your vision of freedom? In his book *GodStories*, H. Stephen Shoemaker suggests that we are story-formed creatures. Any true understanding of freedom or justice must be comprehended and passed on to others as story. We are, says Shoemaker, "*homo narratus*."[1] This is profoundly true in our context today not because it is a clever use of the Latin but because, for too long, freedom has been emphasized and considered in the realm of debate and discussion of the *homo sapiens*. We do far too much thinking and not enough storytelling, and not enough listening or practicing of freedom. Hence, while commenting on these two aspects of the contemporary debates and discussions about freedom, I shall tell stories.

Who gets to decide what freedom is? Modern liberal secularism might proclaim freedom for all as a basic human right. However, what does that look like in the diversity of our contexts? What do we do with those who choose something that we think is less than free? What are the boundaries between freedom and authority? Between freedom and anarchy? Who gets to decide where these boundaries are located? Freedom and power go hand in hand.

A common challenge to liberal secularism contends that its notions of freedom and equality are very Western, rooted in ideas of capitalism and democracy. In this type of critique, freedom becomes something imposed on religious communities that distorts or undermines the convictions of such religious traditions. At one level, it is a fair critique. On what basis do we determine whether the convictions and practices of a religious community impose a limitation on freedom? Conversely, how can we affirm freedom of religion for all traditions while at the same time judging certain practices as oppressive or abusive?

Freedom is not a given—neither in its definition nor in its practice. Catholic theologian Ivan Illich (1926–2002) questioned how our talk about peace often employs language shaped for and by aggression. For example, President John F. Kennedy talked of the "war on poverty"; even the most peace-loving advocate for peace has "strategies"—literally, war plans; and it is common to talk of "freedom fighters." Thus, we face a challenge: how can we talk about a recovery of a true sense of freedom or put freedom into words? As Illich writes, "To me, it seems that each people's freedom [peace] is as distinct as each people's poetry. Hence the translation of freedom is a task as arduous as the translation of poetry. Freedom has a different meaning for each epoch and for each cultural area . . . and within each culture area, freedom means something different both at the centre and on the margins."[2]

We can see the impact of "freedom on the margins" by turning to Luke 4:16–30, one of the texts chosen for study during the 2019 Building Bridges Seminar. According to this narrative, Jesus returns to his hometown of Nazareth and speaks in the synagogue. Everything is going very well for him as he begins to read aloud from a scroll containing the writings of the prophet Isaiah—one of the heroes of Israel: "The Spirit of the Lord is upon me, because he has anointed me to bring good news to the poor. He has sent me to proclaim release to the captives and recovery of sight to the blind, to proclaim the year of the Lord's favor" (Luke 4:18–19, quoting Isa. 61:1–2).

But then, things take an awkward turn. As he explains this text, Jesus decides to go off-piste in his examples. By *off-piste,* I don't mean he just preaches a bad sermon. Rather, he does the unexpected. He applies the text of the promises of Isaiah to outsiders: recalling passages from other parts of the Hebrew Scriptures, he reminds his audience that, in a time of great famine of old, Elijah had intervened to ease the suffering only of a widow at Zarephath in Sidon; and that, among Israel's many lepers, the prophet Elisha had healed only Naaman the Syrian.[3] According to Scripture, Jesus explains, although there were many of God's people suffering from various ailments and famine, it was to these so-called outsiders that God gave the freedom of food for the hungry and healing for the sick. His audience was shocked and horrified! Had members of some other groups indeed received the divine love, freedom, and justice that they had assumed was theirs? In this instance, those at the center—those who thought they knew what it meant to receive God's promises—were required to see God give that freedom to those at the margins.

Most Christians affirm and like the Universal Declaration of Human Rights. It fits nicely with Luke 4:16–30. It is inspiring to read Jesus's proclamation in the gospel: "I have come to proclaim good news to the poor, liberty to the captives, sight to the blind." It is inspiring to read Mary's Magnificat: "God has brought down the powerful from their thrones and lifted up the lowly; he has filled the hungry with good things, and sent the rich away empty." These are powerful words of freedom in the Christian sacred texts. And yet, we who like to quote these texts rarely think of ourselves as the ones with power who will be brought down. Are we not more like those in the synagogue who heard Jesus read from Isaiah and assume those are God's promises of freedom for us? These texts issue a reminder to Christians—and, perhaps, to all of us—that God is the one who defines freedom; God defines the boundaries of justice, which look very different from what we might think they should look like.

Christian and Muslim alike, we members of the Building Bridges Seminar are highly educated. When we think of freedom, most of us probably claim to follow some sort of version of liberation theology. However, we must ask: Whose liberation are we fighting for? Do we not often impose our understanding of the year of God's favor—another reference to Luke 4—onto the poor? But to paraphrase an oft-quoted Latin American quip, "liberation theology opted for the poor; and the poor opted for prosperity." This saying gets at the heart of the question, Who gets to decide what freedom looks like for the other?

A friend of mine from Colombia has been part of a project on refugees, displaced peoples, and the challenges to all sorts of freedoms imposed on the people trapped in such situations. He also takes part in *leitura popular da Bíblia*—a Latin American grassroots method of scripture study. On one occasion, he was with a group of eight women caught up in the migration of displaced peoples in Colombia. The women were reading the Old Testament book of Ruth, a story of restoration and freedom on which my friend had written a commentary. In the practice of *leitura popular*, the group first hears the narrative read out loud. The participants are then invited to indicate the character in the story with whom they most identify. During this particular meeting, as they proceeded in this way, some of the women started to cry. Six of them had lost husbands or sons in the drug wars. In the biblical story, Naomi, Ruth's mother-in-law, had lost her husband and both sons. It was quite easy for those women in Colombia to identify with Naomi.

At the beginning of the story, Naomi and her Moabite daughter-in-law, Ruth, return to Naomi's hometown of Bethlehem. The text reads, "When they came to Bethlehem, the whole town was stirred because of them; and the women said, 'Is this Naomi?'" (Ruth 1:19). As my friend heard this familiar passage in the company of these refugee women, he felt compelled to ask, "Who am I in this story?" The answer, he recalls, hit him like a ton of bricks! He was one of the townspeople who had watched the widow and her widowed and childless daughter-in-law arrive starving—yet did nothing. Those women in that study group had taught him something new about this sacred text that all his learning, all his reading, all his experience of church had not shown him. How often are we Christians, who proclaim the freedom Jesus declares in Luke 4, more like the townspeople who—although they identify the problem and see the captivity—sit by and do nothing?

When addressing a gathering of cardinals in 2013, Jorge Mario Bergoglio (then, archbishop of Buenos Aires; now, Pope Francis) said, "The church is called to come out of itself and go to the margins, not only geographical, but also in human terms, where the mystery of sin, pain, injustice, and ignorance dwells, where there is contempt for religious and for religious thinking, and where there are all kinds of misery."[4] Contemporary debates about freedom must include actual presence at the margins and in the places where there are all kinds of misery. Yet, for us Christian and Muslim scholars who gather as the Building Bridges Seminar, discussions of freedom take place within the context of dialogical study of texts. So I propose a challenge: I ask that we consider for a moment the people in our institutions who are blind, deaf, or mute. How much richer might our debates be if they were to include their points of view on, their readings of the Christian and Muslim writings on which we focus?

By way of illustration, I point to the Universal Declaration of Human Rights. In 1999 it broke the existing record and became the most translated document in the world. According to the UN website, as of 2019 the Declaration has been translated into 527 languages—including American, British, Portuguese, Spanish, and Tetum sign languages.[5] With this in mind, let us recall a portion of Martin Luther King Jr.'s "I Have a Dream" speech of August 28, 1963: "I have a dream that one day even the state of Mississippi, a state sweltering with the heat of injustice, sweltering with the heat of oppression, will be transformed into an oasis of freedom and justice."[6] Dr. King's speech is all about freedom. It is also a speech that draws on the biblical images of slavery, captivity, freedom, and justice. Not surprisingly, in both American and British sign language, the sign for "dream" is different from the sign for "vision." However, I find it interesting that, when King's speech of August 28, 1963, is delivered in either ASL or BSL, the English word *dream* is rendered by the sign for *vision*.[7] Why is this done? It is a recognition that, by "dream," King means a vision of freedom. Visions are more concrete; visions are shared and acted on. What is your vision of freedom?

The Building Bridges Seminar is part of a wider vision of promoting dialogue in various forms. Those of us who participate in it need not only to read and debate our sacred texts but to read them with and through the voices of others—just as happened with the group in Colombia that read the biblical book of Ruth together; just as we learn from ASL and BSL translations of MLK's dream/vision speech. Our discussions of freedom and our attempts at justice have their integrity insofar as we learn to be with and at the margins.

How is our vision of freedom enhanced by the friends we make and the company we keep? Ivan Illich wrote about conviviality (literally, "living together") as an alternative to captivity. He said, "Conviviality refers to a sense of individualized freedom in personal interdependence."[8] One cannot be free alone. True freedom is anything but individualistic.

Samba, typical music from Brazil, is best played or "lived" in a *roda* (circle). Like those early Christians at Pentecost, there is great diversity in the *roda de samba*. Each person has her own gifts and unique talents, but the freedom and beauty of the music happens only when everyone is together in the circle. Without the circle, we are free to blow a whistle or shake a tambourine as much as we wish; but it won't be samba unless we do it alongside others who are also doing their thing. The Building Bridges Seminar is a type of *roda*. The music generated by our conviviality is unique. Our vision of freedom is enhanced by the other even as we acknowledge whose voices are missing at our table of dialogue and consider together how we go from here to join a circle that understands how freedom is realized at the margins.

Notes

1. H. Stephen Shoemaker, *GodStories: New Narratives from Sacred Texts* (Valley Forge, PA: Judson, 1998), xiii.

2. Ivan Illich, "The De-linking of Peace and Development," opening address on the occasion of the first meeting of the Asian Peace Research Association, Yokohama, December 1, 1980. Quoted in Marion Boyars, *In the Mirror of the Past: Lectures and Address, 1978–1990* (New York: Marion Boyars, 1991), 15–16.

3. For the account of Elijah in Sidon, see 1 Kings 17:1–16; for the story of Elisha's healing of the Syrian, see 2 Kings 5:1–14.

4. Jorge Mario Bergoglio, remarks to the General Convention of the Cardinals of the Roman Catholic Church (March 9, 2013), as recalled (in English translation) by Agenzia Info Salesiana in a press release dated March 14, 2017, titled "VATICAN—When Cardinal Bergoglio Proposed 'a Pope Who Would Help the Church to Get Out to the People on the Margins.'" http://www.infoans.org/en/sections/news/item/2854-vatican-when-cardinal-bergoglio-proposed-a-pope-who-would-help-the-church-to-get-out-to-the-people-on-the-margins. Accessed November 28, 2019. For an extended analysis, see Andrea Riccardi, *To the Margins: Pope Francis and the Mission of the Church* (Maryknoll, NY: Orbis, 2018).

5. "About the Universal Declaration of Human Rights Translation Project" (n.d.), https://www.ohchr.org/EN/UDHR/Pages/Introduction.aspx.

6. Martin Luther King Jr., "I Have a Dream," Speech given in Washington, DC, August 28, 1963, https://www.americanrhetoric.com/speeches/mlkihaveadream.htm.

7. For a rendition of King's "I Have a Dream" speech in American Sign Language, see https://www.youtube.com/watch?v=5H2-3O-NJFg. Accessed November 29, 2019.

8. Ivan Illich, *Tools for Conviviality* (New York: Marion Boyars, 2003), 11.

God-Given Freedom

An Islamic Point of View

Tuba Işık

In the ninth century, the development of rational theology involved consideration of the relationship between human freedom and divine predestination. The debates from this classical period constitute the foundation on which today's different Muslim discourses around freedom have developed. In what follows, I provide some foundational information for examining Islamic perspectives on freedom. I then concentrate on the modern period, focusing especially on the question of the freedom of women.

Foundations

Exploration of freedom from an Islamic perspective calls for a look at pre-Islamic religion and the life circumstances of pagan Arabs of seventh-century Mecca. That is, in order to understand more clearly concepts and categories like freedom as they are mentioned in the Qur'an, it is wise to begin with a close look not just at the cultural and historical context but also at the Weltanschauung and the faith of the first listeners. Attention to the language of seventh-century Arabia is crucial as well because it reflects the Weltanschauung of the groups of that time.

The precondition for God's revelation to be comprehensible is that the message revealed by Him must use the common spoken (or written) language of the context into which it will be delivered. To use Ludwig Wittgenstein's term, God must participate in the common language game of the first recipients of the revelation.[1] In the case of the Qur'an, revelation takes into account seventh-century Arabian pagans and their worldview. It recognizes Mecca, a well-known pilgrimage city for polytheists and the center of a powerful priestly caste who tried to control everybody.

In this context, God uses the common language games but modifies them or gives them a new meaning. The Arabic *al-hurriyya* (freedom) is a prime example. The Qur'an's new understanding of freedom not only reflects the Weltanschauung of pagan Arabs but also sets an alternative interpretive pattern for the human being itself. Certainly, among the pagan Arabs, freedom was reserved for clan members and was denied to people of color and slaves. Furthermore, laws could easily be broken directly for one's own benefit.

With the advent of Islam, a fundamental change was introduced into the Arab worldview and conception of freedom. The social order of the era included slavery—an external form of bondage (lack of freedom). The egalitarian attitude imposed by the Qur'an and the Prophet Muhammad questioned not only the institution of slavery but also the perception of the human being in general. According to the Qur'an, each human was granted freedom—which meant that, at the same time, each human was granted dignity. It would not be an exaggeration to say that the bedrock of the Islamic understanding of freedom was then, and still is, the Qur'anic vision of the human being.[2] Each human is a creation of God. God manifests his signs not only on the "horizons" but also within the soul of the human being because God has breathed into the human being God's own spirit (Q 38:72).[3] There is a dimension of divinity within humanity. The human is blessed with intellect and free will and is created in the best of forms (Q 95:4).

From an Islamic point of view, free will does not mean infinite freedom. The self-limitation of freedom for the sake of the freedom of all is reflected in the norms of morality and law, which bind human action to rules in the form of (divine) laws. But still, in the Islamic understanding, the human being enjoys religious liberty. Binding commitments that are not imposed from the outside as compulsion, but chosen, are a product of freedom. This is an attitude God asks of the human being.[4]

In this context, the frequent occurrence in the revelations during the Meccan period of eschatological themes of final judgment is not unimportant. The Qur'an's first listeners are called on to refine their sense of responsibility for their own actions because their actions and behavior have consequences not only in this world but in the hereafter. The close connection between the freedom of the human being and human responsibility in this world and the hereafter aims to strengthen the believer's faith in the direct connectedness of these realities. The phrases about hell draw on vivid images and metaphors to rouse humans and lead them to repentance. Therefore, freedom was associated with (self-)responsibility, which initiated a new and different sense of self-consciousness and human action. However, mere possession of consciousness of freedom is not enough to actually *be* free. That depends on discovering how freedom and bondage—that is, the unconditionality and conditionality of human self—go together. Only in spite of unfreedom, and even within it, does one get an idea of what freedom is.

The Islamic understanding and valuation of freedom is related to a certain understanding of social justice. While, in the seventh century, the concept of social justice had not yet been articulated, the call for liberation (from oppression) of all people was synonymous with it. This idea shaped not only history but also the entrenched social and political structures of pagan Arabs of that era. In this sense freedom meant the liberation of the oppressed from the chains of social inequality, oppression, and injustice. But this liberation also involved religious liberty—specifically, the freedom to worship what one believed in and not what his clan lord forced him to believe in. So it can be stated that Islam in its early times was welcomed as a very tolerant alternative to the rule of violence, oppression, and arbitrariness.[5]

Discourse on freedom (*al-hurriyya*) touches all branches of theology: the jurists are concerned with the rights and liberties that are the outcome of conformity to the divine law (*sharia*); the theologians (*mutakallimūn*) are mainly concerned with the relationship between the human will and the divine will and with the extent to which the latter limits freedom of the former. For the Sufis, freedom primarily means freedom from the desires of the self, a freedom that leads one from dependence on the material world to union with God. Philosophers, on the other hand, mainly assert the reality of human free will and approach it from the standpoint of the political philosophy of al-Farabi (d. 970).

Modern Developments in Islamic Discourse on Freedom

Turning to the modern era, in the late nineteenth and early twentieth centuries, notable new perspectives on freedom developed. While some scholars understood the Qur'an as attributing complete and total power to God, thus downplaying the role of the individual, other modern Muslim thinkers, inspired by a desire for freedom, appealed to Qur'anic passages that provide fertile ground for arguments in support of human free will.[6] The approach of such modernist thinkers was shaped in different ways both by the sociopolitical situation of their home countries and by their experiences and, in some cases, their education in the West. One conviction they all shared, however, was that the Muslim world was in a profound crisis. They saw Muslims as having fallen into a sociopolitical lethargy based both on a limited understanding of human free will and on the belief that, theologically, everything necessary had already been said. Such thinkers wanted to liberate Muslims from sociopolitical and theological stagnation and to admonish Muslims to keep thinking and to recognize their responsibility for their own lives and actions as well as for the welfare of the world.

For a specific example of such an approach, we might consider the Pakistani thinker Muhammad Iqbal (1877–1938), who tried to reconcile Islamic theology with modern thought by referring mainly to questions of spirituality. The goal of his philosophy was to facilitate the emancipatory effect of religion. His new understanding of the Qur'an emphasized human being and the embracing of active responsibility for one's own life, including the search for authentically Muslim solutions to social, political, and economic challenges.[7] For Iqbal, human existence is a call to live the Qur'anic experience now, in the modern world. He believed that this means God limits his own freedom for the sake of human freedom.[8]

Modern science disciplines have also dealt with the disadvantaged situation of Muslim women because modern times continued to bear the fruits of imperialism and colonial power relationships by what established hierarchical power structures maintained. Colonial rulers justified their power with, among other things, the liberation of *other women*.[9] These colonialist interventions were often answered by reorganizations of the gender regimes, which were by no means to the advantage of Muslim women. To the contrary, their colonized brothers became their oppressors. Today, even in modern Western societies, new forms of domination and subordination emerged, such as the racializing of Muslim women in general as inferior and as passive victims in need of white women's liberation.[10] Generally, women's bodies seem to become an ideological battlefield without women being granted more power. In the academic arena, the critical examination of the construction of gender difference and the representation of Muslim women on the political floor as well as the decolonializing of language began with the establishment of postcolonial theory approaches in the late 1970s and early 1980s.[11] Especially, scholars of postcolonial feminism argued that Muslim women suffer from "double colonization": the oppression of colonialism and patriarchy.[12]

The Question of Freedom of Women

As seen above, political and social circumstances through the subsequent centuries had often worked to the disfavor of Muslim women. Predominant traditions of male authority and honor as well as various oppressive practices had made it difficult for women to avail themselves of the rights guaranteed by the Qur'an.[13] Significantly, Muhammad 'Abduh (1849–1905), an Egyptian early modernist thinker, was vocal about the disadvantaged position of women in Muslim societies. He identified the plight of women as the cause of the decay of the Islamic family and society and argued that the Qur'an referred to social practices of its time that needed to be reformulated in the modern period to overcome bias against women.[14] In a similar vein, other thinkers argued that, in its original seventh-century context, Islam had provided women a position of honor and respect, with clearly stated rights and legal protections in the areas of inheritance, marriage, and divorce (which all improved the situation of women considerably).[15]

Although many male scholars acknowledged the reality of gender oppression in Muslim societies and prepared the way for a revolt against the predicament of women, it was ultimately Muslim women who had to speak out loud for themselves. And they did so in a variety of ways.

Many Muslims may see in the demand for freedom for Muslim women a Western construct intended to damage the image of Islam. However, this suspicion must be resisted because the truth is that restrictions on the freedom of women are an ever-bleeding wound in Muslim societies, even today. Muslim women around the world are struggling with various forms of repression, which are justified in particular by theological arguments. In this essay, I introduce a few examples of women who have started a whole new movement in modern Islamic thought and theology. This movement has variously been called gender justice, gender jihad, and Islamic feminism. However, at this point my interest is not with labels but with understanding the key approaches and ideas that constitute the theological framework on which Muslim women are claiming their rights. In what follows, I identify and describe some key issues involved.

Since the middle of the nineteenth century, Muslim women increasingly have taken up the struggle against their largely marginalized position in family and society, (re-)claiming in their writing and "everyday activism" the right to their own *ijtihad* (their own independent reasoning or authority to interpret the Islamic sources for themselves in addressing the issues of the day).[16] The aim of these efforts was to break out of their marginalized positions, which were justified by traditional interpretation of the Qur'an and Hadith, authoritative collections of sayings and actions of the Prophet that have exercised great influence in the Islamic tradition and are the second source for religious reasoning. The motivation for many women certainly lay first in their own experiences of oppressive practices, sexism, racism, and so forth, and second in ethical and moral commitment to Islam.

Educated middle- and upper-class women were the first to introduce new ideas. For example, the Egyptian ʿĀisha ʿAbd al-Rahmān (1913–1998), who held a professorship of Islamic theology in Morocco, based her strong advocacy of women's rights on a contextual interpretation of the Qurʾan and eternal ethical and spiritual values. The Lebanese Nāzira Zayn ad-Dīn (1908–1976) argued for the equality of Muslim women in the Arab world. Her criticisms focused not on the Qurʾan itself but rather on the responsibility of Muslim scholars for women's underprivileged living conditions.[17] Both of these women addressed the textual sources of the Islamic tradition and reflected critically on the reception history of these texts as well as their sociopolitical impact throughout history.[18]

In the twentieth century a number of reforms in Muslim-majority countries have led to improved opportunities for education, for gender equality, and in general to greater emancipation and empowerment for women. However, it should be kept in mind that the needs of Muslim women vary greatly from one culture to another and that failing to recognize this variety of cultural contexts results in the underwriting of cultural and racial hierarchies.[19] While recognizing the universality of gender justice, our approaches must also be culture specific.[20]

In this light, Muslim women scholars, together with a few men, have tried to bring the different experiences of Muslim women into the discussion, seeking recognition for the voices of women and their ways of knowing, alongside those of men, as equally important contributions to the lived reality of Islam. Muslim scholars, some calling themselves Muslim feminists, formulate hermeneutical approaches to the Qurʾan and Hadith in favor of women's rights and against patriarchal systems and structures. While the gender debate focuses mainly on the Qurʾan, there are many hadith texts that have been used to subjugate women, prompting scholars like Fatima Mernissi and Farid Esack to assess the historical credibility of such texts through painstaking examination of their chains of transmission.

Presently, on the one hand, there are secular approaches to Muslim women's rights, such as that of Nasr Abu Zaid. He questions the ontological status of the Qurʾan as divine speech and argues that the Qurʾan itself is the product of culture in the Arabian Peninsula.[21] He seeks to secularize the Qurʾan as a precondition for establishing women's rights.[22] On the other hand, there are theological approaches, such as that of Asma Barlas, who criticizes patriarchal interpretations of the Qurʾan rather than the text itself. For her, the Qurʾan is Divine Discourse, whereas the Hadith is not. She argues further: since access to the Divine Discourse is mediated by humans and in gendered language and since the humans who have interpreted the Qurʾan historically have been men, we can certainly hear male voices and masculinist bias in traditional exegesis.[23] She emphasizes the importance of a liberatory Qur'anic hermeneutics to Muslim women's struggles for rights and equality.[24] Barlas acknowledges that merely holding some concept of freedom is insufficient for making a woman or man capable of liberatory readings. For her, intellectual and ideological differences, as well as sexual difference, might generate divergent concepts of freedom. However, she still affirms the possibility of women and men achieving a shared understanding of freedom.[25]

Perhaps the most prominent Muslim woman scholar in this field is Amina Wadud, who is notable for her political activism as well as her theological approach. Hence, she is known for having taken the controversial step of leading a mixed congregation of Muslims in the Friday prayer in New York City in 2005, and she is celebrated for having initiated a more proactive approach to the gender equality debate, criticizing the continuing hegemonic discourse of male scholars.[26] Wadud pursues a holistic approach to the Qur'an, emphasizing the relationship between text and context and avoiding a narrow, atomistic approach by reading each verse in the light of the wider Qur'anic Weltanschauung, which she defines in terms of the key concepts of the oneness of God (*tawhid*), guidance (*hidaya*), individual responsibility (*mas'uliyya*), and equality (*musawa'*).[27] A major priority in Wadud's work is the careful examination of the grammatical functions and meanings of these key Qur'anic concepts, which enables her to interpret them in ways that support an exegesis of the scripture that is radically liberating for women.

Wadud's claim that the fundamental Islamic belief in *tawhid*, the oneness of God, requires human rights appears to be influenced very much by the South African scholar Farid Esack, who elaborated on the meaning of *tawhid* in apartheid-era South Africa. For Esack, the oneness of God points to the need for true human unity, so the concept of *tawhid* means opposing the divisive structures of apartheid and working actively for the equality of all people.[28] The call for liberation and equality is seen as synonymous with the notion of social justice rooted in the Qur'anic Weltanschauung. This critique in the Qur'an and the prophetic tradition of the social and political structures of the seventh-century pagan Arabs has been deployed by many Muslim activists and scholars to criticize Western countries like Germany and France in which significant Muslim minorities live and where Muslim women encounter discriminations as well. In Western countries, in contemporary cultural debates and battles, the bodies of Muslim women are transformed into representatives and mirrors of the Muslim community, becoming focal points for the projection of collective needs and identities. Veiled Muslim women in particular are disempowered and become the subject of various discourses related to democracy, modernity, and womanhood. They face an unjust social order. The veil is used as a reason to deny and limit their access to educational opportunities, professions such as the law, and the labor market, which all leads to the marginalization of Muslim women from the public sphere as well as to their silencing.[29] So the gender jihad in the West has a certain character and aims, whereas in traditional Muslim countries such as Afghanistan it may have a quite different focus, such as fighting for women's right to enter mosques and to learn how to read the Qurʾan.

Resistance of Authorities

Let me note briefly some of the counterarguments to the various liberative Muslim approaches I have been describing. One common argument against the demand for gender equality is that women are not "the same" as men, and this demand is not compatible with a woman's physical or spiritual nature because women are created in many ways distinctly different from men.[30] From a quite different perspective, there are those who may be personally sympathetic to the outcomes sought by the liberationist approaches I have described but who argue that the Qurʾanic text undeniably has patriarchal elements because it inevitably reflects the cultural realities of its historical context. In other words, all sympathy to Wadud and Barlas, but they face an impossible task in reconciling the Qurʾan with modern understandings of freedom.

More widely, we must recognize the considerable challenge posed by the gender-egalitarian Muslim approaches I have described, with their demand that all Muslims should have the right to read and interpret the Qurʾan for themselves, since the Qurʾan came for everybody (and, in the seventh century, for the mostly illiterate Bedouins) and not exclusively for scholars and jurists. This demand certainly threatens established structures of male authority in Muslim communities. Notably, the authority of traditional Muslim scholars (*ʿulama*) is called into question, which prompts such scholars to emphasize the relevance of a good theological education, access to which (surprisingly enough) is still blocked for women. The intention is to keep the area of authoritative interpretation reserved to men in order to control the social conditions of Muslim women.

Those who believe that Islamic law is a product of human thinking and, as such, is certainly susceptible to rethinking argue that many juridical practices need to be reconsidered. For instance, they argue that punishments like stoning to death are not stipulated in the Qurʾan and need to be rethought. Those in favor of traditional interpretations of *sharia* will at this point quote hadith, which raises a fundamental issue in the debate I am describing: how to understand the relative authority for Muslims today of Qur'an and Hadith. While this important question merits deeper treatment, for the moment we should note that those who defend a traditional approach to *sharia* will typically move from the Qur'an to the prophetic tradition, the Hadith, and from there to the consensus of the community (*ijma'*). To respond that *ijma'* is a sociocultural construct does not really break the circle of oppressive thinking. Anyway, there is a paradox and bias to be noted in the context of hadith. It is well known that among the first in the seventh and eighth centuries to be actively involved in teaching and narrating hadith were many women;[31] "but because they were denied access to the exclusively male medieval study of law and theology, they could not determine its practical application to their own lives."[32]

The Outlook

To conclude, it must be recognized that the *'ulama*, the educated class of legal male scholars, do not take seriously the feminist and other liberationist approaches I have described. They do not hold gender egalitarianism to be a virtuous ideal and instead continue to promote the traditional hierarchical model of gender relations in which men are accorded "a degree" over women in terms of rights and responsibilities.[33] For those Muslims who regret this and who long to see Islam interpreted in ways that take more seriously our God-given freedom, it is important to acknowledge that, in Islamic theology, we Muslims have so far more or less failed to give an account of the relationship between God and humans as a dialogical relationship of freedom. Such an account must be rooted in categories of freedom and thus think of the relationship of God to human beings in reciprocal terms. Such an approach calls us to abandon the traditional/classical metaphysical thinking of God as a self-sufficient, almighty being and to stop using gendered language in relation to God. In this perspective, God does not want to realize the good that He wills in any other way than together with human beings.[34] In my opinion this theological-anthropological approach offers a new, freedom-centered way of understanding the God–world relationship. A basic requirement of such an approach is the consistent affirmation of human autonomy in ethics and respect for the human being as an end in itself. In my view, human freedom is linked to the responsibility for ethical action that makes humans human. Gender ultimately becomes irrelevant within a vision of all human beings flourishing together in the unity and freedom bestowed on them by the One God.

Notes

1. See Toshihiko Izutsu, *God and Man in the Koran: Semantics of the Koranic Weltanschauung* (Tokyo: Keio Institute of Cultural and Linguistic Studies, 1964), 165.

2. See also Abdullah Saeed, "Religious Freedom in Islam: The Witness of the Qur'an and the Prophet," *ABC Religions & Ethics* (blog), October 23, 2018, https://www.abc.net.au/religion/religious-freedom-in-islam/10419798.

3. See Seyyed Hossein Nasr, ed., *Islamic Spirituality: Foundations* (New York: Crossroad, 1997), xv.

4. This strand of thought deserves expanded treatment, but that would take us beyond the parameters of this chapter.

5. See also Rose Wilder Lane, *The Discovery of Freedom: Man's Struggle against Authority* (New York: John Day, 1943).

6. Dimitri V. Frolov, "Art: Freedom and Predestination," in *Encyclopaedia of the Quran*, vol. 2, ed. Jane D. McAuliffe, 267–71 (Leiden: Brill, 2002), 267.

7. See Mohammad Iqbal, *The Reconstruction of Religious Thought in Islam*, ed. M. Saeed Shaikh (Lahore: Institute of Islamic Culture, 1999), 77.

8. See Yasien Mohamed, "Predestination and Free Will in the View of Iqbal and Nursi," *Jurnal Akidah & Pemikiran Islam* 7, no. 1 (December 2006): 93–120, https://ejournal.um.edu.my/index.php/afkar/article/view/13286.

9. See Maria Do Mar Castro Varela and Nikita Dawan, "Feministische Postkoloniale Theorie: Gender und (De-) Kolonisierungsprozesse," *Femina Politica* 2 (2009): 12.

10. For example, the colonial position assumed that (Algerian) veiled women were oppressed by men; this was not necessarily a view shared by Muslim women. See Jenni Ramone, *Postcolonial Theories* (Oxford: Macmillian Education, 2001), 30.

11. See Ritu Tyagi, "Understanding Postcolonial Feminism in Relation with Postcolonial and Feminist Theories," *International Journal of Language and Linguistics* 1, no. 2 (2014): 45.

12. Tyagi, 45.

13. Jane I. Smith, "Women in Islam: Equity, Equality, and the Search for the Natural Order," *Journal of the American Academy of Religion* 47, no. 4 (1979): 517.

14. See Fatma M. Gökçe, "Islam and Gender," in *International Encyclopedia of the Social and Behavioral Sciences*, ed. Neil Smelser and Paul Baltes, 7913–16 (Amsterdam: Elsevier, 2015), 7914.

15. See Smith, "Women in Islam: Equity," 517.

16. *Ijtihad* means effort, zeal, diligence; an independent decision of a legal question based on the interpretation of the sources. See Jawad Haifaa, "Muslim Feminism. A Case Study of Amina Wadud-Muhsin's Qur'an and Women," *Islamic Studies* 42, no. 1 (2003): 107–23. See also Margot Badran, "Feminism," in *The Oxford Encyclopedia of the Modern Islamic World*, ed. John L. Esposito (New York: Oxford University Press, 2001), 19–23.

17. See Muna Tatari, "Gender Justice and Gender Jihād—Possibilities and Limits of Qur'anic Interpretations for Women's Liberation," in *Muslima Theology: The Voices of Muslim Women Theologians*, ed. Ednan Aslan, Marcia Hermansen, and Elif Medeni, 155–66 (Wien: Wiener Islamstudien 3, 2013), 156.

18. For further names and examples, see Leila Ahmed, *Women and Gender in Islam: Historical Roots of a Modern Debate* (New Haven, CT: Yale University Press, 1992).

19. See Elizabeth V. Spelman, *Inessential Woman* (London: Women's Press, 1988), 133–59.

20. Farid Esack, "Islam & Gender Justice: Beyond Simplistic Apologia," in *What Do Men Owe to Women? Men's Voices from World Religions*, ed. John C. Raines and Daniel C. Maguire, 187–210 (Albany, NY: SUNY Press, 2001).

21. See Tuba Işık, "Die Bedeutung des Gesandten Muhammad für den Islamischen Religionsunterricht," in *Systematische und Historische Reflexionen in Religionspädagogischer Absicht* (Paderborn: Schöningh Verlag, 2015), 187–90.

22. See Nasr Abu-Zayd, *Rethinking the Qur'an: Towards a Humanistic Hermeneutics* (Amsterdam: Humanistics University Press, 2005).

23. Asma Barlas, *"Believing Women" in Islam: Unreading Patriarchal Interpretations of the Qur'an* (Austin: University of Texas Press, 2002), 21–22.

24. See Asma Barlas, "Uncrossed Bridges: Islam, Feminism and Secular Democracy," in *Toward New Democratic Imaginaries: İstanbul Seminar on Islam, Culture and Politics*, ed. Seyla Benhabib and Volker Kaul (New York: Springer, 2016), 271–79.

25. See Barlas, *"Believing Women" in Islam*, 20–21.

26. See Tuba Işık-Yiğit, "Conference Report: IV International Congress on Islamic Feminism," *Ilahiyat Studies: A Journal on Islamic and Religious Studies* 1, no. 2 (2010): 282–85.

27. See Amina Wadud, *Qur'an and Woman. Rereading the Sacred Text from a Woman's Perspective* (Oxford: Oxford University Press, 1999), 25–26.

28. See Farid Esack, *Qur'an, Liberation & Pluralism: An Islamic Perspective of Interreligious Solidarity against Oppression* (Oxford: Oneworld, 1997), 92.

29. See Todd D. Nelson, ed., *Handbook of Prejudice, Stereotyping, and Discrimination* (New York: Psychology Press, 2015).

30. See Rukaiyah Hill Abdulsalam, *Women's Ideal Liberation: Islamic versus Western Understanding* (Jeddah: Abdul-Qasim, 1998), 65.

31. Just to mention a few names: Aisha and Asma bint Abi Bakr, Hafsah bin Umar ibn Khattab, Khansa bint Khidam, Umm Salamah, Umm Ayyub, Umm Habibah. See Faqihuddin Abdul Kodir, *Hadith and Gender Justice. Understanding the Prophetic Traditions* (Indonesia: The Fahmina Institute, 2007), 136.

32. Denise Spellberg, "History Then, History Now: The Role of Medieval Islamic Religio-Political Sources in Shaping the Modern Debate on Gender," in *Beyond the Exotic: Women's Histories in Islamic Societies*, ed. Amira El-Azhary Sonbol (Syracuse, NY: Syracuse University Press, 2005), 8.

33. Rumee Ahmed, "Islamic Law and Theology," in *The Oxford Handbook of Islamic Law*, ed. Anver M. Emon and Rumee Ahmed, 105–32 (Oxford: Oxford University Press, 2018), 126.

34. Inspired by Klaus von Stosch, "Barmherzigkeit als Leitkategorie für Islamische Theologie," in *Theologie der Barmherzigkeit*, ed. Mouhanad Khorchide, Milad Karimi, and Klaus von Stosch, 37–53 (Münster: Zeitgemäße Fragen und Antworten des Kalām, 2014), 40.

Freedom in the Contemporary Context

Trends in Intersections of Religion, Development, and Foreign Policy

Azza Karam

My task is to serve as a respondent to excellent and learned essays: "Who Gets to Decide What Freedom Is? A Christian Perspective" by C. Rosalee Velloso Ewell and "God-Given Freedom: An Islamic Point of View" by Tuba Işık.[1] While I am honored to do so, I must qualify at the outset that I approach this task not as a theologian but as a practitioner and scholar of international development and multilateralism and as a scholar of lived religion.

Tuba Işık speaks of freedom in modern or contemporary times (nineteenth and twentieth centuries onward)—not through reading or narrating Qur'anic text but rather through sharing the thinking of theologians such as Muhammad ʿAbduh (1849–1905), Jamal ad-Din al-Afghani (1838–1897), and Muhammad Iqbal (1877–1938) as well as that of analysts of women's lived realities such as Fatima Mernissi and Amina Wadud. Thus Işık references the lens of women interpreters who essentially challenge the jurisprudential status quo by approaches both secular and theological.

For Işık, it would appear that her reading of freedom is through the prism of women having to "face an unjust social order" in which, among other ills, "the veil is used as a reason to deny and limit their access to educational opportunities, professions such as the law, and the labor market, which all leads to the marginalization of Muslim women from the public sphere as well as to their silencing." In her argument, she refers to "gender equality" and "gender-equitable hermeneutics" in referencing the "patriarchal elements of Qur'anic text," which sits ill at ease with those of us practitioners of development and foreign policy who long have argued that *gender* encompasses multiple sexual orientations and socialization. In turn, these would have diverse implications on the perceptions and realities of freedoms, which should not be circumscribed (in a sense) to what women experience. And while Işık clearly notes that cultural context is critical, her own presentation is limited to a largely Middle Eastern–inspired set of realities, which I argue silence South Asian and Southeast Asian Muslim realities by simply ignoring them—in spite of the large numbers of Muslim in those parts of the world.

Nevertheless, Işık makes cogent arguments for the right of every Muslim . . . to read and interpret the Qur'an for themselves, since the Qur'an came for everybody (and, in the seventh century, for the mostly unlettered Bedouins in the desert) and not exclusively for scholars and jurists." She stresses how challenging this would be:

> This demand certainly threatens established structures of male authority in Muslim communities. Notably, the authority of traditional Muslim scholars (*'ulama*) is called into question, which prompts such scholars to emphasize the relevance of a good theological education, access to which (surprisingly enough) is still blocked for women. The intention is to keep the area of authoritative interpretation reserved to men in order to control the social conditions of Muslim women.

Turning now to Rosalee Velloso Ewell's overview from her Christian perspective, it is notable that she begins by insisting that we consider just whose freedom we are talking about, that we ask, Who gets to decide what freedom is?—thereby also implicitly questioning the power dynamics in any given context. Velloso Ewell speaks of a Christian perspective wherein "God is the source of freedom and dignity for all of creation—not just for people but for everything." She also affirms that "God defines the boundaries of justice, which look very different than what we might think they should look like."

I find it helpful that, in her "The Motif of Freedom in New Testament Texts: An Introduction," an essay found later in this volume, Susan Eastman refers to the relational nature of freedom, which she chooses to explain through focusing on scriptures, specifically the New Testament texts. Thus we are able to see, with her, freedom "from," freedom "for," and freedom "by"—through the prism of the textual narration of nascent Christian communities of the Roman Empire. Eastman argues that, for early Christians, freedom is distinct from matters of equality and social status, which neither guarantee nor inhibit freedom. Thus freedom "in the community of believers, dignity, status, worth, and agency derive from belonging to God above all other masters."

Eastman refers to the story, found in Mark 5:1–20, of the man who lived among the graves of the dead and was possessed by demons, whom Jesus interacts with, beginning by asking him his name. I take particular note of that point, for in the act of asking for a name is an act of unique and singular recognition, of reciprocity of humanness. And in the naming of who or what there is, there is a certain liberation from taking prejudices or stereotypes for granted. In being given a name, we are given an identity. In being asked for our name, we are granted a recognition or our existence somehow. It is this act of naming that I will come back to soon. For now, let us return to the story of Jesus.

Having liberated the man who lived among the graves, Jesus urges him to "go and tell what the Lord has done for you." Eastman emphasizes "a restoration of agency, voice, and community, even in the face of real potential social conflict." She goes on to explain that, indeed, "practical freedom has social and economic consequences that are not always welcome in the status quo." Velloso Ewell also refers to a form of status quo and riffs on a wry observation made by one Latin American theologian. In asserting that "liberation theology opted for the poor; and the poor opted for prosperity," he thereby also somehow pulled the rug from under the feet of a status quo inhabited by those who believe themselves to be righteously affirming—and, indeed, struggling—to realize freedom and dignity.

Both Işık and Velloso Ewell speak to notions of freedom as fundamentally challenging the status quo—whether through women-centric exegesis of the Qur᾿an or through asking the very foundational question of who gets to decide what freedom looks like for the other. This leads me to the task of reflecting on freedom in the context of contemporary dynamics of working on/with/about another feature of our status quo: the intersections of "religion and development" in ongoing work.

I cannot provide here a full overview of the more than two decades I have spent working specifically on these intersections in practical ways, primarily as a policymaker. However, I can tell you a story of trying to "do religion" as a practitioner of human development, as a policymaker whose job is to advise fellow policymakers, and as a scholar of international relations and of religion and development. But, above all, I ask you to listen to what I have to share, spoken from the most important space I have: as a woman of faith.

I started working on religious intersections with human rights by interning with a human rights organization that dealt with what were alternately referred to as "Islamists" (those who espoused Muslim ideals and their interpretations of Islamic praxis, in a very deliberate effort to challenge—and take over—political power and government) or "Muslim fundamentalists." The mere fact that these two distinct categories of Muslim realities were often seen by many human rights actors—and especially women's rights activists—as one and the same eventually taught me what I considered to be one of the challenges of "doing religion": that there is a deliberate essentialization of ideas, praxis, scriptures, characters, identities, and even of laws that is constantly taking place by all actors.

This essentialization takes place by governmental entities and nongovernmental organizations (NGOs)—secular or faith-based—at an individual or collective level. We seek to simplify complex realities by placing them into neat categories that fit our own worldviews—a syncretism that refuses to go away. It goes something like this: we policy wonks did "democracy," we did "human rights," we did "terrorism," and now we are doing "religion." The fact that "religion" does not quite lend itself to the same means of comprehension, enactment, realization, and instrumentalization has yet to register. Indeed, this essentialization is a key feature of the current instrumentalization taking place by governmental officials of religion and specifically of religious nongovernmental actors—whether religious leaders, religious NGOs, or religious institutions.

It is, or should be, a huge undertaking for secular government bureaucrats to seek to understand the complexity of faiths. Think of each religious or faith tradition, historical evolutions of each, textual exegesis, contextual cultural dynamics, idiosyncrasies of human lives lived in the name of these traditions, the social, political, economic, financial kaleidoscope of religious discourses. Completion of a serious educational program would be necessary to possess true competence in this. Yet it remains quite interesting, to say the least, how many of these bureaucrats—and now religious counterpart practitioners in both development and diplomatic circles—speak to providing "trainings" in "religious literacy" that do not require in-depth knowledge of the faiths per se. The justification is that we are not studying religions per se but "merely" how religions intersect with development or with foreign policy.[2] Indeed?

In a manner somewhat like the story of the man who was freed of his demons by Jesus and who went to tell his people what his Lord did (Mark 5:1–20), I made the argument that, as secular practitioners and policy wonks, we should not presume to understand the complexities of religion—as a matter of people's faith—by focusing on systems of governance or by limiting our understanding to the discourses of those who claim to speak in the name of this or that religion. For instance, we should not seek to learn about Islam through studying how one Muslim country's development or foreign policy is taking place. Please do not presume to understand the faith through its political or interest-driven institutional praxis, I have argued repeatedly.

For the foreign policy establishment in the Western hemisphere, this argument has largely fallen on deaf ears. The counter argument has been—and is—that we need to understand how these governments are practicing what they claim to be their religiously influenced narratives in order to have, at least, a frame of reference for how "Islam" is being leveraged in political dynamics—particularly ones tinged by fear of so-called Muslim/Islamic terrorism.

There is more than a nugget of truth—and wisdom—in this perspective. The challenges, however, are myriad. When the reverse takes place—that is, when the Jewish and Christian and Hindu religions are seen by others through similar prisms—can we begin to see how we are feeding into a narrative of religious essentialization that will lead to religion being seen through the prism of political interest? Indeed, what is unfolding is a pervasiveness of "religious-centric" political worldviews—apparently increasingly at odds with one another—that are informing our developmental and foreign policy engagements.

Another development is this: because "doing religion" is now increasingly seen as central to our political and overseas development work, governments are increasingly allocating financial resources to their own national institutions (religious and secular) to undertake "religion and . . . [fill in the dots]" projects and programs. As I lived and witnessed in the 1980s and 1990s (a period during which democracy / good governance and human rights initiatives were popular), numerous new initiatives, offices, and NGOs are emerging with supposed expertise in all matters having to do with "religion." As with the democracy and human rights' days, opportunism is rampant, with nouveau expertise increasingly permeating the "market place" of "religion and . . . ."

Using religion this way means we risk attempting to fit "religion" into old approaches to development and foreign policy. This syncretism is, in and of itself, strongly reminiscent of noblesse oblige, "white man's burden," or *la mission civilisatrice*. Colonialism rears its ugly head as many a policymaker reiterates how important it is to work with religious actors since they are "84% of the world's people" (quoting a Pew Research survey of 2012), how realization of sustainable development goals requires engagement of faith-based organizations, and how important it is to work with religious leaders to realize a "moral imperative." Colonialism began with a moral imperative after all.

The underlining subtext is along the following lines: we can use religion to bring about better living standards because faith-based organizations are service providers (so "migrants from over there need not come here"); to assist with counterterrorism by, among other things, gathering intelligence about potential extremist triggers among and within religious communities;

to build peaceful and inclusive societies by enabling religious leaders to be mediators in conflict situations—and so on.

Against this backdrop, a key feature of the foreign policy priorities of Western regimes: religious liberty, often cloaked as "freedom of religion and belief" (FoRB, as it is now referenced in policy circles). Religious actors, it would seem, according to the mantra of government bureaucrats, should prioritize working on freedom of religion and belief because this is now understood as a fundamental or even foundational human right. The emerging industry around FoRB is increasingly de rigueur for all matters religion, particularly on the part of the traditional donors to international development—for example, the United States or Canada, the European Union, and some of its member states.

The fact that these are among the largest donors to development and humanitarian relief and human rights work seems coincidental. But it is not. It means there is a direction and an intentionality behind this. Some of these governments/regimes espousing FoRB are the same ones that have veered somewhat to the right of the political spectrum—in some instances also espousing disturbing populist narratives. Moreover, the fact that the origins of FoRB engagement are almost identical to the origins of the labels and activism around "religious fundamentalism" in the 1980s is unknown to most of the current practitioners or is willfully ignored. Both worldviews emerged from within a cultural context informed by Christian-influenced scholars and interests[3]—and both are flourishing as academic disciplines seeking to influence policy establishments.

I am not arguing that "freedom of religion and belief" is not a critical human rights issue (or, better, series of issues), nor am I arguing that it is unimportant. Far from it! The point here is to appreciate how freedom, as understood and practiced in the spaces I have occupied for decades (that is, the intersections of religion–politics–human rights) is being instrumentalized in a neocolonial context.

This neocolonial syncretism, its accompanying opportunism, and the political conservatism undergirding all presumes that religious leaders, religious NGOs, and the faith of ordinary people can somehow be subjectified and integrated into old molds and frameworks of policymaking, becoming new priorities according to an old process of prioritization, accompanied by usual norms of financing or resource mobilization.[4]

What I consider particularly disturbing, however, is that faith leaders, several religious institutions, and many faith-based organizations are willing parties—indeed, fully complicit—in all of the above. Many of these religious organizations are seeking to syncretize their work on and with FoRB, with their regular praxis of providing services in health, education, sanitation, environment, and even humanitarian relief. Indeed, many faith-based actors are rushing to feature in FoRB meetings, events, and debates, even without fully comprehending "freedom of religion and belief." And many religious actors are engaging without much experience in working in these divisive political spaces in which some government interest (in FoRB) is also part and parcel of broader national security agendas focused on violent extremism.

So rather than using the experience of working with religious actors to question how foreign policy and development are usually done or seeking to use the religious ethos of service to be self-critical about how development and foreign policy can be based more on reciprocity rather than interest, some governments (and governmental entities) are using religion as a relatively new instrument for doing the same old foreign policy and development. But this is taking place in a time when the political regimes, which are now setting the priorities, are far from savory in general. In particular, some of these regimes are zeroing in on FoRB at the same time as they articulate various levels of fear of the "other's religion" (read: Islam) as *the* source of terror, insecurity, and instability in the world. And many religious organizations are rushing to comply and affirm this notion of, and this work on, freedom.

It would thus seem that within this emerging nexus of religion, development, and foreign policy, increasingly funded and determined by specific national interests (rather than the common good of all nations), *freedom* is about FoRB. But this is freedom as viewed from largely ethnocentric perspectives of fear, essentialization, and instrumentalization of religion. In other words, this is a concept of religious freedom dictated by largely Western political regimes setting priorities influenced by their national security concerns. This is not freedom understood as fear of God and thus a need to avoid that which would contradict or lead away from His love (as most Muslims are traditionally taught). Nor is it freedom "derived from belonging to God above all other masters," as Susan Eastman reminds us. Neither is it a freedom derived from conviviality (as Rosalee Velloso Ewell iterates) and focused on those in the margins. Rather, this is a freedom that is conceptualized *from within* the centers of political power—albeit claiming to speak for those on the margins.

My fear is that, while many are now "doing" religion, we are quite possibly losing the sacred in and of and about *faith*. And in losing the sacredness of faith, we become slaves to the oldest of practices: the political abuse of the sacred. By losing sight of faith in God, we are, ironically, losing sight of the freedom of thought, conscience, and belief, which is the fundamental human right meant to be safeguarded.

Notes

1. Passages quoting Tuba Işık, C. Rosalee Velloso Ewell, and Susan Eastman are from their essays in this volume.

2. For example, the United Nations, *Transforming Our World: 2030 Agenda for Sustainable Development*, A/RES/70/1, https://sustainabledevelopment.un.org/content/documents/21252030%20Agenda%20for%20Sustainable%20Development%20web.pdf.

3. "Freedom of religion and belief" started with a concern for Christian minorities—particularly, albeit not only, in Muslim majority countries. It remains a key pillar of interest for Christian Evangelical, Catholic, Protestant, and Mormon communities.

4. Indeed, now the emerging norm, even among international intergovernmental organizations like the United Nations, is to seek "religious funding" from faith-based organizations to fund developmental and humanitarian work. This usually refers to "Islamic financing." So far I appear to be a lone voice speaking against this trend and seeing it as deeply challenging on multiple levels—but this is a subject of a totally different discussion.

Part Two

Islamic Texts on Freedom

Aspects of Human Freedom

Reflections on Selections from the Qur'an and Hadith

Abdullah Saeed

I begin with two observations. First, the way we discuss and debate the notion of human freedom today is quite different from the way the Qur'an appears to address the topic. Moreover, the Qur'an focuses on a wide range of issues concerning human freedom. Therefore, in an introductory essay such as this, it is not possible to give a full account of the Qur'anic discourse. Rather, I can only touch on a few of its aspects. My primary aim in this chapter is, therefore, to introduce the Qur'an and Hadith passages selected for study during the 2019 Building Bridges Seminar without engaging with the post-Qur'anic debates on freedom found in Islamic theology, philosophy, and mysticism.

Second, freedom can be understood in very different ways: as (a) the power of self-determination or the ability to make decisions independent of fate or necessity; (b) the ability to act in accordance with what is true or good; (c) the absence of subjection to political domination or a despotic government, or the achievement of basic liberties, such as freedom of expression, human rights, and democracy; (d) the state of not being imprisoned or enslaved; or (e) the power or right to act, speak, or think in the way we want, without constraint, in everyday life. Other possibilities also exist. For the purpose of this chapter, I have chosen to use a working definition that relates to our experience of freedom in everyday life: the ability to choose one course of action, thing, view, or position over another in the midst of various physical, psychological, environmental, political, legal, social, and economic constraints. After making a few brief remarks on God's freedom, I focus on just two aspects of human freedom in this chapter: spiritual/moral and political/legal.

God's Freedom

The Qur'an presents many texts on God's absolute power, knowledge, and ability to create as well as humanity's dependence on God for its existence. God creates and recreates, and a part of this is the creation of human beings, not just the first person (Adam) but every single one: "Do they not see that God brings life into being and reproduces it? Truly this is easy for God" (29:19). This text and others in the selected texts show the utter dependence of human beings on God, the Ruler who is constantly watching over them. It also emphasizes that God grants His mercy and favors on whom He chooses. God does not need anyone, including human beings; they, as well as creation, are always in need of God (35:15). The Qur'an superimposes this concept of power, knowledge, and control over any freedom that human beings may have been given. Although the vast majority of the Qur'anic texts on freedom are about God's freedom, our focus here is on human freedom.

Human Freedom

In a world that is deterministic, God creates human beings with much of their existence interconnected to this deterministic world. Yet the Qur'an suggests that God created human beings with certain unique characteristics. Human beings were created as honored beings, connected in some way to the very Spirit of God. They are vicegerents of God on Earth, backed by a primordial covenant and given a range of tools that enable them to be faithful to such a covenant. God gave human beings intellect, language, thought, and senses, all of which help them recognize God and be connected to Him. The unique characteristics of human beings, which were not given to other creatures, appear to require at least some kind of freedom and agency (even if severely limited) to function appropriately in this world, with the capacity to be faithful to the primordial covenant, if one chooses to be. We briefly look further at some aspects of this.

Human Beings' Covenant with God and Freedom

Although there are many references to covenants in the Qur'an, the most important is God's primordial covenant with humanity. The Qur'an says, "And [mention] when your Lord took from the children of Adam—from their loins—their descendants and made them testify of themselves, [saying to them], 'Am I not your Lord?' They said, 'Yes, we have testified'" (7:172). God asks all humanity, "Am I not your Lord?" Humanity collectively testifies that He is.

This primordial covenant requires that human beings recognize God and His authority over them, the Oneness of God and the lordship of God over all creation, while serving Him and rejecting the ways of Satan.[1] All human beings are born into this covenant relationship with God, which gives them an innate disposition (*fitra*) toward God. God invites all people to fulfill the covenant and ultimately to achieve salvation. However, failure to follow God's guidance and to adhere to the covenant will result in judgment and punishment. The covenant remains from the beginning to the end of time, making it the foundation of belief and freedom. However, most human beings fail to maintain the covenant and move toward Satan. They reject God and fail to recognize and serve Him.

In the Qur'anic creation story, during the dialogue between Iblis and God, Iblis promises God that he will lead large numbers of human beings—descendants of Adam—astray: "Iblis said, 'I swear by Your might! I will tempt all but Your true servants'" (38:82–83). Instead of preventing Iblis from doing this, God gives him the freedom to act on this promise. It is the job of Iblis to lure human beings away from the covenant; however, it is humanity's free will that allows Iblis to either succeed or fail in this endeavor.

Human Beings as Vicegerents of God

Human freedom appears to be intricately connected to the nature of human beings as vicegerents of God on Earth and their ability to choose to follow (or reject) the primordial covenant with God. The basis of freedom in the Qur'an comes from the notion that human beings are people created and honored by God. It affirms, "He created you all from a single being" (39:6). God breathed His Spirit into human beings, thus giving them a unique status in creation and endowing them with intellect and some degree of freedom to make choices. The Qur'an mentions that God created human beings "in the best of molds" (95:4), bestowed special favors on them, stating, "We have honored the sons of Adam . . . and conferred on them special favors" (17:70), and granted them the intellect to differentiate between right and wrong. This indicates that "who receives guidance, receives it for his own benefit: who goes astray does so to his own loss" (17:15).

When God decided to create human beings, He announced His creation to the angels, saying that He was going to put vicegerents on Earth. Despite the angels' objections and concerns, God went ahead and created these new beings, declaring them vicegerents on Earth. For human beings to function as such, they needed the ability to operate with some degree of freedom and accountability. The vicegerency thus assumes human freedom and agency as its foundation. This "state of moral responsibility" that comes from the covenant is embodied in the vicegerency bestowed on humankind. Those who adhere to the covenant are God's true vicegerents on Earth.[2]

Leading Human Beings Astray and Freedom

An important issue in the Qur'anic discourse on freedom is the notion of God leading human beings astray. The Arabic word associated with this idea is *dalal*. This word and a variety of its derivatives appear in the Qur'an. The opposite of this concept is the notion of *being guided*. The Arabic word *huda* (guidance) and its derivatives are used frequently in the Qur'an.

Many Qur'anic texts also appear to suggest that it is God who decides what happens to human beings by guiding them or leading them astray. For instance, "God points out the right path, for some paths lead the wrong way" (16:9) and "Through it, He makes many go astray and leads many to the right path" (2:26). Again, "If it had been Our will, we could certainly have given every soul its true guidance" (32:13) and "We have assigned a law and a path to each of you" (5:48). Other verses of the Qur'an also affirm this point (for instance, 7:178; 13:33; 45:23). Qur'an 3:74 states that it is God's choice whom He shows His mercy to: "He singles out for His mercy whoever He will."

Continuing with this theme, Qur'an 2:26, for instance, states that God leads astray those human beings He chooses: "He makes many go astray and leads many to the right path." It is God who guides: "God points out the right path . . . if He wished, He could guide you all" (16:9); He guides those whom He is pleased to guide: "Now God leaves straying those whom He pleases and guides whom He pleases" (14:4). In fact, God could have guided everyone: "Had He so willed, He would have guided you all" (6:149; see also 20:99). Several Qur'anic verses appear to say that those people who reject God's invitation are dumb, deaf, and blind; for instance, Qur'an 90:8–10, which rhetorically states, "Did We not give him two eyes, a tongue, and two lips, and we guided him to the two clear ways [of good and evil]?" Others suggest that peoples' hearts are sealed by God so that nothing can enter them, their hearts are hard, or there is a veil between them and the truth, such as Qur'an 45:23: "God has, knowing [him as such], left him astray, and sealed his hearing and his heart [and understanding], and put a cover on his sight." If this is the case, God has essentially determined that certain people will either be guided or led astray. How, then, does human responsibility factor into this?

The Qur'an presents both the act of being led astray and the act of being guided as associated with how human beings respond to the invitation from God to recognize and believe in Him. If, for whatever reason, a person's response is to reject His invitation or to deliberately move away from His invitation, then God leads this person astray. This is emphasized in Qur'an 13:11: "God does not change the condition of a people [for the worse] unless they change what is in their hearts." Conversely, if a person's response to the invitation involves reflection or being prepared at some level to consider the invitation, this may perhaps lead to God's guidance. The key here is not so much that God compels people to move in a certain direction; rather, His actions depend on a person's response to His message or his/her preparedness or willingness to be guided. Qur'an 2:26 says, "But it is only the rebels He makes go astray." Therefore, human preparedness and effort are very important.

Human Agency

While in early Islamic literature there is a clear recognition of human beings' utter inability in the face of God's dominance, power, will, and knowledge, there are also voices that emphasize the room God gives human beings to make choices and to take responsibility for their actions. Therefore, it appears just as important to emphasize human agency, as it concerns going astray or being guided. Several Muslim theologians argued that God's justice demands that human beings are free to decide their fate. The Muʿtazilis argued that human beings have the ability to direct their own actions and they are entirely free to act, whether that be to choose "good" or "evil."[3] For the Muʿtazilis, this position was closely connected to their understanding of God's justice. If God created humankind without free will and then caused them to sin or do evil, then ultimately punishing them for the very same acts would be manifestly unjust. From the Muʿtazilis' point of view, people could not be held morally responsible or accountable for their actions unless they had free will.[4] They could not be justly punished for acts they did not have the freedom to choose to commit.

God's justice therefore requires that human beings have the necessary freedom to act without God moving them in any particular direction. For the Muʿtazilis, human beings have the necessary agency. People are the authors of their own actions. However, this emphasis on the freedom of human beings led them to impose certain constraints on God, which chips away at the knowledge and power of God. Such a view, for example, may suggest that

God does not have complete knowledge of human actions or control over certain aspects of creation as far as human actions are concerned. This was a problematic idea for other theologians and commentators (e.g., those from the Ashʿarī tradition), who argued that this kind of human freedom was incompatible with many Qurʾanic texts.

Many verses of the Qurʾan also suggest that a human being's final destiny is decided on on the Day of Judgment, and it depends on how a human being receives God's invitation and acts in response: "God will admit those who believe in Him and do righteous deeds into Gardens graced with flowing streams, where they will remain forever" (65:11). Furthermore, "all those who believe in God and the Last Day and do good—will have their rewards with their Lord" (2:62). The Qurʾan makes clear the consequences of rejection: "Let those who wish to reject it do so. We have prepared a Fire for the wrongdoers that will envelop them" (18:29).

In response to the tension between the notions of God's absolute power and foreknowledge and human beings' freedom, the Ashʿarīs reached what has been described as an "intermediary position."[5] While they emphasized God's omnipotence and that God is the creator of everything, they also affirmed some level of human agency (and therefore responsibility) when it came to a person's actions. They argued that God created all actions, but people acquired them. Human beings could only acquire what God created because human beings do not have the power to create acts themselves. However, people also have the ultimate responsibility for their actions because they freely choose which acts to acquire.

Belief

As a part of its discourse on freedom, the Qurʾan says human beings have the choice to believe or not to believe in God. Those who wish to reject God may do so—"'Say, 'Now the truth has come from your Lord: Let those who wish to believe in it do so, and let those who wish to reject it do so'" (18:29). Central to these texts is the verse "there is no coercion in matters of faith" (2:256). The Qurʾan considers the matter of belief an individual responsibility, not a collective concern. The rejection of coercion specified in this verse comes through clearly in the Qurʾan. Even Prophet Muhammad was prohibited from forcing others to become Muslim (10:99). His role was simply to communicate the message: "if they turn away, your only duty is to convey the message" (3:20). It was up to individuals to accept or reject his message. The Qurʾan says, "The messenger is not bound to do more than deliver the message" (24:54). It also says, "You [Prophet] are not there to force them" (50:45).

From a Qur'anic point of view, does this mean that every single individual has this freedom? Without entering into Islamic legal debates on this issue, particularly concerning apostasy (*riddah*), we can say that the dominant view in the Qur'an is that all individuals have such freedom—be they Muslim or non-Muslim. All people have the ability to accept or reject faith. Obviously, the Qur'an does not consider the rejection of faith a good or meritorious act. It makes it clear that those who reject faith or God will be punished—but only in the hereafter. It does not seem to specify a worldly punishment for rejecting faith.

Opposition to Slavery

The Qur'an uses a range of words to refer to slaves, such as "what your right hand possesses," *'abd* (slave), *amah* (female slave), and sometimes even *fatayat* (young female slaves). However, a range of modern terms used for slaves and slavery, such as *riqq* or *'ubudiyyah* for slavery, or the opposite of these—*hurriyah*, which means freedom—are not used in the Qur'an.

A slave is a person who is owned by another human being—their master. Masters may sell, free, or keep their slaves. Slavery was an institution that existed in Mecca and Medina at the advent of Islam, and the Qur'an seems to recognize the legitimacy of this institution. It did not prohibit the acquisition of or keeping of slaves; rather, it encouraged their good treatment. It prohibited masters from forcing their female slaves into prostitution (24:33), and it condemned the ill treatment of slaves. The Qur'an appears to have considered slaves to be an extension of a person's family, much like a family member but not necessarily having the same status as other family members. In the very first generation of Muslims, there were those who became Muslim and remained slaves, whereas other slaves who converted to Islam were set free. The fact that these people were former slaves did not affect their status in Muslim societies. Some examples include Salman al-Farsi, Bilal b. Rabah, and even the Prophet's adopted son Zayd b. Thabit. All became prominent leaders in the community.

The main concern of the Qur'an was not complete freedom for slaves; rather, its concern was to confirm the internal freedom they had as human beings. From a Qur'anic point of view, slaves were human beings who had the ability to believe or not believe in God, and they had the capacity to follow or reject God's commandments. They could make these decisions on their own, without their master's help, support, or even consent. Having their humanity acknowledged and recognized was, of course, the starting point. Once this had been acknowledged from a Qur'anic point of view, the legal aspect of being free versus a slave was not much of a concern. The Qur'anic social order was quite comfortable with accepting slaves and free people, but the emphasis appears to have been on the internal aspects of freedom, such as freedom of conscience.

Apart from requiring masters to treat slaves fairly, gently, or well, the Qur'an also asked Muslims to consider releasing a slave, if the slave wanted freedom, in exchange for some form of compensation. To facilitate this, the Qur'an considered the manumission of slaves a noble and virtuous act (90:11–16). It also allocated a portion of *zakat* for this very purpose (9:60). In fact, the Qur'an required Muslims to free slaves as a way of showing repentance for a number of sins (5:89). This seems to suggest that the Qur'an acknowledged the existence of the institution but believed it was better if slavery were eliminated. However, the Qur'an does not explicitly say that the manumission of slaves is one of its objectives. Still, some modern readings of the Qur'anic verses suggest that the ultimate objective of the Qur'an was to free slaves.

Oppression

One of the most important references to the freeing of oppressed peoples is the example of the Children of Israel (the Jewish people) and their deliverance from Pharaoh. Their emancipation is considered one of the greatest of God's favors (14:6). Pharaoh is presented as a person who saw himself as mighty; he divided his people into various groups, slaughtered their children but spared women, and caused corruption on Earth. In response, God decided to favor those who were being oppressed—the Children of Israel—by making them leaders and establishing them in the land (28:3–6). Other texts refer to the people who were oppressed and how God's promise to the Children of Israel was fulfilled because of their patience, perseverance, and adherence to the covenant. The key point here is that oppressed people are in God's sight, and when they persevere, God listens and supports their cause of freedom.

Although the clearest example of this kind of large-scale oppression is the case of the Children of Israel and the oppression and persecution that Pharaoh inflicted on them, there are also other references in the Qur'an to those who are oppressed, weak, or unable to defend themselves, including slaves and women. The Qur'an seems to suggest that people who are oppressed should not give up hope or anticipate suffering forever. Instead, they are encouraged to leave the place where they are oppressed and seek freedom elsewhere. In the case of those who are unable to leave their oppressive situation and have no means at their disposal whatsoever, God knows their situation and will not use it as a reason for punishing them. People who are free to leave a place of oppression must leave, and they should make their departure a priority. God will excuse those who have no means to take refuge elsewhere. What is interesting is that these principles refer not only to believers in God. It seems that anyone who is oppressed—whether or not a believer—must move or try to leave such a situation if they can. If no means are available, then God knows and will excuse these people.

Today the references to the oppressed and the weak in the Qur'an and their encouragement to seek freedom elsewhere are sometimes considered a justification for struggles against exploitation and oppression. Given that the Qur'an does not necessarily differentiate between Muslims and those from other religions who are oppressed, it appears that oppressed people, regardless of their faith, should engage in a struggle to free themselves, because being oppressed transcends such matters. This concern is perhaps one of the most important aspects of the kind of freedom that many people support today.

Law, Boundaries, and Freedom

The idea of human freedom is also closely connected to what the Qur'an refers to as *hudud* (boundaries). Often the phrase "these are God's boundaries, do not transgress them" (2:187) is mentioned. Those who do not adhere to God's limits or boundaries will be chastised and punished. Although the term *hudud* was mainly used in relation to civil matters in the Qur'an, God's boundaries or *hudud Allah* later came to be associated with certain types of penalties under Islamic law, such as flogging or retaliation.

One of the functions of these laws and boundaries is to curb individuals' endless desires. Left unchecked, these competing desires will create havoc in the community, ultimately curtailing whatever freedom individuals may have in this environment. Therefore, placing boundaries that clearly articulate how each individual can function in the midst of many others appears to create more freedom for all, not less. By submitting to God's laws, following His ways, and adhering to His boundaries, a person becomes freer. For the Qur'an, true freedom can only be found by submitting to the One God, which liberates human beings from the burdens others place on them or from the desires of the self.

Conclusion

In summary, I have attempted to reflect on some key aspects of the Qur'anic discourse on human freedom. While some aspects of what I have addressed appear problematic or difficult in the context of contemporary debates on human freedom, considering the multifaceted nature of the Qur'anic discourse is perhaps important. It includes texts that range from appearing to severely curtail human freedom to those that seem to affirm a great degree of leeway. The multifaceted nature of this discourse has obviously led to heated exchanges between Muslim theologians, philosophers, and commentators on the Qur'an over many centuries, and it has produced a vast array of positions among Muslims on human freedom. Detailing these is beyond the scope of this chapter. In light of the importance of the concept of freedom today, particularly when it comes to debates about human dignity and rights, Muslim scholars are involved in projects that aim to appropriate texts of the Qur'an to respond to such contemporary concerns. These scholars use a range of interpretive methods and tools developed for the purpose of making sense of Qur'anic texts on freedom and applying them to our particular context today.[6]

Notes

1. David R. Vishanoff, "Religious Beliefs," in *The Oxford Encyclopedia of Islam and Politics*, vol. 2, ed. Emad El-Din Shahin (Oxford: Oxford University Press, 2014), 321–37.

2. See Vincent J. Cornell, "Fruit of the Tree of Knowledge: The Relationship between Faith and Practice in Islam," in *The Oxford History of Islam* (Oxford: Oxford University Press, 1999), 63–106.

3. Abdur Rashid Bhat, "Free Will and Determinism: An Overview of Muslim Scholars' Perspective," *Journal of Islamic Philosophy* 2, no. 1 (2006): 10; and Massimo Campanini, "The Mu'tazila in Islamic History and Thought," *Religion Compass* 6, no. 1 (2012): 44.

4. Bhat, "Free Will and Determinism," 10.

5. Bhat.

6. See, for example, Wan Fariza Alyati Wan Zakaria, "Qadar in Classical and Modern Islamic Discourses: Commending a Futuristic Perspective," *International Journal of Islamic Thought* 7 (1995): 39–48.

The Qur᾽an and Hadith on Freedom

Selections for Dialogue

The Qur᾽an on God's Freedom

Surat Āl ʿImrān (3):74

He singles out for His mercy whoever He will. His grace is infinite.

Sura Yunus (10):49

Say [Prophet], "I cannot control any harm or benefit that comes to me, except as God wills. There is an appointed term for every community, and when it is reached they can neither delay nor hasten it, even for a moment."

Surat al-ʿAnkabūt (29):19

Do they not see that God brings life into being and reproduces it? Truly this is easy for God.

Sura Fāṭir (35):15

People, it is you who stand in need of God—God needs nothing and is worthy of all praise.

Surat al-Zumar (39):6

He created you all from a single being, from which He made its mate; He gave you four kinds of livestock in pairs; He creates you in your mothers' wombs, in one stage after another, in threefold depths of darkness. Such is God, your Lord; He holds control, there is no god but Him. How can you turn away?

Hadith on God's Freedom

Sahih Muslim 2644: Book 46, no. 3

Hudhaifa b. Usaid reported directly from the Prophet (pbuh) that he said: When the drop of semen has been in the womb for forty or forty-five nights,

In this chapter, all Qur᾽an passages are according to the translation by M.A.S. Abdel Haleem (Oxford University Press, 2010). Reprinted by permission of Oxford University Press. All hadiths have been translated by members of the Seminar.

the angel comes and says: My Lord, will he be wretched or prosperous? And both these things would be written. Then the angel says: My Lord, would he be male or female? And both these things are written. And his actions and choices, his lifespan, his livelihood; these are also recorded. Then his pages are rolled up and nothing in them is increased or lessened.

The Qur'an on Human Freedom

Surat al-Baqara (2):26

God does not shy from drawing comparisons even with something as small as a gnat, or larger: the believers know it is the truth from their Lord, but the disbelievers say, "What does God mean by such a comparison?" Through it He makes many go astray and leads many to the right path. But it is only the rebels He makes go astray.

Surat al-Baqarah (2):62

The believers, the Jews, the Christians, and the Sabians—all those who believe in God and the Last Day and do good—will have their rewards with their Lord. No fear for them, nor will they grieve.

Surat al-Baqara (2):256

There is no compulsion in religion: true guidance has become distinct from error, so whoever rejects false gods and believes in God has grasped the firmest hand-hold, one that will never break. God is all hearing and all knowing.

Surat Āl 'Imrān (3):20

If they argue with you [Prophet], say, "I have devoted myself to God alone and so have my followers." Ask those who were given the Scripture, as well as those without one, "Do you too devote yourselves to Him alone?" If they do, they will be guided, but if they turn away, your only duty is to convey the message. God is aware of His servants.

Surat al-Mā'idah (5):48

We sent to you [Muhammad] the Scripture with the truth, confirming the Scriptures that came before it, and with final authority over them: so judge between them according to what God has sent down. Do not follow their whims, which deviate from the truth that has come to you. We have assigned a law and a path to each of you. If God had so willed, He would have made you one community, but He wanted to test you through that which He has given you, so race to do good: you will all return to God and He will make clear to you the matters you differed about.

SURAT AL-AN'ĀM (6):149

Say, "The conclusive argument belongs to God alone. Had He so willed He would have guided you all."

SURA HŪD (10):99

Had your Lord willed, all the people on earth would have believed. So can you [Prophet] compel people to believe?

SURAT AL-RA'D (13):11

Each person has guardian angels before him and behind, watching over him by God's command. God does not change the condition of a people [for the worse] unless they change what is in themselves, but if He wills harm on a people, no one can ward it off—apart from Him, they have no protector.

SURAT AL-NAḤL (16):9

God points out the right path, for some paths lead the wrong way: if He wished, He could guide you all.

SURAT AL-ISRĀ' (17):13

We have bound each human being's destiny to his neck. On the Day of Resurrection, We shall bring out a record for each of them, which they will find spread wide open.

SURAT AL-KAHF (18):29

Say, "Now the truth has come from your Lord: let those who wish to believe in it do so, and let those who wish to reject it do so." We have prepared a Fire for the wrongdoers that will envelop them from all sides. If they call for relief, they will be relieved with water like molten metal, scalding their faces. What a terrible drink! What a painful resting place!

SURAT AL-SAJDAH (32):13

If it had been Our will, We could certainly have given every soul its true guidance, but My words have come true. "I shall be sure to fill Hell with jinn and men together."

SURA ṢĀD (38):75–83

75God said, "Iblis, what prevents you from bowing down to the man I have
made with My own hands? Are you too high and mighty?" 76Iblis said, "I
am better than him: You made me from fire, and him from clay." 77"Get
out of here! You are rejected: 78My rejection will follow you till the Day

of Judgement!" [79]but Iblis said, "My Lord, grant me respite until the Day when they are raised from the dead," [80]so He said, "You have respite [81]till the Appointed Day." [82]Iblis said, "I swear by Your might! I will tempt all [83]but Your true servants."

Sura Qāf (50):45

We know best what the disbelievers say. You [Prophet] are not there to force them, so remind, with this Qur'ān, those who fear My warning.

Surat al-Dhāriyāt (51):6

I created jinn and mankind only to worship Me.

Surat al-Najm (53):38–41

[38]No one laden shall bear the burden of another; [39]that man will only have what he has worked towards; [40]that his labor will be seen [41]and that in the end he will be repaid in full for it.

Surat al-Ṭalāq (65):11

[He sent] a messenger—reciting to you God's revelations that make things clear—to bring those who believe and do righteous deeds from darkness into light. God will admit those who believe in Him and do righteous deeds into Gardens graced with flowing streams, where they will remain forever—He has made good provision for them.

Surat al-Balad (90):8–10

[8]Did We not give him two eyes, [9]a tongue, and two lips, [10]and we guided him to the two clear ways [of good and evil]?

Surat al-Zalzalah (99):1–8

[1]When the earth is shaken violently in its [last] quaking, [2]when the earth throws out its burdens, [3]when man cries, 'What is happening to it?'; [4]on that Day, it will tell all [5]because your Lord will inspire it [to do so]. [6]On that Day, people will come forward in separate groups to be shown their deeds: [7]whoever has done an atom's weight of good will see it, [8]but whoever has done an atom's-weight of evil will see that.

Hadith on Human Freedom

Abū 'Ubayd, Kitāb al-Amwāl, no. 519

The Compact of Medina (Dustūr al-Madīnah)

. . . The Jews of Bani Awf are [one] community with the Believers—the Jews have their religion [*dīn*], and the Muslims have theirs. The same applies both to them and to their freedmen. The exception will be those who act unjustly and sinfully. By so doing they wrong themselves and their families. The same applies to Jews of Bani al-Najjar, Bani al-Harith, Bani Saeeda, Bani Jusham, Bani al-Aws, Bani Tha'laba, and the Jafna (a clan of the Bani Tha'laba), and the Bani al-Shutayba.[1]

Abū 'Ubayd, Kitāb al-Amwāl, No. 503

The Compact of Najrān

. . . Najran is entitled to the protection of God and the protection of His Messenger, with regard to their lives, their property, their religion [*milla*], their commerce, their monks and bishops, those of them who are present [here] as well as those who are absent, and whatever they have whether small or great. No bishop, church warden or monk or shall be removed from his position. They are not held in contempt and they shall suffer no vengeance killing. They are not required to be mobilized and no army shall occupy their land. If anyone of them makes a claim, justice shall be done between the parties. However, they may not claim interest. For anyone who claims interest on past loans my protection is cancelled. They are obliged to make a good-faith effort regarding what they have received—apart from those who have been wronged or treated harshly.[2]

Musnad Ahmad 18449

Tariq b. Shihab reported: A man asked the Messenger of Allah, peace and blessings be upon him, "What is the best jihad?" The Prophet said, "A word of truth in front of a tyrannical ruler."[3]

Sahih al-Bukhari 6922: Book 88, no. 5

Narrated by Ikrima: Some Zanadiqa were brought to Ali and he burned them. The news of this event, reached Ibn Abbas who said, "If I had been in his place, I would not have burned them, as God's Messenger forbade it, saying, 'Do not punish anybody with God's punishment (fire).' I would have killed them on the basis of the statement of God's Messenger: 'Whoever changes his religion, kill him.'"

The Qur'an on Freeing the Oppressed

Surat al-Baqarah (2):177

Goodness does not consist in turning your face towards East or West. The truly good are those who believe in God and the Last Day, in the angels, the Scripture, and the prophets; who give away some of their wealth, however much they cherish it, to their relatives, to orphans, the needy, travelers and beggars, and to liberate those in bondage; those who keep up the prayer and pay the prescribed alms; who keep pledges whenever they make them; who are steadfast in misfortune, adversity, and times of danger. These are the ones who are true, and it is they who are aware of God.

Surat al-Mā'idah (5):89

God does not take you [to task] for what is thoughtless in your oaths, only for your binding oaths: the atonement for breaking an oath is to feed ten poor people with food equivalent to what you would normally give your own families, or to clothe them, or to set free a slave—if a person cannot find the means, he should fast for three days. This is the atonement for breaking your oaths—keep your oaths. In this way God makes clear His revelations to you, so that you may be thankful.

Surat al-A'rāf (7):137

We made those who had been oppressed succeed to both the east and the west of the land that We had blessed. Your Lord's good promise to the Children of Israel was fulfilled, because of their patience, and We destroyed what Pharaoh and his people were making and what they were building.

Surat al-Tawbah (9):60

Alms are meant [only] for the poor, the needy, those who administer them, those whose hearts need winning over, to free slaves and help those in debt, for God's cause, and for travelers in need. This is ordained by God; God is all knowing and wise.

Surat al-Nūr (24):33

Those who are unable to marry should keep chaste until God gives them enough out of His bounty. If any of your slaves wish to pay for their freedom, make a contract with them accordingly, if you know they have good in them, and give them some of the wealth God has given you. In your quest for the short-term gains of this world, do not force your slave-girls into prostitution when they themselves wish to remain honorable. However, if they are forced, God will be forgiving and merciful to them.

Surat al-Qasas (28):3–6

[3]We recount to you [Prophet] part of the story of Moses and Pharaoh, setting out the truth for people who believe. [4]Pharaoh made himself high and mighty in the land and divided the people into different groups: one group he oppressed, slaughtering their sons and sparing their women [5]he was one of those who spread corruption—but We wished to favor those who were oppressed in that land, to make them leaders, the ones to survive, [6]to establish them in the land, and through them show Pharaoh, Haman, and their armies the very thing they feared.

SURAT AL-DUKHĀN (44):30–31

[30]We saved the Children of Israel from their degrading suffering [31]at the hands of Pharaoh: he was a tyrant who exceeded all bounds.

SURAT AL-BALAD (90):11–16

[11]Yet he has not attempted the steep path. [12]What will explain to you what the steep path is? [13]It is to free a slave, [14]to feed at a time of hunger [15]an orphaned relative [16]or a poor person in distress.

The Qur'an on the Limits of Freedom by the Law

SURAT AL-BAQARAH (2):188

Do not consume your property wrongfully, nor use it to bribe judges, intending sinfully and knowingly to consume parts of other people's property.

SURAT AL-MĀ'IDAH (5):32

On account of [his deed], We decreed to the Children of Israel that if anyone kills a person—unless in retribution for murder or spreading corruption in the land—it is as if he kills all mankind, while if any saves a life it is as if he saves the lives of all mankind. Our messengers came to them with clear signs, but many of them continued to commit excesses in the land.

SURAT AL-SHU'ARĀ' (26):181

Give full measure: do not sell others short.

Hadith on the Limits of Freedom by the Law

SUNAN AL-NASA'I 4891: BOOK 46, NO. 22

It was narrated from Jabir that: A woman from Banu Makhzum stole (something), and she was brought to the Prophet. She sought the protection of Umm Salama, but the Prophet said: "If Fatima bint Muhammad were to steal, I would cut off her hand." And he ordered that her hand be cut off.

Notes

1. Abū 'Ubayd, *Kitāb al-Amwāl*, ed. Khalīl Harrās (Beirut: Dār al-Fikr, n.d.), 266 (#519). See also Ibn Hishām, *al-Sīra al-Nabawiyya*, ed. Muṣṭafā Saqqā (Cairo: Bābī Ḥalabī, 1955/1375), 1/501–4.

2. Abū 'Ubayd, *Kitāb al-Amwāl*, ed. Khalīl Harrās, (Beirut: Dār al-Fikr, n.d.), 244 (#503).

3. Considered authentic by al-Nawawi.

Freedom as a Theme in Islamic Thought

An Introduction to Selected Premodern Texts

Lejla Demiri

The premodern Islamic texts selected for study during the 2019 Building Bridges Seminar come from five different sources written in the eleventh and twelfth centuries. They belong to three scholars quite distinct in their orientations and methods: Abū l-Qāsim al-Qushayrī (d. 1072), Khwāja ʿAbdallāh al-Anṣārī (d. 1089), and Abū Ḥāmid al-Ghazālī (d. 1111).[1] All three come from the Persian-speaking Muslim lands of Central Asia, a region called Greater Khorasan. Qushayrī was originally from Ustuwa (northeastern Iran); Anṣārī, from Herat (in present-day Afghanistan); and Ghazālī, from Ṭūs (in what is now northeastern Iran). Both Qushayrī and Ghazālī studied in the great academic and spiritual city of Nishapur and were Ashʿarī theologians and jurists of the Shāfiʿī school of law, while Anṣārī followed the Ḥanbalī school, reputed for its determination never to stray from the plain sense of scripture. All three were advocates and exponents of Sufism, *taṣawwuf*, a mystical orientation disputed today by fundamentalists but prevalent and indeed normative among Sunni scholars of the medieval period. There is a further Sufi connection linking Qushayrī and Ghazālī, as Ghazālī was a committed student of Qushayrī's major disciple Abū ʿAlī Faḍl ibn Muḥammad al-Farmadhī (d. 1084).

During the 2019 Building Bridges Seminar these texts were not approached chronologically but rather thematically—and that is how they are organized in the chapter that follows this essay. Starting with divine freedom, we move to the paradox of human freedom and are then given a discussion on free will and human responsibility as well as a detailed examination of the subtle relationship that exists between freedom and servanthood to God and ultimately freedom and salvation. The texts are of separate literary genres, representing different Islamic disciplines. Here I offer a few words about each work and the way it relates to our theme.

Ghazālī's al-Maqṣad al-asnā fī sharḥ asmāʾ Allāh al-ḥusnā ("The highest goal in explaining the beautiful names of God")

Abū Ḥāmid al-Ghazālī's book is dedicated to a thorough examination of the ninety-nine names that Muslim scriptural tradition predicates of the deity. Some of you may recall John Taverner's oratorio based on these names, which he found to be not only Islamic but also Christian and even universal. In his own description of his project Taverner explains,

> The 99 Names are universal, insofar as they are theophanies of the eternal Primordial Being. A companion of the Prophet Mohammed said "I never saw anything without seeing God." Man's mission, therefore, is to join the vision of the "Outward" (the tangible) to the "Inward" (the spiritual). This is the aspiration of The Beautiful Names. And perhaps, by doing this in the language of music, one may contribute a little to an inward healing of the appalling strife that permeates the modern world.[2]

Turning to Ghazālī's own twelfth-century exegesis of these names, we find that each of his book's ninety-nine sections begins with a theological meditation on a divine name, followed by a counsel or lesson that a believer can follow in order to assume the character traits of that particular name. This apparently rather Platonic exercise turns out to be very Islamic as well, certified in the hadith literature: the overall intention is to reestablish the *imago Dei* (image of God), or *takhalluq bi akhlāq Allāh* (assumption of the character traits of God), and to do this is a Prophetic command.

With some Names, the human corollary and ground for emulation is evident: God is Merciful, and so should we be; He is just, loving, patient, and so forth; and the creature's virtue is evidently grounded in these predicates of divine perfection. In the case of some of the most majestic and transcendent names, however, we seem to run into a difficulty of incommensurability. For instance, God names Himself in scripture Mālik al-Mulk—King of Absolute Sovereignty. In what possible way can a human being, molded of poor and mortal clay, *ḥamaʾ in masnūn* (Q 15:26), emulate this name?

In Ghazālī's text, freedom is identified with absolute power, sovereignty, and independence. Reflecting on the divine names of al-Qādir (the All-Powerful) and al-Muqtadir (the All-Determiner), our author attributes absolute power, omnipotence, to Almighty God—as He is the only existent entity Who stands in no need of assistance, thanks to His aseity, which is an intrinsic part of the definition of Godhead. Human creatures (descendants of Adam and inheritors of his clay) can attain power in a remarkably slight and temporary modality. This is received and derived entirely from God, for He is "Himself creator of human powers by His power, inasmuch as He puts all the existing causes at the service of man's power"—this being the instantiation of Adam's *khilāfa* or vicegerency (Q 2:30).[3]

Absolute and true liberty is proper to God alone, Who is further named al-Malik (the King), for He has no need of anything, while everything else stands in absolute and eternal need of Him. God is unique in His power, as He is the only one to possess perfect power.[4]

Divine aseity is what makes the Godhead truly free. Yet a human being may, paradoxically, experience a taste of kingship. This cannot be achieved when he is ruled by ego: Pharaoh was certainly no king in this esoteric sense but was ʿabd *hawā* (a slave to his whim). Rather, it is achieved when the human creature is ruled by none other than God, and when he realizes that he is in no need of anything except God. This kingship combines monarchical and caliphal dignity in the order of creation, with the recognition of absolute *islām* (surrender) and *ʿubūdiyya* (servanthood) to the Creator.

Ghazālī also offers a physiological simile, also known in Hellenistic anthropology, which medieval Muslims were happy to appropriate and creatively develop. In Ghazālī's words, "the kingdom proper to him [i.e., the human being] is his own heart and soul, where his soldiers are his appetites, his anger, and his affections; while his subjects are his tongue, his eyes, his hands, and the rest of his organs. If he rules them and they do not rule him, and if they obey him and he does not obey them, he will attain the level of a king in this world."[5] For Ghazālī, this true dignity, of real Adamic self-mastery and kingship over oneself, is the level of the prophets and the religious scholars, the inheritors of the prophetic legacy. Here human freedom is defined as detachment from worldly needs and passions, for in Ghazālī's words, "kingship lies in being free and able to dispense with everything."[6]

In sum, our first text speaks of absolute and true freedom, which is possessed by God alone, and a human freedom that is ultimately dependent on God, which can be attained by cleansing the heart from everything other than God.

Ghazālī's Kitāb al-Tawḥīd wa-l-tawakkul ("Faith in divine unity and trust in divine providence")

Our second text is taken from Book 35 of the *Iḥyāʾ ʿulūm al-dīn* ("The revival of the religious sciences"), Ghazālī's much celebrated magnum opus. The *Iḥyāʾ* consists of four "quarters," each divided into ten books or chapters. The first quarter, titled *ʿibādāt* (worship of God) deals with the creed, ritual purity, prayer, and devotion. The second quarter concerns what the author calls the *ʿādāt* (social customs), thus dealing with such matters as eating habits, marriage, traveling, and many other normal practices of human life. The third quarter, titled *muhlikāt* (vices of character leading to perdition), focuses on the purification of the heart from spiritual pollution. The fourth quarter, on *munjiyāt* (virtues leading to salvation), deals with a set of scriptural virtues proper to the mystical life, such as patience, gratitude, trust in God, and love of God.

The text chosen for study by the Building Bridges Seminar forms part of this last quarter and deals with the notoriously paradoxical question of the human freedom to act in a universe radically subject to Divine knowledge and power. If faith in divine unity requires the recognition that there is no true agent other than God, then how can we hold a human being responsible for his actions, asks Ghazālī. Would this not lead to what early Muslim theology anathematized as a principle of coercion or compulsion (*jabr*)? If so, then what is the purpose of reward or punishment, divine anger (*ghaḍab*) or approval (*riḍā*)? Ghazālī asks, How can God be angry at His own deed? Conversely, if we consider human beings as agents, how do we explain divine agency? Or are we to be dualists, attributing some actions to God, and others to human beings and perhaps to other living things?

This is a famously subtle and complex matter, and we can do no more than point to Islamic theology's solutions here, bearing in mind that for Ghazālī, the "secret of Divine destiny" is discernible through mystical unveiling rather than through the reductive categories of scholastic analysis. Ghazālī opens his formal discussion by noting that the principle of agency has different meanings, which allow us to attribute human acts to God as well as to human beings, according to different definitions. God is agent in the sense that He is the originator of all existing things, while a human being is an agent as he is the locus or substrate (*maḥall*) in which knowledge, will, and power are created. Human will and power are fully contingent and dependent on the will and power of God.[7] In Ghazālī's view, the term *agent* signifies the one who originates, "but [in that sense] there is no agent but God, so the term belongs properly to Him and metaphorically to whatever is other than Him."[8]

As it was in the first text above, here also freedom is related to power and power to self-subsistence. "Everything except God is empty,"—that is, "everything which does not subsist in itself, but has its subsistence from another, . . . is nothing." God "subsists essentially [*bi-dhātihi*] while everything that is other than He subsists by His power. So, He is the truly Real One [al-Ḥaqq] and all that is other than He is nothing," writes Ghazālī.[9] Divine actions are defined by His knowledge and wisdom, for God's treatment of His servants is unqualifiedly just with no injustice in it; nothing is "more fitting, more perfect, and more attractive within the realm of possibility."[10] What humans experience as free choice is part of this divine perfection; but that perfection is not circumscribed by human experience.

Ghazālī's Kitāb Qawāʿid al-ʿaqāʾid ("The principles of the creed")

Kitāb Qawāʿid al-ʿaqāʾid is the second book of the first quarter of Ghazālī's *Iḥyāʾ*. It offers an introduction to his *kalām* (systematic theology). Part of the *Qawāʿid* consists of a treatise written in Jerusalem explaining the ʿaqīda and is known as *al-Risāla al-Qudsiyya* ("The Jerusalem Epistle").

This text also emphasizes divine sovereignty, as all existent entities owe their existence to God. Ghazālī writes, "Every contingent thing in the universe is His act, His creation, and His design. . . . He created humankind and its deeds, and gave being to its power and motion. All the actions of His creatures are created by Him and dependent on His power."[11]

God's omnipotence requires that He be the Creator of His servant's actions and govern the motions of His servants' bodies. But then the needful question of human responsibility is raised again. In his response, Ghazālī proposes the Ashʿarī theory of *kasb*: "Although God is the sole creator of humankind's deeds, they are still under each person's power by means of acquisition."[12] Human deeds are thus the object of God's power as creation and the object of a person's power through acquisition.

Human free will is, on the plane of human empirical experience, a reality, but it remains created by God, as He creates both the power and the deed and creates the choice (*ikhtiyār*) and the chosen (*mukhtār*). Ghazālī follows the Ashʿarī maxim that "What God wills comes to pass, and what He does not will does not."[13] Thus he writes,

> Although the servant's deed is acquired by him, this does not mean it is not willed by God. Nothing happens in the worldly kingdom or the realm of spiritual domain, not even the blink of an eye, a fleeting thought, or a passing glance, except by God's ordainment (*qaḍāʾ*) and determination (*qadar*), and by His desire (*irāda*) and will (*mashīʾa*). From Him are good and evil, benefit and harm, . . . error and guidance, obedience and disobedience. . . . God sends astray [thereby] whom He wills and guides whom He wills.[14]

To claim that God sits back from events in creation when they are the work of human hands is to set a limitation on the sovereignty of God, which would reduce Him to weakness and incapacity, and this is exactly what Ghazālī aims to avoid. To be meaningfully omnipotent, God determines all things; but by the mystery of the *rūḥ*, the divine secret breathed into Adam's clay by God, and which obligates the angels to bow down to the first man, the human soul acquires acts that God has made. This crucial distinction, which is perhaps ultimately mystical, occupies volumes of analysis in the classical manuals of Islamic ontology, and, as I indicated, I can do no more than offer a brief account here.

al-Risāla al-Qushayriyya fī ʿilm al-taṣawwuf ("Epistle on Sufism")

The *Epistle on Sufism* by Abū l-Qāsim al-Qushayrī is considered one of the most popular and authoritative Sufi manuals. Written in 1045, it has served as a primary textbook for many generations of Sufis down to the present. It consists of three major parts: Sufi Biographies; Sufi Terminology; and Major Stations (*maqāmāt*) of the Mystical Path. Qushayrī's views on *hurriyya* (freedom) appear in this third section.

Freedom is considered as one of the stations of the seeker in the path of God. It is defined as emptying one's heart of everything other than God. Freedom means, for Qushayrī, that "the servant of God does not allow himself to become enslaved by [other] creatures, nor is he subject to the power of originated things (*mukawwanāt*)." Thus, one has to become a slave of God in order to attain true freedom. Freedom can be achieved through the perfection of one's servanthood (*ʿubūdiyya*). When one's servanthood before God is sincere, one's heart is free from attachment to anything other than God.[15]

In Sufi parlance, freedom implies "that one is not bound by any mundane attachments or fleeting things of this world nor those of the Hereafter."[16] The Sufi's sole devotion to God detaches him from worldly as well as otherworldly thoughts and aspirations. Qushayrī emphatically writes that freedom can be attained by constant devotion to the service of God. He then takes a step further claiming that "the greatest kind of freedom lies in serving the poor." This he associates with the prophetic statement, "The master of a people is their servant."[17]

Anṣārī's Munājāt-nāma ("Intimate conversations with God")

Khwāja ʿAbdallāh al-Anṣārī's *Munājāt-nāma* ("litanies," or "intimate conversations with God") is considered a masterpiece of Persian literature. Here the treatment is reminiscent in some way of the perspective of Qushayrī, which we have just outlined. Face to face with human inability, helplessness and weakness, God is All-Powerful. Yet human beings can raise themselves to be monarchs if they accept divine power and recognize that all will is God's.

The motif of freedom through servanthood is to be found here too, as Anṣārī prays: "There is no freedom except in bondage to you. . . . O God, Give us courage to place the ring of slavery to You in our ears."[18] Freedom can be achieved by emptying oneself of the ego and its desires, as he prays: "Give me deliverance from the bonds of my self, O Lord. Give me freedom from my evil self, O Lord. I am a stranger: Make me know myself. Give me knowledge of myself, O Lord."[19]

Conclusion

Although these texts emanate from different authors and diverse genres, they share five interconnected ideas and principles. First, human freedom is not absolute but radically dependent on God. Second, freedom is conditioned on the acknowledgment of one's categoric and necessary neediness toward God. Third, true freedom, a supremely liberative experience, can be attained by servanthood to God. Fourth, freedom defines not only a human being's relationship with God but also with *His* creation. Fifth, freedom leads one to care for God's creation and ultimately to salvation.

In all these textual examples, we note a very distinctive theistic understanding of freedom, shaped according to the humble theological wisdom that recognizes God's sovereignty and human contingency and dependence. This topic provokes intriguing questions. For instance, does the Ashʿarite idea of *kasb* (acquisition), so apparently paradoxical, supply a better basis for theories of human agency and dignity than the strongly deterministic tendencies observable in modern science, particularly physics, neuroscience, and genetics? To what extent can metaphysics explain the radically contingent nature of the physical world in ways that do not abuse the limits of language, with its built-in assumptions about the reality of causality and the passage of time? Does the notion of a freedom consisting in liberating ourselves from worldly and self-oriented desires make us exiles from the modern Enlightenment universe, with its near-idolatry of the will of the individual? These are but three questions. Undoubtedly, there are others. As we study these examples of premodern Islamic thought on freedom, let us find comfort in the knowledge that our outcomes are safe in God's keeping; but we remain accountable to Him for the responsible way in which we convey His truth.

Notes

1. For al-Qushayrī's biography, see the translator's introduction to Abū 'l-Qasim al-Qushayri, *Al-Qushayri's Epistle on Sufism | Al-Risala al-qushayriyya fi ʿilm al-tasawwuf,* trans.

Alexander D. Knysh, reviewed by Muhammad Eissa (London: Garnet Publishing, 2007), xxi–xxvii.

2. John Taverner, "Composer's Note," *The Beautiful Names* for solo tenor, double choir and orchestra (London: Chester Music Ltd, 2004). © 2004 Chester Music. All Rights Reserved. International Copyright Secured. Used by Permission of Hal Leonard Europe Limited.

3. Al-Ghazālī, *The Ninety-Nine Beautiful Names of God | Al-Maqṣad al-asnā fī sharḥ asmāʾ Allāh al-ḥusnā*, trans. David B. Burrell and Nazih Daher (Cambridge: Islamic Texts Society, 1992), 132.

4. Al-Ghazālī, 57–58.

5. Al-Ghazālī, 58.

6. Al-Ghazālī, 59.

7. Al-Ghazālī, *Faith in Divine Unity and Trust in Divine Providence | Kitāb al-Tawḥīd waʾl-Tawakkul | Book XXXV of The Revival of the Religious Sciences | Iḥyāʾ ʿUlūm al-Dīn*, trans. David B. Burrell (Louisville, KY: Fons Vitae, 2006), 40.

8. Al-Ghazālī, 43.

9. Al-Ghazālī, 44.

10. Al-Ghazālī, 46.

11. Al-Ghazālī, *Kitāb Qawāʿid al-ʿAqāʾid | The Principles of the Creed | Book 2 of the Iḥyāʾ ʿulūm al-dīn | The Revival of the Religious Sciences*, trans. Khalid Williams with an introduction and notes by James Pavlin (Louisville, KY: Fons Vitae, 2016), 75.

12. Al-Ghazālī, 76.

13. Al-Ghazālī, 77.

14. Al-Ghazālī, 76–77.

15. Al-Qushayrī, *Al-Qushayri's Epistle on Sufism*, 230.

16. Al-Qushayrī, 230.

17. Al-Qushayrī, 231.

18. Kwaja Abdullah Ansari, *Intimate Conversations*, trans. Wheeler M. Thackston (New York: Paulist Press, 1978), 195, 205.

19. Ansari, 206.

Premodern Islamic Writings on Freedom

Selections for Dialogue

Abu Hamid Muhammad al-Ghazālī, (c. 1056–1111)

The Ninety-Nine Beautiful Names of God
al-Maqṣad al-asnā fī sharḥ asmā' Allāh al-ḥusnā

4. Al-Malik—the King—is the one who in His essence and attributes has no need of any existing thing, while every existing thing needs Him. There is nothing among things which can dispense with Him concerning anything—whether in its essence or its attributes, its existence or its survival; but rather each thing's existence is from Him or from something that is from Him. Everything other than He is subject to Him in its essence and its attributes, while He is independent of everything—and this is what it is to be king absolutely.

Counsel. The creature cannot be conceived of as being king absolutely, for he cannot dispense with everything; indeed he will always be needy with regard to God the most high, and would be even if he were able to dispense with all but Him. Nor can one conceive of a creature having everything in need of him, since most existing things have no need of him. But to the extent that it is conceivable for one to be free from some things while other things need him, one may have a taste of kingship.

For a king among people is one whom no-one rules but God the most high, and who does not need anything except God—great and glorious. And with that he rules his kingdom insofar as his soldiers and his subjects obey him. Yet the kingdom proper to him is his own heart and soul, where his soldiers are his appetites, his anger, and his affections; while his subjects are his tongue, his eyes, his hands, and the rest of his organs. If he rules them and they do not rule him, and if they obey him and he does not obey them, he will attain the level of a king in this world. And if that be coupled with the fact that he is independent of all people, yet all people are in need of him for their life now and in the future, he will be an earthly king.

This is the level of the prophets—may God's blessings be upon all of them. For they have no need of direction to the next life from anyone except God—great and glorious—while everyone needs it from them. They are followed in this kingship by religious scholars, who "inherit the legacy of the prophets." Their kingship, however, is proportional to their ability to guide the people, and to their lack of need for asking for guidance.

By means of these attributes man comes close to the angels in qualities, and by means of them approaches God the most high. This kingship is a gift to man from the true king whose sovereignty has no competitor.

One of the "knowers" [*'ārifūn*] was right to respond to a prince who said to him: "Ask me for what you need," by saying: "Is that the way you speak to me when I have two servants who are your masters?" When he said: "Who are these two?" the knower answered: "Greed and desire: for I have conquered them yet they have conquered you; I rule over them while they rule you." And one of them said to a certain shaykh: "Advise me," and he said to him: "Be a king in this world and you will be a king in the next." When he said: "How might I do that?" the shaykh answered: "Renounce this world and you will be a king in the next." He meant: detach your needs and your passions from this world, for kingship lies in being free and able to dispense with everything.

69–70. Al-Qādir, Al-Muqtadir—the All-Powerful, the All-Determiner—both mean "one who possesses power," but "the All-Determiner" is more emphatic. Power is equivalent to the intention by which a thing comes into existence according to a determinate plan of will and knowledge, and in conformity with both of them. The All-Powerful is one who does what he wills, or does not act if he so wills, and is not so conditioned as to will necessarily. So God is all-powerful in that He could bring about the resurrection now, and He would bring it about were He to will it. So if He does not bring it about, that is because He has not willed it, and He does not will it to happen now inasmuch as His knowledge had previously fixed its appointed time and moment according to plan, which hardly detracts from His power. The absolutely powerful is He who creates each existent individually without needing assistance from anyone else, and this is God most high.

So far as man is concerned, he is possessed of power in a general sense but deficiently so, for he only attains some possibilities. It is not within his power to create, yet God the most high is Himself creator of human powers by His power, inasmuch as He puts all the existing causes at the service of man's power. But a book like this one is not able to probe below this depth.

84. Mālik al-Mulk—the King of Absolute Sovereignty—is the one who carries out what he wills in his kingdom, in the manner that he wills and as he wills it, bringing into being and destroying, perpetuating and annihilating. Al-Mulk here means "kingdom," and al-Mālik means the powerful one with perfect power. All existent things form a single kingdom, and He is their king and the one holding power over them. All existent things form one kingdom only because they are connected one with another, so even if they are many in one respect, they are one in another. This is much like the human body, which is like a kingdom for the essence of man; many different members cooperating, as it were, in realizing the goal of one manager, and so forming a single kingdom. In that way, the entire world is like one person, with the parts of the world like his members, cooperating toward one goal, and its existence represents the highest possible realization of the good, as divine generosity requires. Because its parts are arranged in an orderly ranking and linked together by a single bond, they form one kingdom with God the most high as its sole king. The kingdom of each man is his own body. For if what he wills is accomplished in the qualities of his heart and in his limbs, then he is king of the kingdom of himself according to the measure of power given to him.[1]

Abu Hamid Muhammad al-Ghazālī

Faith in Divine Unity and Trust in Divine Providence
Kitāb al-Tawḥīd wa'l-Tawakkul

Now you may object: how can there be any common ground between faith in divine unity and the *sharia* [religious law]? For the meaning of faith in divine unity is that there is no agent but God Most High, and the meaning of the law lies in establishing the actions proper to human beings [as servants of God]. And if human beings are agents, how is it that God Most High is an agent? Or if God Most High is an agent, how is a human being an agent? There is no way of understanding "acting" as between these two agents. In response, I would say: indeed, there can be no understanding when there is but one meaning for "agent." But if it had two meanings, then the term comprehended could be attributed to each of them without contradiction, as when it is said that the emir killed someone, and also said that the executioner killed him; in one sense, the emir is the killer and, in another sense, the executioner. Similarly, a human being is an agent in one sense, and God—Great and Glorious—is an agent in another. The sense in which God Most High is agent is that He is the originator of existing things [*al-mukhtari' al-mawjūd*], while the sense in which a human being is an agent is that he is the locus [*maḥall*] in which power is created after will has been created after knowledge has been created, so that power depends on will, and action is linked to power, as a conditioned to its condition. But depending on the power of God is like the dependence of effect on cause, and of the originated on the originator. So everything which depends on a power in such a way as it is the locus of the power is called "agent" in a manner which expresses that fact of its dependence, much as the executioner and the emir can each be called "killer," since the killing depends on the power of both of them, yet in different respects. In that way both of them are called "killer," and similarly, the things ordained [*maqrūrāt*] depend on two powers.

In accordance with that, God Most High in the Qur'an sometimes attributes actions to angels and sometimes to human beings, and at other times applies the very same attributions to Himself. So God Most High says of death: *Say [O Muhammad] "the angel of death who has charge of you"* [32:11], while the Great and Glorious One also says: *at the point of death God takes human souls* [39:42]; and yet again, in relation to us, *Have you considered the soil you till?* [56:63], yet also: *We have sent the rain in copious downpours and broken up channels in the ground, bringing forth grain there* [80:25–28]. The Great and Glorious One says [of Maryam]: *Then We sent to her Our Spirit who came to her in comely form* [19:17], and then: *We breathed into her of Our Spirit* [21:91]. (But the one breathing [into her] was Gabriel—peace be upon him—as the Most High says: *as We recite it, follow its recital* [75:18]; for it is said in the commentary that this means "when Gabriel recited it to you.") Again, the Most High says: *Kill them! God will punish them by your hands* [9:14], so connecting the killing with them [who carry it out] and the punishment with Himself, yet the killing and the punishment are the same. So the Most High clarifies it, saying: *You [Muslims] did not kill them, but God killed them*, and further: *You [Muhammad] did not throw when you threw, but God threw* [8:17]. On the surface this amounts to a denial and an affirmation together, but its meaning is: you did not throw in the sense in which the Lord can be said to throw, since you threw in the sense in which it belongs to a human to throw—and the two senses are different. . . .

So it is that "acting" is fraught with different senses, and these meanings are not contradictory once you understand [that fact]. . . . Anyone who relates all there is to God Most High is unquestionably one who knows the truth and the true reality, while whoever relates them to what is other than Him is one whose speech is laced with figurative expressions and metaphors. Figurative expression is on one side while true reality is on another, yet the author of language determined the term "agent" to mean the one who originates [*mukhtari*ʿ], so those supposing human beings to be originators call them "agents" according to their power. For they suppose that human beings actualize [*taḥqīq*], so they imagine [*tawhīm*] that "agent" is attributed to God Most High metaphorically, as the killing was attributed (in the example) to the emir, yet metaphorically so when contrasted with that attributed to the executioner.

You may still object: It is now clear that all is coerced [*jabr*]. But if so, what can these mean: reward or punishment, anger or complete approval [*riḍā*ʾ]? How can He be angry at His own deed? You should know that we have already indicated the meaning of that in the Book of Thanksgiving [Book 32 of the *Iḥyā*ʾ], so we will not proceed to a long repetition here. For this has to do with the divine decree [*qadar*], intimations of which we saw with respect to the faith in divine unity which brings about the state of trust in divine providence, and is only perfected by faith in the benevolence and wisdom [of God]. And if faith in divine unity brings about insight into the effects of causes, abundant faith in benevolence is what brings about confidence in the effects of the causes, and the state of trust in divine providence will only be perfected, as I shall relate, by confidence in the trustee [*wakīl*] and tranquility of heart toward the benevolent oversight of the [divine] sponsor. For this faith is indeed an exalted chapter in the chapters of faith, and the stories about it from the path of those experiencing the unveiling go on at length. So let us simply mention it briefly: to wit, the conviction of the seeker in the station of faith in divine unity, a conviction held firmly and without any doubt. This is a faith deemed to be trustworthy and certain, with no weakness or doubt accompanying it: that when God—Great and Glorious—created all human beings according to a reason greater than reason and a knowledge greater than their knowledge, that He also created for them a knowledge that would sustain each one of them, and bestowed on them a wisdom that they would never cease describing. In like manner, He enhanced knowledge, wisdom, and reason in a great number of them, and then unveiled for them the effects of things [*al-*ʿ*awāqil al-umūr*], apprising them of the secrets of the intelligible world, teaching them the subtleties of speech and the hidden springs of punishment, to the point where they were thus informed regarding what is good and evil, useful or harmful. Given that He had bestowed reason and wisdom [on them], He then commissioned them to administer the visible and invisible worlds. Even though all of them required direction, it was nonetheless manifest and evident to Him that this would add—may He be praised—to God's direction of creation, in this world and the next. And that direction continues: whether or not the number of atoms be increased or diminished, sickness or evil eye, weakness or poverty or harm will not be removed from those afflicted by them; nor will health, beauty, wealth, or advantage be taken away from those whom God has blessed with them. Indeed, of everything which God Most High created in heaven and earth, if human beings would but turn their eyes to it all and prolong their gaze, they would not see diversity or discontinuity in it. For everything which God Most High distributes among His servants: care and an appointed time [*ajal*], happiness and sadness, weakness and power, faith and unbelief, obedience and apostasy—all of it is unqualifiedly just with no injustice in it, true with no wrong infecting it.

Indeed, all this happens according to a necessary and true order, according to what is appropriate as it is appropriate and in the measure that is proper to it; nor is anything more fitting, more perfect, and more attractive within the realm of possibility. For if something were to exist and remind one of the sheer omnipotence [of God] and not of the good things accomplished by His action, that would utterly contradict [God's] generosity, and be an injustice contrary to the Just One. And if God were not omnipotent, He would be impotent, thereby contradicting the nature of divinity. Indeed, all need and harm in the world, while it represents a deficiency in this world, nonetheless spells an enhancement in the next, and everything which amounts to a deficiency in the next world for one person spells a benefice for another. For if there were no night one would never know the reach of daylight, and absent sickness one would not enjoy good health when one had it; or if there were no hell, the inhabitants of paradise would not know the extent of their blessing. And just as there is no wrong if one is required to sacrifice animal lives as the price of human lives, so the fact that perfection takes precedence over diminishment is proper to justice. Similarly, amplifying blessing on behalf of the inhabitants of paradise while increasing the punishments of the inhabitants of hell, so that the price of the people of faith is paid by the people of unbelief, is quite proper to justice. If diminishment had not been created, the dignity of human beings would not be evident, for perfection and diminishment become evident in relation to one another, so it belongs to generosity and wisdom to create perfection and diminishment together. Just as it is just to cut off an extremity once gangrene has set in, to prolong one's life, because the less perfect is sacrificed to the more perfect, so it is with the order of differences which exist among people in the divisions within this world and the next. All of that is just with no injustice in it; true with no jest in it [cf. 21:16,44:38].[2]

Abu Hamid Muhammad al-Ghazālī

The Principles of the Creed
Kitāb Qawāʿid al-ʿAqāʾid
Chapter 3: The Jerusalem Epistle
The Third Pillar of Faith: Knowledge of the Acts of God

This pillar has ten foundations.

The First Foundation is knowledge that every contingent thing in the universe is His act, His creation, and His design. They were created by none other than Him, and given being by none other than Him. He created humankind and their deeds, and gave being to their power and motion. All the actions of His creatures are created by Him and dependent on His power, as is confirmed in His words, *God is the Creator of all things* [39:62]; *While God created you and what you do* [37:96]; and again, *And conceal your speech or publicize it; indeed, He is Knowing of that within the breasts. Does He who created not know, while He is the Subtle, the Acquainted* [67:13–14].

He commanded His servants to be cautious in their words, deeds, secrets, and thoughts, because He knows the sources of their actions. This infers knowledge about creation. How could He not be the Creator of His servant's actions, when His omnipotence is complete and without deficiency, and governs the motions of His servants' bodies? The movements are homogeneous in nature, and His omnipotence governs them all intrinsically. What would keep it from governing some of them and not others, when they are homogeneous in nature? How could animals monopolize design? The spider, the bee, and all the animals produce such subtleties of design as to make intelligent men marvel; how could they achieve such design alone without the aid of the Lord of Lords, when they do not even know the details of what they do? Far be it! These creatures are weak and lowly, and all sovereignty and dominion belong to the Compeller (*al-Jabbār*) of earth and heaven.

The Second Foundation: Although God is the sole creator of humankind's deeds, they are still under each person's power by means of acquisition. God creates both the power and the deed, and creates the choice (*ikhtiyār*) and the chosen (*mukhtār*). The power is a quality of the servant and a creation of the Lord not acquired by Him. The deed is a creation of the Lord and a quality of the servant, being acquired by him. It has been created as the object of a power, which is a quality of his; the deed has a relation to another attribute called "power," and with respect to this relationship it is called "acquisition."

How could it be absolute compulsion, when [every man] necessarily grasps the difference between a predestined action and an involuntary shiver? And conversely, how could it be created by the servant when he does not have comprehensive knowledge of the details of all aspects of his acquired deed, nor their number?

Since both extremes have been shown to be false, there remains only the way of moderation in creed, namely that deeds are the object of God's power as creation, and the object of a person's power in another kind of relationship which is called acquisition. It is not necessary that the connection of power to its object be through creation alone, since God's power was connected to the world from all eternity, even before the world was created; and then when creation occurred, it was connected to it in another way. This shows that the relationship of power is not limited to the actual creation of its object.

The Third Foundation: Although the servant's deed is acquired by him, this does not mean it is not willed by God. Nothing happens in the worldly kingdom or the realm of spiritual domain, not even the blink of an eye, a fleeting thought, or a passing glance, except by God's ordainment (*qaḍāʾ*) and determination (*qadar*), and by His desire (*irāda*) and will (*mashīʾa*). From Him are good and evil, benefit and harm, Islam and disbelief, recognition and denial, victory and defeat, error and guidance, obedience and disobedience, idolatry and faith. Nothing can rebuff His ordainment, nor amend His judgment. God sends astray [thereby] whom He wills and guides whom He wills. *He is not questioned about what He does, but they will be questioned* [21:23].

Transmitted reports indicate this, such as the unanimous statement of the Muslim community that "What God wills comes to pass, and what He does not will does not"; as well as God's words *had God willed, He would have guided the people* [13:31], and *if We had willed, We could have given every soul its guidance* [32:13].

Rational proofs also indicate this, such as the observation that if God hated sins and crimes and did not desire them, and if they were naught but the will of the Devil (*iblīs*), may God curse him, who is an enemy of God, this would mean that the enemy's will would be more successful than the will of God Himself.

Upon my word, could any Muslim permit himself to reduce the sovereignty of the All-Compelling (*al-Jabbār*), the Sublime and Generous, to a level that even a village leader would not accept for himself? If the leader's enemy had more control over the village than the leader did, he would disdain his own leadership and resign his position. Now disobedience is the prevalent state for humankind, and according to the heretics this all takes place against the will of the Truth (*al-Ḥaqq*), which would reduce Him to the depths of weakness and incapacity—and the Lord of Lords, Most-Lofty and Great, is ever exalted above the claims of the unjust! In any case, the more apparent it becomes that the deeds of humankind are created by God, the more clearly it is established that they are also willed by Him.[3]

Abū l-Qasim ʿAbd al-Karim ibn Hawazin al-Qushayrī (986–1073)

Epistle on Sufism
Al-Risāla al-qushayriyya fī ʿilm al-taṣawwuf

God—may He be great and exalted—said: "[They] prefer others to themselves even though poverty be their portion [Q 59:9]." He [i.e., al-Qushayrī] explained: "They have preferred others to themselves, because they have freed themselves from that which they have given up and preferred." . . .

He [i.e., al-Qushayrī] said: "Freedom means that the servant of God does not allow himself to become enslaved by [other] creatures, nor is he subject to the power of originated things (*mukawwanāt*). The sign of its soundness is that his heart is no longer capable of distinguishing different things to such an extent that everything he sees looks equal to him." . . .

Know that the True Reality of freedom lies in the perfection of one's servanthood (*ʿubūdiyya*). When one's servanthood before God is sincere, one's freedom is cleansed from attachment to anything other than God. Those who fathom that the servant may occasionally remove the bridle of servanthood and turn his sight away from [God's] commands and prohibitions in the realm of the Divine Law (*dār al-taklīf*), while being of sound mind, [are deluded,] for this is nothing but forfeiting one's religion.

God—praise be to Him—said to His Prophet—may God bless and greet him: "Serve thy Lord until the Certitude comes to you [Q 15:99]." All commentators agree that [the Certitude] here means one's appointed time [of death] (*ajal*). When the folk (*qawm*) speak of freedom they imply that one is not bound by any mundane attachments or fleeting things of this world nor those of the Hereafter. This man devotes himself solely to God and is subject to neither the transitory things of this world, nor to the fulfillment of his desires, nor to the promptings of aspirations; he has no requests, no goals, no need, and no fortune. . . .

Sufi masters have discoursed profusely on freedom. Thus, al-Husayn b. Mansur [al-Hallaj] said: "Whoever aspires to freedom, let him devote himself constantly to the service [of God]!". . . Bishr al-Hafi said: "Whoever wants to taste the flavor of freedom and to find rest from servanthood must purify the secret (*sarīra*) between himself and God Most High."

Al-Husayn b. Mansur said: "When the servant has fulfilled all the stations of servanthood, he becomes free of the hardship of servanthood. He then [becomes capable of] acquiring servanthood without any effort or self-exertion on his part. This is the station of the prophets and the truthful (*siddīqūn*)." That is, he is being borne (*maḥmūl*) [toward his goal]; no difficulty attaches itself to his heart, even though [outwardly] he remains adorned by [the injunctions of] the Divine Law. . . .

Know that the greatest kind of freedom lies in serving the poor. I heard the master Abu ʿAli al-Daqqaq—may God have mercy on him—say: "God Most High revealed to [the prophet] David—peace be upon him: 'If you see anyone who seeks Me, be his servant!'" The Prophet—may God bless and greet him—said: "The master of a people is their servant." . . . I heard Ibrahim b. Adham say: "One who is noble and free withdraws from this world before he is removed from it [by God]." Ibrahim b. Adham also said: "Keep the company of none except one who is noble and free: he will listen, but will not speak [to others]." [4]

Khwāja ʿAbdallāh al-Anṣārī (1006–1088)

Intimate Conversations
Munājāt

O God,
When I look upon you,
I see myself a king among kings,
A crown on my head.
When I look upon myself,
I see myself among the humble,
Dust on my head.

. . .

O God,
I am aware of my own inability.
I bear witness to my own helplessness.

All will is yours. What can I will?
I want not eternal life from you,
I want not the good things of this life,
I want not my heart's desire or my soul's repose.
What I desire of you is whatever is your pleasure.

. . .

O God,
Since all is as you will,
what do you desire of this helpless weakling?

. . .

O God,
We rejoice in the grief that comes of loving you:
we flourish in the plunder of your tribulations.
O God,
There is no joy without pain from you;
there is no freedom except in bondage to you.

. . .

O God,
The agony of loving you is a calamity.
Calamity from the hand of the beloved is a boon,
and to complain of a boon is wrong.

. . .

O God,
Give us courage to place the ring of slavery to you in our ears,
give us courage to taste the bitterness of your wisdom.

. . .

Give me deliverance from the bonds of my self, O Lord.
Give me freedom from my evil self, O Lord.
I am stranger: Make me to know myself.
Give me knowledge of myself, O Lord.

. . .

O God,
If you would but once call me your slave,
My joy would surpass the Throne of Heaven.

. . .

O God,
You made Creation gratis.
You provided sustenance gratis.
Have mercy on us gratis:
You are God, not a merchant!

. . .
O God,
I come to your gate as a slave—
my lips full of repentance,
my tongue asking forgiveness.
If you will, ennoble me by your generosity.
If you will, demean me,
for I am ashamed and you are the Lord.
. . .
I have bound myself to you to the exclusion of all else.
If you would have me, I will worship you.
If you would have me not, I will worship myself.
Make me not despondent: Take my hand![5]

Notes

1. From Abu Hamid Muhammad al-Ghazālī, *The Ninety-Nine Beautiful Names of God | al-Maqṣad al-asnā fī sharḥ asmā' Allāh al-ḥusnā*, trans. David B. Burrell and Nazih Daher (Cambridge: Islamic Texts Society, 1992), 57–59, 131–32, 139.

2. From Abu Hamid Muhammad al-Ghazālī, *Faith in Divine Unity and Trust in Divine Providence | Kitāb al-Tawḥīd wa'l-Tawakkul*, trans. David B. Burrell (Louisville, KY: Fons Vitae, 2001), 40–41, 43–46.

3. From Abu Hamid Muhammad al-Ghazālī, *The Principles of the Creed | Kitāb Qawā'id al-'Aqā'id*, trans. Khalid Williams, ed. James Pavlin (Louisville, KY: Fons Vitae, 2016), 75–77.

4. Alexander D. Knysh, trans., *Al-Qushayri's Epistle on Sufism | Al-Risāla al-qushayriyya fī 'ilm al-taṣawwuf* (Doha, Qatar: Center for Muslim Contributions to Civilization, 2007), 229–32.

5. Victor Danner and Wheeler M. Thackston, trans., *The Book of Wisdom* by Ibn 'Ata'llah and *Intimate Conversations* by Kwaja Abdullah Ansari (New York: Paulist Press, 1978), 184, 189, 193, 195, 196, 205, 206, 208, 211, 212. Used by permission.

Modern Muslim Elucidations and Contentions on Freedom

An Introduction to Texts for Dialogue

Martin Nguyen

It is impossible to capture the true range of thought that has emerged in the modern Muslim world with respect to Islamic conceptions of freedom. The conceptual horizons that have developed across the world and centuries are staggeringly broad and diverse. Yet the Building Bridges Seminar was determined to include examples from the modern era among the texts on freedom to be studied during its 2019 gathering, confident that—although the selection would provide only a small window into that panoply—it would be a window nonetheless capable of revealing some of the major threads and themes that have emerged from and continue to recur in contemporary Muslim communities. Hence, ten pieces of modern Islamic thought on freedom were read closely by the 2019 Building Bridges Seminar and compose this volume's chapter titled "Islamic Thought in the Modern Period: Texts for Dialogue about Freedom." Eight of these texts were authored individually by notable Muslim thinkers. Four of these focus on freedom and human nature, while the other four turn to human liberation. The remaining two texts are collective declarations of consensus on particular aspects of religious freedom—statements jointly made by a significant cohort of Muslim thought and policy leaders.

All ten excerpts come from texts that continue to speak to Muslim audiences today. It is important to keep in mind, however, that they were all originally written—sometimes spoken—by thinkers immersed in the particularities of their respective historical and social circumstances. Therefore, this chapter's objective is to contextualize these passages in such a way that can both widen and deepen the reader's theological engagement with them, privileging voices that seem both historically influential and broadly representative of the main currents. In what follows, I introduce the authors of these items in chronological order within each grouping, endeavoring to share as concisely as possible the life and legacy of each. I then describe the specific work that has been excerpted, highlighting particular themes or trajectories of thought that underlie and inform the passage under study.

Freedom and Human Nature in Islam

We begin with four authors who interrogate the concept of freedom as an aspect of human nature situated within a larger cosmological order.

Muhammad Iqbal (d. 1938)

The South Asian philosopher and poet Muhammad Iqbal was born in 1877 in Sialkot to a Kashmiri family. Living under British rule, Iqbal studied philosophy, law, and English literature. He was also a prolific and celebrated poet in Urdu and Persian. Eventually he traveled abroad to Germany to earn his doctorate—and to England as well. In 1922 he was knighted by King George V. During his lifetime, he famously argued for the creation of a Muslim state in northwest India. While he did not live to see the end of British rule in India or the county's subsequent partition, he is widely regarded as a founding figure of modern-day Pakistan.

The Seminar studied a passage from Iqbal's English-language philosophical work, *The Reconstruction of Religious Thought in Islam*, which might be his best-known work in the Euro-American academy. Six of its seven chapters were originally delivered as lectures in Madras, Hyderabad, and Aligarh in 1930. The seventh chapter was added upon the book's publication in 1934. In the introduction to book, Iqbal discloses the rationale for the work: "In these Lectures . . . I have tried to meet, even though partially, this urgent demand by attempting to reconstruct Muslim religious philosophy with due regard to the philosophical traditions of Islam and the more recent developments in the various domains of human knowledge."[1] Faced with mounting intellectual challenges precipitated by British colonial rule, Iqbal's work of reconstruction can be understood as an endeavor to place the intellectual traditions of Islam in critical conversation with modernity and Western philosophy.

We have chosen a passage in which Iqbal speaks at length of the ego—the term he uses to translate the Persian term *khudi* (the concept of self). He makes two significant points. First, he argues that freedom is a necessary aspect of human existence because freedom is instrumental in how we navigate the mental world that the human ego constructs. Second, he argues that this idea is precisely in line with the Qur'anic worldview. By divine design, humans have the ability to freely choose truth from falsehood and good from evil. Moreover, the rituals of the faith—prayer, in this case—are also designed to foster and sustain that freedom. More than an abstract concept, freedom for Iqbal is also an embodied practice within Islam.

Ali Shariati (d. 1977)

The Iranian sociologist and revolutionary intellectual Ali Shariati was born in 1933 in Mazinan village in northeastern Iran. His family had long fostered a line of Shiʿa religious scholars. Shariati, for his part, studied at the Teacher's Training College in Mashhad and became a high school teacher. In 1955 he received his bachelor's degree from the University of Mashhad. Living under the regime of the US-backed shah of Iran, Shariati became part of Mohammad Mosaddegh's political organization, the National Front of Iran. After the American-orchestrated coup that deposed Mosaddegh, Shariati joined the underground National Resistance Movement.

A few years later, Shariati departed for France to pursue his doctorate in sociology at the Sorbonne. His five years of graduate study in France coincided with the Algerian revolution across the Mediterranean. Connecting this North African struggle for independence with the struggle against the shah's regime back home, Shariati began working with the Algerian National Liberation Front in 1959 where he came to be deeply influenced by the work of the psychiatrist and revolutionary philosopher from Martinique, Frantz Fanon (d. 1961). Shariati would later translate several of Fanon's works into Persian, the most famous of which being *The Wretched of the Earth*.[2] When Shariati returned to Iran in 1964, he was arrested for a short time for activities abroad that had been perceived as subversive at home.

Shariati would go on to teach at the University of Mashhad before moving to Tehran, where he became a popular speaker critical of the shah and Western encroachment. Joining together religion and protest in his speeches, he gathered a significant following especially when he was temporarily granted a platform at the Hosseiniyeh Ershad religious center. His revolutionary rhetoric, however, landed him in jail, where he was placed in solitary confinement until his release in 1975. In 1977 he traveled to England, where he died only a few weeks after his arrival. His supporters claimed his death occurred under mysterious circumstances; several speculated that the shah's regime was behind his death.

While not formally a religious scholar, Shariati's lectures and writings have been likened to a form of liberation theology grounded in the religious narratives of the Imami Shiʿa tradition. In Shariati's thinking, religion could serve as an engine for revolution, especially when unhindered by the burdensome traditions of religious clericalism. One popular opus titled *Man and Islam* is a collection of seven lectures that he had delivered at various universities in Iran. Our selection comes from the first chapter, where Shariati articulates a theological anthropology based on the role of vicegerency that human beings have over creation. According to his English translator, Fatollah Marjani, Shariati maintains that the human being is "a responsible being who stands between the two poles of Satan and God [who] is free to choose either of these two directions" because of her free will.[3]

In our excerpt, Shariati focuses on the concept of will, with the freedom of that will being implicit in his discussion. In his view, the possession of free will is a unique characteristic of humankind. The human being's ability to choose her course of action is what makes her human, even if that course of action goes against her best interests or nature. Shariati couples this idea with vicegerency—namely, that God has placed human beings as His trustees on Earth over His creation and that these two things together, human will and the responsibility of God's trusteeship, disclose the equality of human beings to one another regardless of race or gender and the superiority of human beings over angels and other creatures.

Murtaza Mutahhari (d. 1979)

One of seven children, Murtaza Mutahhari was born in Fariman, Iran, in 1919 into a line of religious clerics. His training took place primarily in Qom, where he had the opportunity to study ethics, spirituality, and, later, jurisprudence under Ruhollah Khomeini (d. 1989).[4] He also studied jurisprudence, legal methodology, and Islamic philosophy with the noted Iranian cleric and philosopher Muḥammad Husayn al-Tabataba'i (d. 1981).

In the years leading up to the Iranian Revolution in 1979, Mutahhari became an important religious thinker serving as a vocal activist and organizer in opposition to the shah. In 1965, with several others, he cofounded Mu'assasih-yi Taḥqiqāti va Ta'limati-yi Ḥusayniyih-I Irshad (Hosseiniyeh Ershad Institute for Research and Education). The institute was a "modern cultural complex" for religious activism, organizing, and education.[5] It was during his early involvement with the institute that he invited Ali Shariati to speak there, despite the latter's persistent critique of religious clerics.[6] While both acknowledged the need for clerical reform, Mutahhari believed that such change should originate from among the religious clerics themselves. Rising tensions over the matter eventually led to Mutahhari's departure from the institute and a general disenchantment with nonclerical intellectuals. Shortly after the revolution, Mutahhari was assassinated on May 1, 1979, by Forqan, an anticlerical radical Islamist group.

Our collection includes an excerpt from Mutahhari's *Jihād: The Holy War of Islam and Its Legitimacy in the Qur'an*, which he wrote between 1970 and 1971.[7] As Mutahhari's biographer Mahmood Davari explains, "during this period, he was seriously considering practical methods for political action."[8] Specifically, he was writing against secular and Marxist ideologies believing it "necessary to revitalize Islamic epic terms like *jihād* and *shahādat*: [stating] 'Of course it requires an intellectual, verbal . . . and practical *jihād*.'"[9] Mutahhari, like Iqbal and Shariati, is concerned with unpacking the meaning of human freedom. In the passage we have chosen, he distinguishes between "freedom of thought" and "freedom of belief," emphasizing the critical need to examine the foundations of one's belief. In Mutahhari's view, the latter is a prerequisite for the former. True freedom of thought cannot be exercised if one's beliefs are rooted in blind imitation and uncritical tradition.

Mahmoud Mohammed Taha (d. 1985)

The Sudanese Muslim reformer Mahmoud Mohammed Taha was born in either 1909 or 1911 in a small town along the Blue Nile in Sudan.[10] He studied engineering early on and worked for a time for Sudan Railways. He was active in the nationalist struggle for independence, founding the Republican Brotherhood, which worked to resist colonial rule. As a result of his efforts, Taha found himself in and out of prison. His student Abdullahi Ahmed An-Naim reports, "It was during this second term of imprisonment, and the subsequent period of self-imposed religious seclusion (*khalwah*) in his home town of Rufa'h, that Ustadh Mahmoud undertook the rigorous program of prayer, fasting, and meditation that led to his insights into the meaning of the Qur'an and the role of Islamic law. These he subsequently articulated as the 'second message' of Islam."[11] This pivotal period of seclusion ended in October of 1951.

As An-Naim summarizes, Taha's "vision of the future of Islam was God-given and not the result of purely rational secular thinking."[12] He attempted to build a utopian community modeled around his understanding of Islam.[13] Taha's opposition to the regime of President Jaafar Nimeiry (d. 2009) late in his life led to his arrest. Charged with apostasy, based on the state's interpretation of his reformist religious views, Taha was executed on January 18, 1985.

Taha's major work, *The Second Message of Islam*, was translated from its original Arabic by his student Abdullahi Ahmed An-Naim. The translation of the text began in 1980 at Taha's request, although the effort was not completed and published until after Taha's death.[14] When looking at the period of revelation, traditionally demarcated as the Meccan and Medinan periods, Taha understands the Meccan revelations as "where the Prophet preached equality and individual responsibility between all men and women without distinction on grounds of race, sex, or social origin."[15] In other words, the universal and prevailing message of Islam lies with the Meccan period, whereas the later Medinan period represents modifications and abrogations made necessary by historical circumstance—thus suitable at that time but not representing the original, universal truth embodied in the Meccan revelations. The Medinan revelations, then, represent the particular.

In the excerpt taken from *The Second Message of Islam*, Taha speaks of the concept of freedom explicitly. He discusses it as having primarily to do with responsibility and duty rather than entitlement and right. He speaks of degrees of freedom and the different needs and mechanisms that a community or society may need to ensure freedom. For Taha, the greater form of freedom is the freedom that is anchored to a righteous sense of communal responsibility, one that is implicitly religious rather than a freedom rooted in the whims of the individual.

Islam and Human Liberation

While our first four authors discussed freedom in relation to human nature, we now turn to four authors who understand freedom as a religious resource or even force for liberation within society.

Muhammad ʿAbduh (d. 1905)

Muhammad ʿAbduh was born in the middle of the nineteenth century into a family of Egyptian notables from Lower Egypt. He moved to Cairo for his studies, eventually spending eight years at al-Azhar University. In 1868, prior to his time at this august religious institute, he met and became a devoted student of the Muslim revivalist thinker Jamal al-Din al-Afghani (d. 1897), who strongly advocated and articulated a form of pan-Islamism in the reaction to European colonialism. During a period of exile later in his life, ʿAbduh would travel to Lebanon, England, and France. While residing in the last of these countries, he would collaborate closely with al-Afghani.[16] ʿAbduh returned to Egypt in 1888, and in 1899 he was appointed grand mufti of Egypt, a position he would hold until his death in 1905 in Alexandria.

ʿAbduh was a deeply influential Muslim thinker in his own right. He articulated a sharp critique of *taqlid* (blind imitation), which he understood as an overreliance on the historic textual tradition. He argued instead that persons ought to employ critically and robustly their God-given intellects since Islam, in his estimation, was a thoroughly rational religion, if not the most rational of them. Indeed, in his view, equal rights could be both properly understood and provided to humankind through a proper understanding and implementation of Islam.

While ʿAbduh's endeavors in Qurʾanic commentary arguably represents his most well-known work, the text studied by the Building Bridges Seminar comes from one of his earliest publications, *Risalat al-Tawhid* (Epistle on Monotheism), which has been translated into English as *The Theology of Unity*.[17] During his exile in Beirut, ʿAbduh developed the work as a series of lectures to be delivered at the Madrasat al-Sulṭaniyya.[18] In 1897 these lectures were compiled and published in book form, which ʿAbduh revised on several occasions during his lifetime.

Our focus is on a passage from chapter 13, "The Islamic Religion, or Islam." In it ʿAbduh examines the religion of Islam as a liberating force in the history of humankind. He focuses on the epistemological shift that transpires from paganism to Islam, a common trope in the religious literature. The Islam he is outlining here, however, is not the historical instantiation that occurs during the life of the Prophet Muhammad. Rather, ʿAbduh is rooting Islam genealogically in the paradigmatic life of the prophet Abraham, the first of the Muslims (Q. 6:163). Moreover, ʿAbduh offers the reader insight into precisely from what humanity is being freed—namely, the delusions and divisions associated with false belief and idolatry. His conception of idolatry, like his conception of Islam, is broader and more dynamic than conventionally understood. For ʿAbduh, idolatry is not necessarily reserved only for objects of worship or imagined divinities other than God. It also encompasses misplaced faith in sovereigns and other human possessors of earthly power. In ʿAbduh's view, divine unity or *tawhid* (monotheism)—by which he means singular service to God—is the force that frees humankind.

Sayyid Qutb (d. 1966)

Sayyid Qutb was born in 1906 in a village in Asyut province in Upper Egypt. In 1929 he moved to Cairo for his studies. Formally, he became an educator and would eventually work for the country's Ministry of Education.[19] Complementing this line of work, however, was his deep engagement with literature, which had begun at an early age. Qutb eventually developed into a recognized author and literary critic and composed two early works that analyzed the literary dimensions of the Qurʾan.[20] He also played an important role in advancing the early career of the Egyptian Nobel Laureate Naguib Mahfouz (d. 2006).

Beginning in 1948 Qutb's thinking shifted and he grew increasingly attracted to the social and political program of the Muslim Brotherhood. By this time the Muslim Brotherhood, driven by a pan-Islamist vision, had developed a reputation for its opposition to British rule and then the Egyptian monarchy that followed it. Qutb, in a demonstration of his increasing affinity for the organization, composed *al-'Adala al-ijtima'iyya fi al-Islam* (Social justice in Islam) in 1948. Later that same year he would depart for the United States to undertake a study of the country's different systems of education.[21] During his two-year visit, Qutb became highly critical of the racism, materialism, and individualism (among other perceived deficiencies) that he witnessed in American society. As a result, his disillusionment with the West and its philosophical ideals deepened further.

In 1952, after returning to Egypt, Qutb joined the Muslim Brotherhood and quickly became one of its most outspoken voices. When President Gamal Abdel Nasser (d. 1970) came to power that same year, the Muslim Brotherhood had a falling out with the new Arab nationalist regime. In 1954 Qutb was arrested and imprisoned for several years, enduring torture and witnessing the execution of his fellow Muslim Brotherhood members. It was during Qutb's imprisonment that he composed *Ma'alim fi al-tariq*—or, *Milestones*, which was published after he was released from jail in 1964. As noted by William Shepard, in *Milestones,* Qutb "openly declared that the existing order in all countries, including so-called 'Muslim' ones, was anti-Islamic, and called on Islamic activists to prepare themselves to replace the present Jahili (i.e., barbaric and ignorant) order."[22] After an eight-month period of respite, Qutb was imprisoned again. He would remain so until his execution in 1966.

The influence of *Milestones* has been discussed by numerous scholars. This book articulates a Manichaean view of the world, in which the term *Jahiliyya,* which is usually understood as the moral, cultural, and religious "ignorance" of the Arabs prior to the historic advent of Islam, is radically reinterpreted to encompass all that is deemed un-Islamic in contemporary societies, even in ostensibly "Muslim" ones. Shepard identifies a clear theme of "theocentrism" building in Qutb's works, such that "God alone, by virtue of His being God and the only God, has ultimate authority, or sovereignty, over all human affairs."[23] While this theme is strongly present in Qutb, it is far from original to him. In fact, Qutb drew heavily on the thought of one of the other Muslim authors included here, the Pakistani religious thinker Abul Al'a Maududi (d. 1979), whose works began to appear in Arabic in the 1950s and to whom Qutb refers in his own writings.[24]

Furthermore, like Muhammad 'Abduh, Qutb envisions Islam as a defining force for human liberation, if not *the* defining force. In fact, when set in comparison to 'Abduh, Qutb's critique is both more incisive and more explicit in its articulation. His words overtly indict the modern society and world in which he abides, and his rhetoric is framed as one of revolt and immediate action. Yet, as he concludes in the passage selected for study by the 2019 Building Bridges Seminar, his message is not for Arabs alone; rather, it is for all human societies that face a similar ultimatum of choosing between persons of authority and God.

Abul Al'a Maududi (d. 1979)

Born in 1903 in British-ruled India, Maududi received religious training in his early life but eventually turned to journalism. It was through his journalistic writing that he began to explore and refine his political thinking. In 1941 he founded the Islamist political movement Jamaʿat-i-Islami with a vision of establishing a Muslim state guided by Islamic principles. These principles were understood to be grounded on a constitution founded on the Qur'an and the Sunna (the tradition of the Prophet Muhammad). When Maududi moved to Muslim-majority Pakistan after the partition of India in 1947, he became increasingly politically active. While his efforts were focused first and foremost in South Asia, his writings spread well beyond the subcontinent.[25]

The 2019 Building Bridges Seminar studied a passage from Maududi's *Political Theory of Islam*, which was in circulation by 1960. While this passage does not explicitly address freedom, it does discuss its conceptual opposite: servanthood or enslavement. The first part of the text is entirely concerned with defining the parameters of the human–God relationship. Building on the Qur'anic discourse, the human being is described as fundamentally a servant or slave of God. Servanthood, however, is not a relationship of subjugation or oppression but one of potential fulfillment. In the second part of the text, Maududi pivots to examine the cause of evil, which again lies with servanthood or enslavement—but as it manifests between human beings. An intentional contrast is presented. Goodness is tied to servanthood to God, while evil emerges out of servanthood in the human realm. Furthermore, Maududi translates the abstract into the concrete by looking at different forms of problematic human-to-human servanthood in the modern world. Where freedom is mentioned, Maududi is careful to connect it to obedience to God.

Farid Esack (b. 1959)

Born in 1959 in Cape Town, South Africa, Farid Esack is a scholar and activist who spent his early years living under and in opposition to the apartheid regime. As a young boy he joined the Tablighi Jamaat, eventually traveling to Pakistan for eight years to complete the Dars-i-Nizami course of traditional religious education. He returned to South Africa in 1982 and became actively involved in organizing Muslims to take part in the anti-apartheid movement.

In 1990 Esack began his pursuit of advanced doctoral work in western Europe, studying theology and then biblical hermeneutics in England and Germany, respectively. After the end of apartheid, President Nelson Mandela appointed Esack as a commissioner of gender equality. Since then, Esack has also become an advocate of Positive Muslims, a group seeking to support HIV-positive Muslims across the continent. Presently, he also heads the Boycott, Divest and Sanctions (BDS) movement in South Africa, which pursues an array of modes of boycott in order to compel Israel to comply with international legal obligations.[26]

Esack's *Qur᾽ān, Liberation & Pluralism: An Islamic Perspective of Interreligious Solidarity against Oppression,* published in 1996, relates the interpretive Qur᾽anic framework that he developed while working alongside various religious communities during his involvement with the antiapartheid movement. The passage excerpted by the 2019 Building Bridges Seminar is useful when examining the social realities of the present because Esack advocates an engaged interpretation of the Qur᾽anic notion of the oppressed. Working in the context of apartheid South Africa, he articulates, in my opinion, the most explicit theology of liberation of the writers we are surveying here. Esack is not addressing the Muslim community alone when he imagines the "oppressed." Through the application of his "Qur᾽anic hermeneutic of pluralism," he is also including a broader swath of society that is explicitly inclusive of the religious other.

Collective Statements concerning Freedom and Islam

In addition to passages from the works of eight influential twentieth-century Muslim authors, our examples of modern Islamic thinking on freedom include two public statements issued collectively by a significant segment of Muslim thought and policy leaders. These documents may be viewed as communal efforts at reframing the discourse on freedom. Yet this reframing is not an entirely internal endeavor. They also represent, simultaneously, a particular reactionary mode of engagement with the liberal West and the structures of power that it wields and possesses.

Cairo Declaration on Human Rights in Islam (August 5, 1990)

The Cairo Declaration was formulated by the member nations of the Organization of Islamic Cooperation (OIC) during its Conference of Foreign Ministers on August 5, 1990. The OIC today consists of fifty-seven member states, not all of which are Muslim-majority countries. For instance, several

West African nations with significant Muslim minority populations are included in the organization. Additionally, all the member of the OIC, with the exception of Palestine, are members of the United Nations.

The OIC argues, however, that the Cairo Declaration is not a rejoinder but a complement to the UN document. As a result, the Cairo Declaration employs universalistic language in order to address Islamic particularities. Specifically, the declaration defines human rights within the bounds of the sharia.

In excerpting this lengthy pronouncement, we have included the preamble material of the declaration so that the premises of the document are both accessible and explicit. Following this are Articles 1, 11, 24, and 25, which were selected because they contain language in which the universal and particulars regarding freedom are made to stand side by side.

Marrakesh Declaration Executive Summary (January 27, 2016)

The Marrakesh Declaration on the Rights of Religious Minorities in Predominantly Muslim Majority Communities was issued on January 27, 2016, in defense of the rights and freedoms of religious minorities in predominantly Muslim countries. The document emerged from a conference co-organized by King Mohammed VI of Morocco and the Ministry of Endowments and Islamic Affairs and the Forum for Promoting Peace in Muslim Societies based in the United Arab Emirates. The impetus for the document is rooted in the persecution of Christians and Yazidis by the Islamic State in Iraq and Syria, which began around 2014. The Marrakesh Declaration, the drafting of which was led primarily by Shaykh Abdallah Bin Bayyah, the president of the Forum for Promoting Peace, was cosigned by over 250 religious scholars and leaders from more than 120 countries.

Of interest in this text is not only the parties addressed (religious scholars, religious educational institutions, politicians and policymakers, culture producers, and religious groups and organizations in general) and the policies recommended for each of them but also the dynamics of power that compelled such a declaration to come into being in the first place. As you read the Executive Summary, consider this question: What sort of freedom is being imagined, expressed, and ensured in such a document?

Conclusion

Such is the array of texts gathered for the 2019 Building Bridges Seminar and reproduced here in the chapter to follow. These modern Muslim elucidations of and contentions about the concept of freedom model a multitude of avenues of inquiry. Nonetheless, a notable theme binds these modern Muslim texts together: they all emerge from the crucible created by disparities in power. These disparities may differ in form—nationalist authoritarianism, European imperialism, Western encroachment and colonialism, apartheid—but a climate of worldly disempowerment informs to a significant degree the context of each text, or so I would argue. An engagement with modern Muslim conceptions of freedom, then, should not overlook the reasons for the emergence of freedom as a concept in need of careful religious elucidation or incisive contention.

Notes

1. Muhammad Iqbal, *The Reconstruction of Religious Thought in Islam*, ed. M. Saeed Sheikh (Stanford, CA: Stanford University Press, 2012), xlv.

2. Ali Shariati, *Man and Islam*, trans. Fatollah Marjani (Houston: Free Islamic Literature, 1981), x.

3. Shariati, xix.

4. Mahmood T. Davari, *The Political Thought of Ayatullah Murtaża Muṭahhari: An Iranian Theoretician of the Islamic State* (London: RoutledgeCurzon, 2005), 15.

5. Davari, 41–42.

6. Davari, 43.

7. Davari, 66.

8. Davari, 66.

9. Davari, 66.

10. Mahmoud Mohamed Taha, *The Second Message of Islam*, trans. Abdullahi Ahmed An-Na'im (Syracuse, NY: Syracuse University Press, 1987), 2.

11. Taha, 4.

12. Taha, 4.

13. Taha, 7.

14. Taha, 1.

15. Taha, 21.

16. He was expelled by the British for his support of the 'Urabi revolt that took place in 1879. Muhammad 'Abduh, *The Theology of Unity (Risālat al-Tauḥīd)*, trans. Isḥāq Musa'ad and Kenneth Cragg (Kuala Lumpur: Islamic Book Trust, 2004), 10.

17. While 'Abduh began the *Tafsir al-manar*, his disciple Rashid Rida (d. 1935) is largely responsible for completing the Qur'an commentary.

18. 'Abduh, *Theology of Unity*, 27.

19. William E. Shepard, *Sayyid Qutb and Islamic Activism: A Translation and Critical Analysis of Social Justice in Islam* (Leiden: Brill, 1996), xiv–xv.

20. Among these works are *al-Taswir al-fanni fi al-Qur'an* (Artistic Portrayals in the Qur'an) published in 1944–45 and *Mashahid al-Qiyama fi al-Qur'an* (Testimonies to the Resurrection in the Qur'an). Shepard, *Sayyid Qutb and Islamic Activism*, xv–xvi.

21. Shepard, xvi.

22. Shepard, xvii.

23. Shepard, xxvi.

24. Shepard, xxv; and Leonard Binder, *Islamic Liberalism: A Critique of Development Ideologies* (Chicago: University of Chicago Press, 1988), 174.

25. According to Leonard Binder in his treatment of Sayyid Qutb, "there is little doubt Qutb served as a transmitter of the ideas of Mawdudi." Binder, *Islamic Liberalism*, 174.

26. See the BDS website, https://bdsmovement.net/.

Islamic Thought in the Modern Period

Selections for Dialogue

This chapter presents excerpts from ten sources of modern Islamic thought (nine from the twentieth century, one from late in the nineteenth century).

Freedom and Human Nature in Islam

The following four readings are by four Muslim authors who interrogate the concept of freedom as an aspect of human nature situated within a larger cosmological order.

Muhammad Iqbal (1877–1938)

The Reconstruction of Religious Thought in Islam

The truth is that the causal chain wherein we try to find a place for the ego is itself an artificial construction of the ego for its own purposes. The ego is called upon to live in a complex environment, and he cannot maintain his life in it without reducing it to a system which would give him some kind of assurance as to the behaviour of things around him. The view of his environment as a system of cause and effect is thus an indispensable instrument of the ego, and not a final expression of the nature of Reality. Indeed in interpreting Nature in this way the ego understands and masters its environment, and thereby acquires and amplifies its freedom.

Thus the element of guidance and directive control in the ego's activity clearly shows that the ego is a free personal causality. He shares in the life and freedom of the Ultimate Ego who, by permitting the emergence of a finite ego, capable of private initiative, has limited this freedom of His own free will. This freedom of conscious behaviour follows from the view of ego-activity which the Qur'an takes. There are verses which are unmistakably clear on this point:

> *And say: The truth is from your Lord: Let him, then, who will, believe; and let him who will, be an unbeliever. (18: 29)*

> *If ye do well to your own behoof will ye do well; and if ye do evil against yourselves will ye do it. (17: 7)*

Islam recognizes a very important fact of human psychology, i.e., the rise and fall of the power to act freely, and is anxious to retain the power to act freely as a constant and undiminished factor in the life of the ego. The timing of the daily prayer which, according to the Qur'an, restores "self-possession" to the ego by bringing it into closer touch with the ultimate source of life and freedom, is intended to save the ego from the mechanizing effects of sleep and business. Prayer in Islam is the ego's escape from mechanism to freedom.[1]

Ali Shariati (1933–1977)

Man & Islam

The only superiority that man has over all other beings in the universe is his will. He is the only being that can act contrary to his nature, while no animal or plant is capable of doing so. It is impossible to find an animal which can fast for two days. And no plant has ever committed suicide due to grief or has done a great service. Man is the only one who rebels against his physical, spiritual, and material needs, and turns his back against goodness and virtue. Further, he is free to behave irrationally, to be bad or good, to be mudlike or Divine. The point is that possession of "will" is the greatest characteristic of man and it throws light upon the kinship between man and God.

Is it not true that God breathed His spirit into man and appointed him as His trustee? Then man is a vicegerent and "relative" of God on earth and the spirit of both quench their thirst from the same fountain of virtue-possession of will. God, the only being in the universe who possesses an absolute will and can do whatever He wishes, even to work contrary to the laws of nature, breathed His spirit in man. And so, man is capable of working like God (not on par with Him, only resembling God), or acting against the physiological laws of his own nature. Therefore, what can be inferred from man's nature and the philosophy of creation are as follows:

> Not only are all men equal, they are brothers. The disparity between equality and brotherhood is quite obvious; equality is a legal term while

brotherhood is an announcement of the identical nature of all men who have, despite their colors, emerged from a single source.

Contrary to all the past philosophies, male and female are of the same nature, and were created simultaneously by God. They are of the same race, they are brothers and sisters.

The superiority of man over angels and the whole universe is scientific, due to the fact that man has learned the names. And angels, despite their superiority in race and nature, bowed down to Adam.

Above all, man is located between mud and providence, he is free to choose either as his will dictates. Possession of will and freedom creates responsibility. And so, from the Islamic point of view, man is the only creature who is responsible not only for his own fate but also has a mission to fulfill the Divine Purpose in the world. Thus, he is a trustee in the universe.[2]

Murtaza Mutahhari (1919–1979)

Jihad: The Holy War of Islam and Its Legitimacy in the Quran

Another point which should be stressed here is that there exists a difference between "freedom of thought" and "freedom of belief." Human beings are endowed with the faculty of thought which enables them to make decisions on the basis of thought, logic and reason. But belief entails a strong tie to the object of belief. And by the way, numerous are the beliefs that are not based on thought, but are sheer imitation, a result of upbringing and habits, and which even molest human freedom. What we say, looking at things from the point of view of freedom, is that what mankind must have, is freedom of thought. Yet there are some beliefs which are not in the least rooted in thought; they have their root in the mere dormancy and stagnation of the spirit, handed down from generation to generation; they are the essence of bondage, so that war fought for the sake of eliminating such beliefs is war fought for the freedom of humanity, not war fought against it. If a man prays for his needs to a self-made idol, then, in the words of the Quran, that man is lower than an animal. This means that the act of this man is not based at all on thought. A little bit of thinking would not allow him to engage in such an act. What he does is merely a reflection of the stagnation and dormancy which have appeared in his heart and in his soul, and which are rooted in blind imitation. This person must be forcibly freed from the internal chains which shackle him, to enable him to think. So, those who recommend the freedom of imitation and apparent freedoms which in fact enchain the souls such as the freedom of belief are in error. What we advocate, in accordance to the verse "la ikrāha fī-l-dīn,"[3] is the freedom of thought. . . .

That religion must not be imposed on the individual and that people must be free in their choice of religion is one thing. That belief, however, in the current phraseology, must be free, is quite another. In other words, whereas freedom of thought and choice is one thing, freedom of belief is quite another. Many beliefs have "thought" for a foundation, meaning that many beliefs have been discerned and found to be true and have been freely chosen. The alignment and commitment of an individual's heart to his beliefs in many cases is built on discernment and selection, but are all human beliefs built on thought, discernment and selection? Or are the majority of mankind's beliefs no more than alignments and commitments of the human soul that have not the slightest relationship to thought at all, that have a mere sentimental basis? An example the Quran cites on the subject of imitation by one generation of the previous generation is: "Verily we found our fathers on their creed and verily we are followers of their footsteps" (43:23). The Quran puts great stress on this point, and the same applies to a belief that is formed by the imitation of the patricians of society. In such places, the phrase freedom of belief is completely without meaning, for freedom means the absence of obstacles to the activities of an active and advancing force, whereas this type of belief is a kind of constriction and stagnation.

Freedom in constriction is equal to the freedom of a prisoner condemned to eternal imprisonment, or of a man chained in heavy chains, and the only difference is that he who is physically enchained senses his condition, while he whose spirit is in chains is unaware of it. This is what we mean when we say that freedom of belief based on imitation and environmental influences, rather than on freedom of thought, is totally meaningless.[4]

Mahmoud Mohamed Taha (1909–1985)

The Second Message of Islam

Thus, freedom in Islam is absolute: every individual has the right to achieve it, regardless of religion or race. But it is a right which corresponds to a duty and must be earned through proper use, namely, discretion in the exercise of freedom. Freedom does not become limited except when the free person is unable to properly discharge his [or her] duty, whereby he [or she] must forfeit his [or her] freedom to the extent of his [or her] failure. In such a situation. freedom is limited through laws that are consistent with the constitution, that is to say, laws that are capable of reconciling the needs of the community for total social justice with the needs of the individual for absolute individual freedom. These laws neither sacrifice the individual for the sake of the community, nor sacrifice the community for the sake of the individual, but maintain the proper balance between the two. When implemented, such laws achieve; in one system and at every level of their application, the interest of the individual and the interest of the community. . . .

Thus it is clear that freedom in Islam is of two levels: the level of freedom limited by laws consistent with the constitution, as explained above, and the level of absolute freedom. A free person at the first level is one who thinks as he wishes, speaks in accordance with his thinking, and acts in accordance with his speech, on condition that his exercise of freedom of speech, or action, does not interfere with the freedom of others. If he so interferes, then his freedom is justly limited by laws which are consistent with the constitution.

A free person at the second level is one who thinks as he wishes, speaks what he thinks, and acts in accordance with what he says, and yet the consequences of his exercise of all these freedoms is only goodness, blessings, and kindness to all people. The lowest degree of the first level is fairness, while the lowest degree of the second level is forgiveness.[5]

Islam and Human Liberation

In this section, we have four works from the late-nineteenth or twentieth century by Muslim authors who discern freedom as a religious source or force for liberation within society.

Muhammad ʿAbduh (1849–1905)

"The Islamic Religion, or Islam"
The Theology of Unity
Risalat al-Tawhid

Thus Islam uprooted paganism and all kindred attitudes, whatever the distinctions within them of form and image, word and term—differences which do not obscure an identity in fact. And in consequence, the minds of men were purged of the corrupting fantasies inseparable from that vain creed. Their souls were likewise liberated from the evil forces belonging with their delusions and found release from the divisions that raged about objects of worship. Thus the whole level of humanity was lifted: human values responded to the new sense of human dignity implicit in worshipping none but the one creator of heaven and earth, the master of all men. Men everywhere could now say with Abraham—indeed were duty bound to say: "I turn may face to Him who created the heavens and the earth, as a true worshipper (*ḥanīf*): I am not one of those who take other gods for God and profess as the Prophet commanded. My prayer, my devotion, my life and my death are God's, the Lord of the worlds. He has none like unto Him. So am I commanded: I am the first of the Muslims" (Surah 6.163).

So man came blessedly to see himself free and honourable: his will was freed from the bonds that tied him to the will of others, whether of fellow men supposedly also an offshoot of the Divine, or of rulers and masters, or fictitious entities to which imagination attributed powers of will, and stones, trees and stars and the like. So man's initiative was released from the captivity to mediators, intercessors, divines, initiates, and all who claimed to be masters of "hidden" cults and pretended to authority over the relations men have with God through their works. These "mediators" set themselves up as disposers of salvation with the power of damnation and bliss. In sum, man's spirit found freedom from the slavery of deceivers and charlatans.

By the doctrine of Divine unity Man came to serve God's purpose only. He was no longer in bondage to another. He now had the right of one free man among free men; there were no inequalities of high and low, in respect of these rights. There was no "inferior" and "superior." The only distinction between men was in their deeds: the only pre-eminence lay in intelligence and breadth of knowledge. The only drawing near to God was by the path of utter purity of mind, with sincerity and integrity of deed. Men thereby could possess their possessions, saving only the obligations to the poor and needy and the claims of public good, and unharassed by worthless people who laid claim to them, not out of any work or service they did but from sheer position or status.[6]

Sayyid Qutb (1906–1966)

Milestones

Ma 'alim fi al-Tariq

The true religion is in fact a universal declaration of man's freedom from the servitude to other men and to his own desires, which, too, are a form of human servitude. This declaration is, in fact, a natural corollary to the declaration that sovereignty rests with God alone and that He is the Lord and Cherisher of the entire universe. This means that religion is an all-embracing and total revolution against the sovereignty of man in all its types, shapes, systems, and states, and completely revolts against every system in which authority may be in the hands of man in any form or in other words where he may have usurped sovereignty under any shape. Any system of governance in which the final decision is referred to human beings and they happen to be the source of all authority, in fact defies them by designating "other than God," as lords over men. But once this declaration has been made that sovereignty and authority were exclusively meant for God alone, it is tantamount to restoring God's usurped authority again to Allah, from the usurpers who by their homemade legislations and devised law wanted to rule over others, thus elevating themselves to the status of lords and reducing others to the position of slaves. In short, proclamation of the sovereignty of Allah and the declaration of His authority connotes the wiping out of human kingship from the face of the earth and establishing thereon the rule of the Sustainer of the world. . . .

This religion is not for the freedom of Arab people only, nor its message confined to the Arabs alone. The subject of this religion is "Man"—the whole human species—and its sphere of activity is earth—the whole of it. Allah, Most High, is not the Sustainer of Arabs only; nor is His providence confined to those people who have embraced the faith of Islam. Allah Most High, is the Sustainer of all the people of the world. This religion wishes to revert all the people to their Creator and Nourisher. It wants them to be free from the worship of others than God.[7]

Abul Alʾa Maududi (1903–1979)

The Political Theory of Islam

The Arabic word *ilah* stands for *maʿbud* (i.e., the object of worship) which is derived from the word *ʿabd*, meaning a servant or slave. The relationship that exists between man and God is that of "the worshipper" and "the worshipped." Man is to offer *ʿibadat* to God and is to live like His *ʿabd*. And *ʿibadat* does not merely mean ritual or any specific form of prayer. It means a life of continuous service and unremitting obedience like the life of a slave in relation to his Lord. To wait upon a person in service, to fold one's hands in reverence to him, to bow down one's head in acknowledgment of his elevated position, to exert oneself in obedience to his commands, to carry out his orders and cheerfully submit to all the toil and discipline involved therein, to humble oneself in the presence of the master, to offer what he demands, to obey what he commands, to set one's face steadily against the causes of his displeasure, and to sacrifice even one's life when such is his pleasure—these are the real implications of the term *ʿibadat* (worship or service) and a man's true *maʿbud* (object of worship) is he whom he worships in this manner.

And what is the meaning of the word *rabb*? In Arabic, it literally means "one who nourishes and sustains, and regulates and perfects." Since the moral consciousness of man requires that one who nourishes, sustains, and provides for us has a superior claim on our allegiance, the word *rabb* is also used in the sense of master or owner. For this reason, the Arabic equivalent for the owner of property is *rabb al-mal* and for the owner of a house, *rabb al-dar*. A person's *rabb* is one whom he looks upon as his nourished and patron; from whom he expects favors and obligations; to whom he looks for honor, advancement, and peace; whose displeasure he considers to be prejudicial to his life and happiness; whom he declares to be his lord and master, and lastly, whom he follows and obeys. . . .

If you were to look at the matter from this angle, you will find that the root cause of all evil and mischief in the world is the domination of man over man, be it direct or indirect. This was the origin of all the troubles of mankind and even this day it remains the main cause of all the misfortunes and vices which have brought untold misery on the teeming humanity. God, of course, knows all the secrets of human nature. But the truth of this observation has also been confirmed and brought home to humanity by the experiences of thousands of years that man cannot help setting up someone or other as his god, *ilah*, and *rabb*, and looking up to him for help and guidance in the complex and baffling affairs of his life and obeying his commands. This fact has been established beyond question by the historical experience of mankind that if you do not believe in God, some artificial god will take His place in your thinking and behavior. It is even possible that instead of one real God, a number of false gods, *ilahs*, and *rabbs* may impose themselves upon you. Even today man is enchained in the slavery of many a false god. May he be in Russia or America, Italy or Yugoslavia, England or China, he is generally under the spell of some party, some ruler, some leader or group, some money-magnate or the like in such a manner that man's surveillance of man continues unabated. Modern man has discarded nature-worship, but man-worship he still does. In fact, wherever you turn your eyes, you will find that one nation dominates another, one class holds another in subjection, or a political party having gained complete ascendancy, constitutes itself as the arbiter of men's destiny; or again in some places a dictator concentrates in his hands all power and influence setting himself up as the lord and master of the people. Nowhere has man been able to do without an *ilah*. What are the consequences of this domination of man by man, of this attempt by man to play the role of divinity? The same that would follow from a mean and incompetent person being appointed a police commissioner or some ignorant and narrow-minded politician being exalted to the rank of a prime minister. For one thing, the effect of godhood is so intoxicating that one who tastes this powerful drink can never keep himself under control. Even assuming that such self-control is possible, the vast knowledge, the keen insight, the unquestioned impartiality and perfect disinterestedness, which are required for carrying out the duties of godhood will always remain out of the reach of man. That is why tyranny, despotism, intemperance, unlawful exploitation, and inequality reign supreme, whenever man's overlordship and domination (*uluhiyyat* and *rabubiyya*) over man are established. The human soul is inevitably deprived of its natural freedom and man's mind and heart and his inborn faculties and aptitudes are subjected to such vexatious restrictions that the proper growth and development of his personality is arrested.[8]

Farid Esack (b. 1959)

Qur'ān, Liberation & Pluralism: An Islamic Perspective of Interreligious Solidarity against Oppression (1996)

Having noted the popularity and broad use during the South African liberation movement of Qur'an 28:4–8—a portion of a chapter that, in telling of the Israelites's flight from Egypt (thus from subjugation under Pharaoh), has much to say about al-mustad'afun *(the oppressed)—Esack asserts that these verses are an indication of God's preferential option for the poor. He then relates this to the struggle against apartheid in South Africa.*

The most significant text of the South African qur'anic discourse on liberation was undoubtedly Qur'an 28:4–8. This particular text was quoted with unceasing regularity at rallies of virtually every Islamist organization—both fundamentalist and progressive—during the uprisings of the 1980s, as well as in their magazines, newspapers and pamphlets. The text reads as follows:

> And it is Our will to bestow Our grace upon the *mustad'afun* on the earth, to make them the leaders, and to make them heirs, and to establish them firmly on the earth, and to let Pharaoh and Haman and their hosts experience through those [the Israelite] the very thing which they sought to protect themselves. (28:5)

The use of *mustad'afun* in this text was applied to all the oppressed people of South Africa, irrespective of their religious background, as is evident from the following two quotations:

> O *mustad'afun* of our land, the system that we have fought against for so long and paid for so dearly in life, blood, and property is evil and rotten to the core. (Qibla n.d., *One Solution, Islamic Revolution*, p. 2)

> [The task of the Muslim community is] to join forces with the progressive streams among the *mustad'afun* . . . to contribute towards the unity of the *mustad'afun*, . . . to declare clearly to the oppressors: "If you rise against the oppressed or stand in the path of the oppressed, we are commanded by God to defend ourselves against injustice and oppression." (Solomon 1985, p. 6)

"The people" in South Africa were transformed into a mass of *mustad'afun* under a vicious system which not only meant separation, but an existence of discrimination and the criminalization of any attempt to escape from it. The engaged interpreter in South Africa may certainly ask, "If God regards the Israelites as His people and demands that His prophets become of them, destroy their oppressors and lead them into freedom, then why would He treat the people of South Africa any differently?"

The need for interpreter both to place himself or herself among the marginalized and within their struggles, as well as to interpret the text from the underside of history, is based on the notion of the divine and prophetic preferential option for the oppressed. Those committed to liberation in South Africa have thus argued that a similar bias must be exercised by anyone approaching the Qur'an and who wants to bring its basic spirit to life. This is a conscious denial of "objectivity." In its place is offered a subjectivity which enables one to walk in the path of the prophets.

The engaged interpreter approaches the text with a conscious decision to search for meaning, which responds creatively to the suffering of the *mustad'afun* and holds out the most promise for liberation and justice. It is within a context of oppression that the interpreter is called upon to bear witness to God. A commitment to humankind and active solidarity with the *mustad'afun* results in a re-reading of both social reality and the text from their perspective. This re-reading and the engagement in social analysis from that point of departure shapes the search for a qur'anic hermeneutic of pluralism for liberation. The objective of this search is an effective qur'anic contribution to the ongoing struggles for justice on the part of the country's people; a struggle whose participants are mainly the religious Other, for they are the overwhelming majority of the *mustad'afun*.[9]

Collective Statements concerning Freedom and Islam

Cairo Declaration on Human Rights in Islam (August 5, 1990)

The Member States of the Organization of the Islamic Conference, reaffirming the civilizing and historical role of the Islamic Ummah which Allah made as the best community and which gave humanity a universal and well-balanced civilization, in which harmony is established between hereunder and the hereafter, knowledge is combined with faith, and to fulfill the expectations from this community to guide all humanity which is confused because of different and conflicting beliefs and ideologies and to provide solutions for all chronic problems of this materialistic civilization.

In contribution to the efforts of mankind to assert human rights, to protect man from exploitation and persecution, and to affirm his freedom and right to a dignified life in accordance with the Islamic sharia.

Convinced that mankind which has reached an advanced stage in materialistic science is still, and shall remain, in dire need of faith to support its civilization as well as a self motivating force to guard its rights;

Believing that fundamental rights and freedoms according to Islam are an integral part of the Islamic religion and that no one shall have the right as a matter of principle to abolish them either in whole or in part or to violate or ignore them in as much as they are binding divine commands, which are contained in the Revealed Books of Allah and which were sent through the last of His Prophets to complete the preceding divine messages and that safeguarding those fundamental rights and freedoms is an act of worship whereas the neglect or violation thereof is an abominable sin, and that the safeguarding of those fundamental rights and freedom is an individual responsibility of every person and a collective responsibility of the entire Ummah;

Do hereby and on the basis of the above-mentioned principles declare as follows:

Article 1:

(a) All human beings form one family whose members are united by their subordination to Allah and descent from Adam. All men are equal in terms of basic human dignity and basic obligations and responsibilities, without any discrimination on the basis of race, colour, language, belief, sex, religion, political affiliation, social status or other considerations. The true religion is the guarantee for enhancing such dignity along the path to human integrity.

(b) All human beings are Allah's subjects, and the most loved by Him are those who are most beneficial to His subjects, and no one has superiority over another except on the basis of piety and good deeds. . . .

Article 11:

(a) Human beings are born free, and no one has the right to enslave, humiliate, oppress or exploit them, and there can be no subjugation but to Allah the Almighty.

(b) Colonialism of all types being one of the most evil forms of enslavement is totally prohibited. Peoples suffering from colonialism have the full right to freedom and self-determination. It is the duty of all States and peoples to support the struggle of colonized peoples for the liquidation of all forms of colonialism and occupation, and all States and peoples have the right to preserve their independent identity and control over their wealth and natural resources. . . .

ARTICLE 24:

All the rights and freedoms stipulated in this Declaration are subject to the Islamic Shariʿah.

ARTICLE 25:

The Islamic Shariʿah is the only source of reference for the explanation or clarification of any of the articles of this Declaration.[10]

The Marrakesh Declaration

The Marrakesh Declaration on the Rights of Religious Minorities in Predominantly Muslim Majority Communities was the outcome of a summit, January 25–27, 2016, organized by His Majesty King Mohammed VI in conjunction with the Forum for Promoting Peace in Muslim Societies. It makes eight key points, each supported by the Qurʾan:

1. *God bestowed dignity to all human beings regardless of their race, color, language, or belief, for God breathed His spirit into their forefather Adam, upon him be peace. [Q. 17:70]*
2. *This dignity requires that humans are granted freedom of choice. [Q. 2:256, 10:99]*
3. *All people—regardless of their different natures, societies, and worldviews—share the bonds of brotherhood and sisterhood in humanity. [Q. 49:13]*
4. *God established the heavens and the earth on the basis of justice and made such justice the standard for all human interaction in order to ward off resentment and enmity, and He encouraged benevolence between people in order to nurture love and harmony. [Q. 16:90]*
5. *Peace is the hallmark of Islam and the primary purpose of Sacred Law for society. [Q. 2:208, 8:61]*
6. *God Almighty sent Prophet Muhammad, upon him peace and blessings, as a mercy to the worlds. [Q. 21:107]*
7. *Islam calls for treating others kindly, regardless of whether they share the same beliefs or not. [Q. 60:8]*

8. *Islamic Sacred Law strongly emphasizes honoring contracts, covenants, and conventions that ensure peace and coexistence between peoples. [Q.5:1, 16:91]*

Here follows the official executive summary of the declaration:

In the Name of God, the All-Merciful, the All-Compassionate

WHEREAS, this situation has also weakened the authority of legitimate governments and enabled criminal groups to issue edicts attributed to Islam, but which, in fact, alarmingly distort its fundamental principles and goals in ways that have seriously harmed the population as a whole;

WHEREAS, this year marks the 1,400th anniversary of the Charter of Medina, a constitutional contract between the Prophet Muhammad, God's peace and blessings be upon him, and the people of Medina, which guaranteed the religious liberty of all, regardless of faith;

WHEREAS, hundreds of Muslim scholars and intellectuals from over 120 countries, along with representatives of Islamic and international organizations, as well as leaders from diverse religious groups and nationalities, gathered in Marrakesh on this date to reaffirm the principles of the Charter of Medina at a major conference;

WHEREAS, this conference was held under the auspices of His Majesty, King Mohammed VI of Morocco, and organized jointly by the Ministry of Endowment and Islamic Affairs in the Kingdom of Morocco and the Forum for Promoting Peace in Muslim Societies based in the United Arab Emirates;

AND NOTING the gravity of this situation afflicting Muslims as well as peoples of other faiths throughout the world, and after thorough deliberation and discussion, the convened Muslim scholars and intellectuals:

DECLARE HEREBY our firm commitment to the principles articulated in the Charter of Medina, whose provisions contained a number of the principles of constitutional contractual citizenship, such as freedom of movement, property ownership, mutual solidarity and defense, as well as principles of justice and equality before the law; and that,

The objectives of the Charter of Medina provide a suitable framework for national constitutions in countries with Muslim majorities, and the United Nations Charter and related documents, such as the Universal Declaration of Human Rights, are in harmony with the Charter of Medina, including consideration for public order.

NOTING FURTHER that deep reflection upon the various crises afflicting humanity underscores the inevitable and urgent need for cooperation among all religious groups, we

AFFIRM HEREBY that such cooperation must be based on a "Common Word," requiring that such cooperation must go beyond mutual tolerance and respect, to providing full protection for the rights and liberties to all religious groups in a civilized manner that eschews coercion, bias, and arrogance.

BASED ON ALL OF THE ABOVE, we hereby:

Call upon Muslim scholars and intellectuals around the world to develop a jurisprudence of the concept of "citizenship" which is inclusive of diverse groups. Such jurisprudence shall be rooted in Islamic tradition and principles and mindful of global changes.

Urge Muslim educational institutions and authorities to conduct a courageous review of educational curricula that addresses honestly and effectively any material that instigates aggression and extremism, leads to war and chaos, and results in the destruction of our shared societies;

Call upon politicians and decision makers to take the political and legal steps necessary to establish a constitutional contractual relationship among its citizens, and to support all formulations and initiatives that aim to fortify relations and understanding among the various religious groups in the Muslim World;

Call upon the educated, artistic, and creative members of our societies, as well as organizations of civil society, to establish a broad movement for the just treatment of religious minorities in Muslim countries and to raise awareness as to their rights, and to work together to ensure the success of these efforts.

Call upon the various religious groups bound by the same national fabric to address their mutual state of selective amnesia that blocks memories of centuries of joint and shared living on the same land; we call upon them to rebuild the past by reviving this tradition of conviviality, and restoring our shared trust that has been eroded by extremists using acts of terror and aggression;

Call upon representatives of the various religions, sects and denominations to confront all forms of religious bigotry, vilification, and denigration of what people hold sacred, as well as all speech that promote hatred and bigotry; AND FINALLY,

AFFIRM that it is unconscionable to employ religion for the purpose of aggressing upon the rights of religious minorities in Muslim countries.

Marrakesh

January 2016, 27th[11]

Notes

1. Muhammad Iqbal, *The Reconstruction of Religious Thought in Islam* (London: Oxford University Press, 1934), 86–87.

2. Ali Shariati, *Man & Islam*, translated from Persian by Fatollah Marjani (Houston: Free Islamic Literature, 1981), 5–6.

3. 2:256 "Let there be no compulsion in religion."

4. Murtaza Mutahhari, *Jihad: The Holy War of Islam and Its Legitimacy in the Quran*, trans. Mohammad Salman Tawhidi (Houston: Islamic Propagation Organization, 1988), 29–30, 34–35. See also Ahl al-Bayt Digital Library, https://www.al-islam.org/organizations/dilp/index2.htm.

5. Mahmoud Mohamed Taha, *The Second Message of Islam*, trans. Abdullahi Ahmad An-Naim (Syracuse, NY: Syracuse University Press, 1996), 64–65, 67.

6. Muhammad ʿAbduh, *The Theology of Unity*, trans. Ishaq Musaʿad and Kenneth Cragg (London: Allen & Unwin, 1966; Selagor, Malaysia: Islamic Book Trust, 2004), 124–25. Arabic title: *Risalat al-Tawhid* (Epistle of Monotheism).

7. Sayyid Qutb, *Milestones* (New Delhi: Islamic Book Service, 2006), 227–28, 229.

8. Sayyid Abul Alʾa Maududi, *The Political Theory of Islam* (Karachi, Pakistan: Islamic Research Academy, 1976), 265, 268.

9. Farid Esack, *Qurʾān, Liberation & Pluralism: An Islamic Perspective of Interreligious Solidarity against Oppression* (Oxford: Oneworld, 1996), 102–3. Used by permission.

10. Authored by the Islamic Conference of Foreign Ministers, published by the Organization of the Islamic Conference, August 5, 1990.

11. Marrakesh Declaration, http://www.marrakeshdeclaration.org/declaration/. Reprinted with permission of the Forum for Promoting Peace in Muslim Societies (Abu Dhabi, UAE).

Part Three

Christian Texts on Freedom

Freedom in the Hebrew Bible

From Exodus to Ezekiel, by Way of Reba McEntire and Rage against the Machine

Christopher M. Hays

Freedom is one of those words like *justice* or *literally* that gets bandied around without much clarity about precisely what one denotes thereby. Consider how the term is used in popular music, especially in the North Atlantic, anglophone context. For many musicians, freedom is about self-determination and self-expression, as in Nicki Minaj's song "Freedom," George Michael's "Freedom 90," or the greasy Kid Rock's "Born Free." This notion of freedom easily slides into libertine hedonism, as on display in Pitbull's party single "Freedom." In that piece, the rapper—with the soul of a frat boy and the vocabulary of a second-grader—declares, "I'm free to do what I want and have a good time. Now somebody, anybody, everyone say." Dido's gentle ballad "No Freedom" (2013) was originally about freedom in romantic relationships, but it was quickly adopted by Syrian rebels because of its chorus: "No love without freedom, no freedom without love."[1]

The Syrian reception of Dido bespeaks the political potency of the notion of freedom. Indeed, numerous artists locate themselves rhetorically downstream from Martin Luther King Jr., composing songs titled "Freedom" in order to resist contemporary forms of oppression. Under this title, Beyoncé indicted the unjust treatment of Black Americans; Rage Against the Machine decried the murder of African American and Native American populations; and Pharrell Williams took aim at diverse forms of global injustice. From the opposite end of the political spectrum, this construal of freedom as a counterpoint to oppression probably stands behind the rhetoric of much American country music, such as Reba McEntire's pro-veteran song "Freedom." The operating assumption of such music is that the United States possesses a unique sort of freedom (shaped in response to British colonialism, with begrudging acknowledgment of French influence), a freedom that is perpetually besieged by foreign entities, entities that in the past decades are increasingly identified as Muslim—as witnessed by the post-9/11 resurgence of "God Bless the USA" by Lee Greenwood, with its telling lines " 'Cause the flag still stands for freedom and they can't take that away. And I'm proud to be an American where at least I know I'm free."

This review of my Spotify account highlights how multifaceted a concept freedom can become, a complexity that should alert us to the possibility that what we mean by *freedom* may not map neatly onto the moral vision of the Hebrew Bible.[2] In point of fact, there is no obvious Hebrew word that means "freedom" in the way that *eleutheria, libertas, liberté,* or *Freiheit* do. In the *Theological Dictionary of the New Testament*'s fifteen-page article on *eleutheros* and cognates (the words for "freedom" in Greek), there is not a single paragraph dedicated to the Old Testament or extra-biblical Judaism.[3] A smattering of terms appear in the Hebrew Bible to cover some of the pertinent semantic range, but none of them encompasses what *freedom* does in English.

All of this should prepare us for the possibility that *freedom* in the Hebrew Bible may be quite different from what comes to mind for a reader like me, from the twenty-first-century West.[4] In the brief survey of texts that follows, I outline how freedom is presented in the Tanakh. We will see that the Hebrew Bible presents liberation from Egyptian domination as the foundation of the nation of Israel's free choice to submit themselves to service of God alone, which in turn precluded the enslavement of their own brethren; nonetheless, the texts argue that Israel's obstinacy impeded their free submission to the Mosaic covenant and resulted in their resubjugation to foreign nations such that the Israelites, both individually and collectively, required a transformation of the heart in order to enable free submission to their liberating God.

The Exodus: The Touchstone of Israelite Liberation and Submission

Freedom from Egypt

We begin with Exodus 6, in which Moses presents to the Israelites God's intention to free them from their current enslavement under Pharaoh. God proposes to liberate Israel from Egypt precisely because he had previously made a deal, a covenant, with the patriarchs (Exod. 6:3–4), promising to give the land of Canaan to the descendants of Abraham;[5] God now intends to make good, to free and redeem the Israelites from Egypt, and to take them as his people.[6] But in making this offer, God makes it clear that, while the Israelites will be freed from Egypt, they will not therefore be without a master; rather, they will belong to him.

When Yahweh says, "I will take you as my people, and I will be your God" (v. 7), he is using a covenant-making formula, expressing that the Israelites are now entering into a religious contract with God, an agreement that will entail both obligations and benefits. The benefits are nothing to shake a stick at (vv. 6–8): rescue from Egyptian domination and bestowal of a land all their own—once they kill off the current inhabitants! The antecedent obligations, however, are not insignificant: Yahweh expects to be their God, and, as we will see forthwith, that comes with strings attached.

Freedom in Order to Obey

Let us jump forward to Exodus 19. After God made good on his promise to free the Israelites from Egypt, the nation made its way to Sinai; there Moses ascends the mountain and God once again offers the Israelites the choice of being his people, saying, "*If* [*'im*] you obey my voice and keep my covenant, you shall be my treasured possession out of all the peoples. Indeed, the whole earth is mine, but you shall be for me a priestly kingdom and a holy nation" (Exod. 19:5–6). As the conditional sentence structure reveals, this is a real, free choice;[7] God previously had made covenant with their ancestors, but this generation gets to choose for itself whether it wants out. Yet if they sign up for being Yahweh's covenant people, the perks are attractive. In addition to the land God already promised to give them, God says that they will become a priestly kingdom, a holy nation. As a "holy nation," they are called to be like the God who is definitionally holy and are set apart for further divine purposes.[8] Those purposes are construed in terms of being a "kingdom of priests," a vocation that entailed representing God and mediating God's presence to the world so as to be a blessing to all nations.[9] Note how holiness and priesthood are democratized in these texts: all Israelites, not just the Levites, have this role, which is no small honor. Still, this honor does not come cheap. If they are holy, set apart for God, it means that they are not their own. Quite the contrary, they are to belong to God, as his "treasured possession"; treasured, yes, but a possession no less. Then again, verse 5 reminds the Israelites that God already owns all the nations; the Israelites just have the opportunity to receive pride of place among the nations. Nonetheless, that pride of place comes with a cost: unwavering obedience to God's covenant (v. 5).

Freedom and Obedience, or Consequences

Deuteronomy 6 fleshes out further what sort of expectations God has for the Israelites. In this chapter Moses reminds the people how God had spoken to him from the great fire that engulfed the top of Mount Sinai and explained how to "follow exactly the path that the Lord your God has commanded you, so that you . . . may live long in the land that you are to possess" (Deut. 5:22–33). That path is defined, in the first place, with the great commandment of Deuteronomy 6: utter and exclusive devotion to Yahweh. "The Lord is our God, the Lord alone. You shall love the Lord your God with all your heart, and with all your soul, and with all your might" (Deut. 6:4–5). On the heels of that exclusive commitment to Yahweh, the text goes on to demand, "Keep these words that I am commanding you today" (v. 6) and "You must diligently keep the commandments of the Lord your God, and his decrees, and his statutes that he has commanded you" (v. 17). In other words, the love of and exclusive fidelity to Yahweh is inseparably fused to obedience to the commandments of Yahweh.

Once again, this covenant dynamic is rooted in the anterior action of God's deliverance of Israel "out of the house of slavery" (*mibêt ʿăbādîm*) in Egypt (v. 12), and again the text is quite clear that the purpose of liberating the Israelites from slavery in Egypt is so that they will serve (*taʿăbôd*) Yahweh alone (v. 12). Here and in many passages in Exodus (see, e.g., Exod. 3:12; 7:16; 8:1, 20; 9:1, 13; 10:3, 7), the same root *ʿbd* is used to describe Egyptian slavery and service to Yahweh precisely because Israel is freed from Egyptian slavery in order to be God's treasured possession and servant.[10]

Naturally, the Pentateuch makes it clear that being God's slave is a good gig. Doing what God commands will result in occupying the land sworn to their ancestors via a summary eviction of its current inhabitants (vv. 18–19), in order to prevent future enslavement by the Canaanites. Nonetheless, their land and freedom from pagan oppression are blessings conditional on covenant fidelity, and these blessings can be withdrawn if Israel should violate the terms of their contract by following other gods (v. 14);[11] if Israel crosses that line, "The anger of the Lord your God would be kindled against you and he would destroy you from the face of the earth" (v. 15).[12]

In sum, the exodus event, setting God's people free from slavery in Egypt, was the foundation of Israelite faith and identity.[13] The notion of freedom in the Hebrew Bible is rooted in an experience of liberation from foreign domination. But, as Americans are fond of saying, freedom ain't free. For the Israelites, freedom from Egypt comes at the cost of slavery to God and obedience to God's covenant, and Israel has the freedom to choose whether to submit herself to that covenant. The benefits of land and protection that come with being God's people are surely worth it (especially since all people already belong to God), but freedom does come at a price. As Georg Sauer put it, "Freedom and obligation belong together . . . : the exodus events and the conquest on the one hand, and the experience of the revelation of the will of God and the obligation to act on the other."[14] The book of Leviticus explains further what that obligation to act entailed.

The Moral Imperative toward Liberation

Leviticus and the Legislation of Liberation

Leviticus 25 plays out one facet of the covenant with Yahweh that is especially closely linked to the fact that the Israelites had been freed from Egypt: to wit, it prohibits the reduction of fellow Israelites to the status of slaves, specifically as a result of economic hardship.[15]

It was common in the ancient Near East for poverty or famine to drive people to mortgage their land or take loans they could not repay, which would eventually require them to cede ownership of their land or enslave themselves or a family member in order to repay their debts.[16] Various texts of the Pentateuch guard against such devastating dynamics; in particular, Exodus and Deuteronomy instate the practice of the Sabbath year, according to which every seven years Hebrew slaves are to be released from their servitude (Exod. 21:2; cf. Jer. 34:8) and debts are to be forgiven (Deut. 15:2).

Leviticus 25, however, takes a slightly different approach. In verses 1–7 debt remission and slave emancipation do not take place in the Sabbath year (rather, the Sabbath is simply conceived as a year to leave the land fallow); instead, these liberating actions take place after every *seventh* Sabbath year: "you shall hallow the fiftieth year and you shall proclaim liberty [*dĕrôr*[17]] throughout the land to all its inhabitants. It shall be a jubilee for you: you shall return, every one of you, to your property and every one of you to your family" (v. 10, cf. 41). That is to say, every fifty years, Leviticus commands not only that debts be forgiven and slaves be freed but also that land that had been mortgaged because of financial hardship *also* be returned to its original owners, such that they would have the means to sustain themselves upon emancipation and not fall back into debt and slavery.[18]

What is especially interesting for the present study is the way that the Jubilee year is grounded in the exodus experience.[19] Verses 39–42 explain why Israelite slaves should be released in the Jubilee year and why the Israelites, upon handing themselves over to creditors, should not be treated like slaves but rather as hired hands. The reason is because the Israelites are already God's slaves (*kî ăbāday hēm*) insofar as God brought them out of slavery in Egypt; since they belong to God, they should never be enslaved to anyone else (v. 42).[20] Verse 55 makes the case emphatically: "For the sons of Israel are slaves [*ăbādîm*] *to me*;[21] they are *my* slaves [*ăbāday*] that I brought out of the land of Egypt. *I* am the Lord their God."[22] Modern translations, such as the NRSV, tend to render *ăbādîm* as "servants," understandably, given modern repulsion at the institution of slavery and, by extension, the notion that God would enslave God's people. Nonetheless, the translation of this word as "servants" obscures the logic of the passage: they are no longer slaves to Egypt; now they are slaves to God, and that is precisely the reason why they cannot be enslaved to any other person.[23] Moreover, being God's slave has pretty significant benefits (so also Isa. 65:13–14; Ps. 123:2–3), according to the Hebrew Bible, such that it is not contemplated that the people of Israel would object greatly to the idea.[24]

In the Pentateuch, freedom is not an absolute good. In the biblical view, all nations belong to God in reality, whether or not they also belong to other peoples. Israel's best-case scenario is to be enslaved *only* to God as his treasured possession because in that way they receive the benefits of their ancestral covenant, in particular, their own land and freedom from oppressors—both foreign and domestic.

Liberation from Oppression in the Moral Vision of the Prophets

The concern for liberation of one's fellow man does not peter out after Leviticus; quite the contrary, it finds a full-throated endorsement in prophets such as Isaiah. For example, Isaiah 58:6–7 calls the Israelites to demonstrate their commitment and submission to Yahweh, not first through forms of piety such as fasting but rather through practices of mercy toward the indigent (v. 7) and especially the liberation of the oppressed: for example, letting the oppressed go free and breaking every yoke (*môṭāh*; v. 6).[25] The text of Isaiah 58 most likely has as its primary focus liberation from debt slavery or debtors' prison, as a consequence of the economic dynamics described above.[26] But the text chooses to describe that sort of oppression in terms of a *yoke* (*môṭāh*), an image that was used in Leviticus to describe slavery in Egypt (Lev. 26:13) and in Jeremiah to describe the exile in Babylon (Jer. 27:2, 10, 12–13; cf. Deut. 28:48).[27] As in Leviticus 25, Isaiah affirms that Israel's experience of liberation from slavery has normative ramifications for the treatment of others who are not free.

> The nation remembers the bondage which it endured itself, and the release that followed. . . . What God promised to Israel, and she had experienced, resulted in a new value being attached what we call freedom. Now, helping to restore a person's freedom is more pleasing to God than the practice of mortifying one's flesh.[28]

Isaiah 61:1–3 likewise construes the Isaianic servant's vocation precisely in terms of bringing freedom to captives and prisoners. Whether one reads these verses as referring simply to the sorts of economic oppression that result in slavery or imprisonment (as in Isaiah 58 and Leviticus 25) or in relation to liberation of the people of Israel living under foreign domination depends on a whole host of other interpretive decisions that need not be sorted in the present text.[29] It is pertinent to note, though, that this act of declaring liberty and release is construed as proclaiming "the year of the Lord's favor" (v. 2), which is of course an allusion to the proclamation of the Jubilee year (Lev. 25:10). The vision of the Leviticus Jubilee, irrespective of any debates about whether it was actually practiced at any point in history, becomes paradigmatic for the ministry of the prophets and, by subsequent extension, the ministry of Jesus.[30] And the consequence of this covenant fidelity, specifically manifested in extending freedom to the captives, is that Israel is not only freed from foreign domination but in fact served *by* foreigners, who feed their flocks and till their land for them (v. 5) so that the Israelites can in turn serve as "priests of the Lord" and "ministers of our God" (v. 6), as Exodus 19:6 indicates that God had always intended. In other words, the experience of past liberation by God becomes the hoped-for pattern of future liberation by God, in accordance with Israel making liberation her paradigm for the treatment of economically oppressed brothers and sisters. (We shall skim over the unpleasant fact that, in this vision, foreigners are subjected to working on behalf of the Israelites!)

Free Choice and Individual Responsibility

The texts previously mentioned are decidedly corporate in their focus, addressing the nation of Israel as a collective. Other texts of the Hebrew Bible, however, layer in more attention to the moral responsibility of the individual for his or her own free choices and thus one's attendant state of freedom or servitude.

Human Responsibility and Freedom in the Garden

The creation and fall narratives of Genesis 2–3 foreshadow the dynamics of the covenant relationship with God, complete with benefits and obligations, which are played out in detail in the Pentateuchal books that follow. The man and woman are placed in the garden—that is, given the benefit of land to cultivate (Gen. 2:15)—and told "You may freely eat [*'ākol to'kēl*] of every tree of the garden;[31] but of the tree of the knowledge of good and evil you shall not eat, for in the day that you eat of it you shall [be doomed to] die [*môt tāmût*]" (2:16–17).[32] In this text the covenant dynamics of blessing, commandment, and choice are proleptically intertwined, representing the irreducible nature of God's way of being with humanity. Humanity is offered blessing by God, within certain parameters (i.e., not taking knowledge of good and evil for themselves) and has the freedom to choose whether to obey the commandment or to sabotage its own blessing.[33] The consequences of rejecting the commandment are clear: certain death.

Perhaps predictably (at least from a dramatic perspective), the woman and man violate the commandment. They choose "to pursue the one thing God had expressly withheld from him: that [they] should be independent of God to determine for [themselves] what is 'good and evil.'"[34] This exercise of their free will, in order to acquire greater moral autonomy, has the consequence that God exiles them from the garden (Gen. 3:23–24), at the center of which is the tree of life (2:9; 3:22), and in so doing dooms them to certain death. The expulsion of the man and woman from the garden foreshadows the later dynamics of Israel's exile for covenant violation, as delineated graphically in Deuteronomy 28:15–68.[35] Abuse of freedom, shirking submission to God, results in death. While subsequent philosophy and culture have exalted libertarian freedom as a preeminent good, the Hebrew Bible is not so categorically sanguine about the good of freedom. Freedom of the will is good only insofar as it is applied in accordance with and submission to the will of God. Freedom apart from submission to God is not good; rather, it is death. From the perspective of Genesis 2–3, Karl Barth was correct to observe,

> [One] is a free man when he thinks and decides and acts at peace with God, when his decision is simply and exclusively the repetition of the divine decision. If this is not enough for him, if he wants to make a primary decision where the decision of God and therefore the divine knowledge of good and evil has already preceded him, this involves a foolish over-estimation of himself. . . . This desire means that man renounces the obedience in which he cannot even toy with the idea that there may be another choice than that which God has made or decision which is not a repetition of His decision, in which he cannot even want to know the opposite of the good which God has set before him, in which he can only wish to adjust himself to what God has already chosen and decided in His knowledge of the one good and its opposite, as the only possible Judge in this matter. And this desire means finally that at once and irrevocably man loses his freedom. He has already left the protective home of peace with God.[36]

Individual Responsibility and Volitional Transformation

Turn and Live: Against Collective Fatalism

The dynamics of free will are addressed in more explicitly individual terms in Ezekiel 18, when many members of the nation of Israel found themselves in exile precisely because of a violation of their covenant with Yahweh.[37] The audience addressed in chapter 18 is the second generation of exiles; because they were not the ones expelled from the land of their ancestors, they had come to conclude that their suffering in exile was simply the fault of their parents. Thus, they spoke to each other the proverb, "The parents have eaten sour grapes, and the children's teeth are set on edge" (Ezek. 18:2), effectively asserting that they were living with the consequences of their parents' sin.[38] The attitude reveals a combination of fatalism about the future and casting blame on their parents for their current suffering.

Without denying that the exile was precipitated by the prior generation's actions, Ezekiel rejects the perspective represented in the proverb. The prophet explains that all people, all lives from each generation belong to God, and that God will deal with each person in accordance with his or her own actions (18:4, 20).[39] The inference is therefore that the second-generation exiles are capable of charting a new course for themselves.[40] Ezekiel argues that the future of the people will depend on their own actions, and so he calls them to repent so as to find new life rather than to continue to languish under the judgment of exile (18:30–31).

In verse 19 the audience reveals its incredulity, asking, "How is it that the son does not suffer for the iniquity of the father?"[41] (This is probably a better translation than the NRSV, which says, "Why should not the son suffer for the iniquity of the father?") That is to say, *pace* the impression one gets from the NRSV, the Israelites are not opining that they *should* suffer for the iniquities of their fathers but rather expressing that, in their lived experience, they were indeed suffering for the sins of their fathers.

In defense of the exiles' skepticism, much of the previous experience of the nation of Israel and of God's own self-descriptions seems to fly in the face of Ezekiel's message that each person and generation could captain their own destiny. For example, in Exodus 34:7, God actually names Godself "the Lord, the Lord, a God merciful and gracious. . . . Yet by no means clearing the guilty, but visiting the iniquity of the parents upon the children and the children's children, to the third and the fourth generation." (See similarly Jer. 32:18). Both iterations of the Ten Commandments include affirmations that God will punish the children, grandchildren, and great-grandchildren for the sins of their progenitors (Exod. 20:5; Deut. 5:9).[42] It is true that the principle of intergenerational retribution is never carried over into Israelite law;[43] on the contrary, God says, in Deuteronomy 24:16 that, as a legal principle, children should not die for their father's sins, and vice versa (cf. 2 Kgs. 14:6; 2 Chr. 25:4).[44] But by the Torah's own previous construal, God was reputationally committed to revisiting the punishment of one generation upon another. As such, this declaration by Ezekiel marks a development in the theology of the Hebrew Bible, as Ezekiel indicates that what had already been the operating assumption of the law would now also be the principle guiding divine justice: each person is to be judged for his or her own actions.[45] Accordingly, the exiles are exhorted to repent of their own sins so as to avoid an even more dire future punishment:

> Cast away from you all the transgressions that you have committed against me, and get yourselves a new heart and a new spirit! Why will you die, O house of Israel?[46] For I have no pleasure in the death of anyone, says the Lord GOD. Turn, then, and live. (vv. 31–32)

Without wanting to deny the collectivist suppositions that still undergird much of this text, Ezekiel 18 makes significant affirmations not only about the freedom of discrete generations but also about the free will and moral responsibilities of individuals.[47] "God also calls upon each individual in every generation to take responsibility for her or his present state, to respond with commitment and passion to God's invitation, and to live."[48]

I Will Make You Follow My Statutes

If Ezekiel 18 focuses on the present state of the exiles, Ezekiel 36 straddles the present, looking both backward at the events that landed the Israelites in exile and forward to when God will deliver them from exile. The prophet underscores that the Israelites did indeed go into exile because of their violation of the covenant, specifically for wanton bloodshed and for worshipping other gods (v. 18).[49] Consonant with the fact that Ezekiel was a priest in his former life, and thus highly attentive to purity concepts, he describes the behavior of his people as defiling the entire land much as if they were collectively a menstruating woman (v. 17).[50] But he goes on to explain that, just as God exiled his people because they had dishonored him with their idolatry, so God will return them because he had come to be dishonored by the fact that his people were in exile (vv. 20–22). The profanation of the land prior to the exile, owing to human bloodshed and idolatry, had come to be multiplied; in the exile, the name of God was again being profaned by the very fact of their exile, insofar as the nations understood it as evidence of Yahweh's impotence.[51] This shows how far the Israelites had fallen from their vocation to be a holy nation and kingdom of priests. In the words of Christopher Wright, "Far from being the royal priesthood of Yahweh in the midst of the nations, they were roving profaners of his name."[52]

In light of this sorry situation, Yahweh reveals that he will take his people out of exile because the current state of affairs was so disastrous for his reputation (v. 22).[53] God declares that he will sanctify his name once again. Exodus 19:6 had declared that Israel was to be a holy people among the nations, but they dropped the ball and were driven into exile among the nations; thus, in Ezekiel God intervenes and decides to sanctify his name among the nations, vindicating his honor precisely by reprising his previous successful strategy: repeating the exodus, taking the people out of exile (v. 24)—a fulfillment of Deuteronomy 30:3–5.[54]

Nonetheless, the divine decision to reverse the exile leaves God with a problem: Israel has not changed her ways yet (as is clear in God's declaration in verse 22, "It is not for your sake, O house of Israel, that I am about to act"), so why should God think that Israel will not turn around and defile the land and defame God once again with her wickedness? God explains that he will cleanse them from their current impurity, replace their hearts, and indwell them with his spirit (vv. 25–27).[55] As a result of this purification and transformation, God will renew his covenant relationship with his people, a point made when verse 28 reiterates the covenant formula from Exodus 6:7: "you shall live in the land that I gave to your ancestors; and you shall be my people, and I will be your God" (v. 28).[56]

For the purposes of the present study, the key image from this passage and from Ezekiel 18 is that of the new heart; this is key because the heart (*lēb*) in the view of the Hebrew Bible is not just a cipher for emotions but in fact the seat of the personality and the volition.[57] Ezekiel diagnoses the problem of the exiles as that of having a heart of stone (v. 26), that is, having a will and disposition that are rebellious toward God.[58] The motif of needing to alter Israel's heart is nothing new: Jeremiah 31:33 says that God's law would be inscribed on Israel's heart; Deuteronomy 30:6 says that Israel's heart needed to be circumcised. But Ezekiel sees the situation as more drastic and suggests that the exiles need a full-blown heart transplant.[59]

Accordingly, in Ezekiel 18 the Israelites are called to repent, to "get yourselves a new heart and a new spirit" (18:31), a phraseology that emphasizes the application of the human will toward its own repentance and transformation. By contrast, in Ezekiel 36:26–27,[60] God is the heart surgeon whose transplant will allow Israel to be faithful to the covenant:

> A new heart I will give you, and a new spirit I will put within you; and I will . . . remove from your body the heart of stone and give you a heart of flesh. I will put my spirit within you, and *make you follow* my statutes and be careful to observe my ordinances.[61]

Notice the emphatic language of verse 27: "*I will make you* [*ʿāśîtî*] follow";

God's agency is front and center in Ezekiel 36.[62] How does one square Ezekiel 18 and 36?[63] Do humans change their hearts, or does God? Were this an essay on philosophy, I would venture a defense of compatibilism, but since this chapter focuses on the Hebrew Bible, it suffices to say that the veracity of both affirmations is essential to any account of divine agency and human responsibility that is worthy of being called biblical.[64] God changes hearts and humans change their hearts; the alignment or cooperation of agencies is essential, for without God's action or without human action, the transformation will not be forthcoming. The scriptures hold together these two agencies through canonical diversity, not through reflections on primary and secondary causes or prevenient grace or anything along those lines (not to deny the value of those philosophical maneuvers).

Here we see a key feature in the Hebrew Bible's construal of freedom. On the one hand, Ezekiel emphasizes the agency of individual exiles in changing their hearts (18:31) and submitting themselves to the God whom they belong (18:4), lest, by following their own inclinations, they die (18:31–32).[65] On the other hand, the human, of her own accord, is not free to submit to God and thus requires God to override her rebellion, transform her heart, and *make her follow* God's statutes (36:26–27). Corrupt free will must be overcome through submitting oneself to a divine override, such that one might come to freely desire God's will. Anything else, according to Ezekiel, is death. Gerard Manley Hopkins captures this dynamic in the sonnet "Patience, hard thing! the hard thing but to pray!," saying, "we hear our hearts grate on themselves: it kills / To bruise them dearer. Yet the rebellious wills / Of us we do bid God bend to him even so."[66]

I Shall Walk at Liberty

The tone of the Hopkins sonnet may perhaps play into a Western postmodern view that submitting oneself to the will of another is an act of self-betrayal. But the consistent witness of the Hebrew Bible is that such submission of human freedom to the divine will is in point of fact *life* (Deut. 6:18; Ezek. 18:32), and doing anything else is tantamount to death (Gen. 3:22–23; Deut. 6:15; Ezek. 18:31). This perspective is on jubilant display in Psalm 119, a postexilic text most likely from the Persian period.[67]

The psalmist declares his unbridled delight in God's commandments, saying that he *loves* them (Ps. 119:47–48). Much as Deuteronomy 6 commands Israel to love God, the psalmist loves the Torah as the expression of God's will.[68] The law is likewise a source of hope (v. 43), and obeying the commandments of God ensures the psalmist's liberty (*răḥābāh*) (v. 45). The term translated *liberty*, *răḥābāh*, is from *rḥb*, denoting "wide, broad" spaces.

The notion seems to be that the psalmist has the freedom to go where he will (contrast the "straits" feared in v. 143), because of his fidelity to the law, insofar as observing the covenant means that he enjoys the blessing of unimpeded life in the land.[69]

Later in the psalm, the author turns from freedom to oppression. In verse 133 he asks God to protect him from falling into sin: "Keep my steps steady according to your promise, and never let iniquity have dominion over me." Sin is here personified as a malevolent force, perhaps reflecting both ancient demonology and the psalmist's awareness of the rebellious tenacity of the human heart.[70] So the psalmist begs God to protect him from walking in a way that would violate the covenant, from allowing his will to succumb to iniquity. On display is the recognition of the vulnerability of the human volition and the tendency of free will to collapse into sin, apart from divine intervention.

Finally, then, the psalmist asks God to "redeem me from human oppression, that I may keep your precepts" (v. 134; cf. 119:122). Effectively, between verses 133 and 134 we see the full circle of the dynamics of covenant violation and fidelity. The author asks to be protected from sin so that he would not incur divine punishment (namely, being conquered by Israel's enemies), which would in turn impede his full practice of the commands of God; then, shifting into the role of the subjugated Israelite, he asks to be redeemed from his enemies in order to live according to God's precepts, which are to him a source of hope and life. His free desire is thus to have his volition aligned with the will of the one to whom he is enslaved, precisely because he has come to understand that submission to his Master is life.[71]

Conclusion

In the final analysis, the Hebrew Bible's notion of freedom may not line up neatly with what Nicki Minaj raps about; perhaps Bob Dylan's "Gotta Serve Somebody" is more on point. However, a particular view of freedom is definitely interwoven deeply in the salvation-historical and moral vision of the Tanakh. Israel's identity is grounded in the experience of having been freed from human oppression by God, thereby exchanging a mortal master for a divine one who will, in contrast to their Egyptian rulers, provide them with land and honor them with the role of being a holy kingdom of priests in the world. Still, the holiness of being a priestly people entails obligation since those who would choose to be God's people must also choose to commit themselves to one God and to treat their neighbor to the same sort of liberative care that God showed them. These covenant responsibilities are at once encroachments on freedom and yet liberating insofar as the covenant expresses life as God created his people to live. That is why later rabbis could say, "When the Torah came into the world, freedom came into the world" (*Gen. Rab.* 53:7).[72]

The great problem the Hebrew Bible confronts is that God's people repeatedly exercise their freedom to choose death, and exile, such that Yahweh eventually decides to transform their wills, give his people new hearts, so that they will finally freely choose submission to their Master's law and live in free submission. Once again, Karl Barth captures the dynamic powerfully:

> Freedom cannot be equated with neutrality . . . but is capable of only the one positive meaning that it is freedom which is exercised in the fulfillment of responsibility before God. . . . It is certainly freedom of choice. But . . . it is the freedom of a right choice. The choice is right when it corresponds to the free choice of God. . . . In the free choice of man, which is really made in exercise of the freedom given by God, it is clear that only thanksgiving to the God of grace . . . and the acceptance of responsibility before him can be chosen. What does the free man choose? He chooses himself to fulfill this responsibility. . . . Hence the freedom of man is never freedom to repudiate his responsibility before God. It is never freedom to sin. When man sins, he has renounced his freedom.[73]

Freedom is freedom to choose rightly. And with a transformed heart, Ezekiel foresees that the people of God will freely choose to keep the Law, for it is hope and love and life. Perhaps this is what Pitbull was trying to say all along as he theologized, "I'm free to do what I want and have a good time. Now somebody, anybody, everyone say."

Notes

1. Mark Savage, "Dido Interview: 'I am the sound of conflict,'" *BBC News*, February 26, 2013.

2. And malleable too; Dirty Heads' song "Freedom" seems to combine construals of freedom in terms of self-determination, social resistance, and recreational drug use.

3. Gerhard Kittel, ed., *Theological Dictionary of the New Testament*, vol. 2 (Grand Rapids, MI: Eerdmans, 1977), 487–502; this is a point made by Bruce Francis Vawter, "Tale of Two Cities: The Old Testament and the Issue of Personal Freedom," *Journal of Ecumenical Studies* 15, no. 2 (1978): 268, who nonetheless insists that "this does not mean that the concept [of freedom] did not exist, but rather that it need not be named, since it was taken for granted." This is a rather stark example of the way in which Western suppositions about freedom influence our reading of a text: even as Vawter recognizes that there is no word for freedom in the Hebrew Bible, he assumes that the concept must be so pervasive that it

was taken for granted.

4. Since I am, properly speaking, a *Neutestamentler*, I am deeply grateful to my Hebrew Bible colleagues whose guidance was invaluable in composing this chapter, especially Dr. Casey Strine, Dr. David Baer, and Dr. Carly Crouch. Naturally, however, even the best of colleagues can do only so much to ensure the quality of a publication, such that any shortcomings that appear in this chapter can be ascribed only to me.

5. It was not merely the fact that Israel was oppressed that moved God to save her but also because of God's previous covenant with the patriarchs. "There were, no doubt, other peoples in the ancient world . . . who groaned under their bondage and cry to heaven for deliverance, but Yahweh responded only to the Israelites, because of his covenant with their fathers ([Exod.] 2:24; 6:5)"; John E. Goldingay, "The Man of War and the Suffering Servant: The Old Testament and the Theology of Liberation," *Tyndale Bulletin* 27 (1976): 85. God affirms the covenant and land promise to each of the patriarchs: Abraham (Gen. 15:18–21; 17:4–14), Isaac (Gen. 26:3), and Jacob (Gen. 28:13–16).

6. The language of redemption, "I will redeem you," often referred to reclaiming property. It occurs frequently in Exodus precisely because the point is that the freedom from Egypt does not mean that the Israelites are set loose to do as they will but now belong to God. Paul L. Schrieber, "Liberation Theology and the Old Testament: An Exegetical Critique," *Concordia Journal* 13, no. 1 (1987): 33.

7. J. Gerald Janzen, *Exodus*, Westminster Bible Companion (Louisville, KY: Westminster John Knox, 1997), 133.

8. This "holy nation" language also is picked up and applied to Christians in 1 Peter 2:9. Cf. Deuteronomy 7:6, which also calls Israel a "treasured possession." Holiness as a concept has ritual, ethical, and personal entailments; "God is intrinsically holy and calls his people to be holy, providing for them the standard of obedience whereby that holiness may be maintained. . . . Thus, the Priestly tradition requires the cleanness of proper ritual and the maintenance of separation; the prophetic tradition demands the cleanness of social justice; the wisdom tradition stresses the cleanness of inner integrity and individual moral acts." William VanGemeren, ed., *New International Dictionary of Old Testament Theology & Exegesis* (hereafter, *NIDOTTE*), vol. 3 (Grand Rapids, MI: Zondervan Academic, 2012), 882–83.

9. This "kingdom of priests" language gets picked up again in Isaiah 61:6; and in the New Testament, 1 Peter 2:9, 5:10; Revelation 1:6. See Janzen, *Exodus*, 134; cf. Victor P. Hamilton, *Exodus: An Exegetical Commentary* (Grand Rapids, MI: Baker, 2011), 304. Read this in the light of Genesis 12:3, a covenant promise that is here beginning to be fulfilled; so also John H. Stek, "Salvation, Justice and Liberation in the Old Testament," *Calvin Theological Journal* 13, no. 2 (1978): 144; and Goldingay, "Man of War," 85.

10. Schrieber, "Liberation Theology," 33; and Goldingay, "Man of War," 91–92. "In Deuteronomy Moses continually reminds the children of Israel that Yahweh staged the exodus to deliver them from slavery into the privileged state of being God's own possession (4.20, 32–37; 5.15; 6.12, 21–23; 7.8, 18–19; 8.14–16; 9.26; 10.19; 11.2–7; etc.)." Lyle M. Eslinger, "Freedom or Knowledge: Perspective and Purpose in the Exodus Narrative (Exodus 1–15)," *Journal for the Study of the Old Testament* 16, no. 52 (1991): 43–60.

11. Georg Sauer, "Vom Exoduserleben zur Landnahme: Theologische Erwägungen," *Zeitschrift für Theologie und Kirche* 80, no. 1 (1983): 30–31.

12. See similarly the threat of Hosea 8:13, 9:3, to the effect that, if they forget God, they will return to slavery in Egypt. Ralph W. Klein, "A Liberated Lifestyle: Slaves and Servants in Biblical Perspective," *Currents in Theology and Mission* 9, no. 4 (1982): 214.

13. Robert Alter, *The Five Books of Moses: A Translation with Commentary* (New York: Norton, 2004), 340; similarly, Goldingay, "Man of War," 83. On the debated historicity of the exodus event and its theological ramifications, see Christopher B. Ansberry, "The Exodus: Fact, Fiction, or Both?," in *Evangelical Faith and the Challenge of Historical Criticism*, ed. Christopher B. Ansberry and Christopher M. Hays (Grand Rapids, MI: Baker, 2013), 55–73.

14. Sauer, "Vom Exoduserleben zur Landnahme," 32, translation mine.

15. Cf. Klein, "Liberated Lifestyle," 212–13.

16. See, for example, 2 Kings 4:1; Nehemiah 5:1–5.

17. The term translated *liberty*, *dĕrôr*, in the NRSV can be used to describe the liberation from debt, captivity (Isa. 61:1), or slavery (thus, Jer. 34:8–9) and, in this context, the return of ancestral lands; *NIDOTTE* 1:986–87. W. H. Bellinger, *Understanding the Bible Commentary Series: Leviticus, Numbers* (Grand Rapids, MI: Baker, 2001), 149. It does not evoke as wide a range of meaning as *liberté* might (Alter, *Five Books*, 654) and may well be best translated *emancipation* or *remission* in some contexts, to avoid anachronistic interpretations; cf. Niels-Erik A. Andreasen, "Festival and Freedom: A Study of an Old Testament Theme," *Interpretation* 28, no. 3 (1974): 295. Jeremiah 34:8–15 is especially intriguing in the present connection, given that it uses the phrase *proclaim liberty* to describe the Sabbath liberation of slaves in the time of King Zedekiah; people freed their Hebrew slaves and then subsequently rescinded their emancipation and reenslaved them. God therefore "proclaims liberty" to the Israelites, a liberty unto the sword, pestilence, and famine (v. 17)! The consequences of violating the covenant conditions regarding emancipation are thus on clear display in this passage.

18. The Promised Land was divided to tribes, and each allotment was to be a permanent inheritance of a given family line; see, for example, Numbers 36:9.

19. In point of fact, even the Sabbath day is grounded in the experience of liberation from Egypt. Deuteronomy 5:14–15 dictates that one should keep the Sabbath holy precisely because the Israelites had been slaves in Egypt; the text also underscores, for that reason, that the Sabbath benefits should be extended to one's own servants/slaves. Andreasen, "Festival and Freedom," 283–84, 93.

20. Interestingly, when Deuteronomy 15:18 speaks of liberating the Hebrew slave in the Sabbath year, it indicates that the slave had *not* been paid: "It shall not seem hard to you when you let him go free from you, for at half the cost of a hired worker he has served you six years." This reveals, most likely, that the expense of feeding and maintaining an indentured servant amounted to half the cost of paying a laborer. Alter, *Five Books*, 957. Although verses 13–14 indicate that when he goes he should be liberally furnished with livestock, grain, and wine, that would not likely amount to several years' worth of wages; this may

be a contributing factor to why verses 15–17 include provisions for the slave to remain with their master permanently; although the stated reason is that he loves his master, it may also be that, apart from the Jubilee provision for the restoration of land, the emancipated slave would have no means by which to support himself. Christoph Bultmann, "Deuteronomy," in *The Oxford Bible Commentary*, ed. John Barton and John Muddiman, 135–58 (Oxford: Oxford University Press, 2001), 147.

21. The preposition and first-person singular suffix *lî* are frontloaded in the Hebrew clause precisely to add emphasis to God's divine ownership (*lî* is a dative of possession).

22. Note: *ăbāday* has been frontloaded in the clause for emphasis. Translation mine; italics added to reflect the emphasis implied by the Hebrew pronominal suffix.

23. Contrast the astonishing lexical clumsiness of Klein, "Liberated Lifestyle," 212: "While the Old Testament uses one word, *'ebed*, for both slave and servant, it radically differentiates between these words, with negative connotations when it refers to slaves and positive connotations when it refers to servants." Cf. Scott Bader-Saye, "The Freedom of Faithfulness," *Pro Ecclesia* 8, no. 4 (1999): 446–47. See Alter, *Five Books*, 658; and N. H. Snaith, *Century Bible: Leviticus and Numbers* (London: Thomas Nelson, 1967), 167–68.

24. Klein, "Liberated Lifestyle," 215–16.

25. Note that Isaiah 58:6–7 shows up again repeatedly in the New Testament: Matthew 5:4; 25:35; Luke 4:18; 6:20–21; 7:22.

26. The term for the *free*, *ḥāfšîm*, is used in Exodus 21:2, 5; Deuteronomy 15:12–13, 18, and so on, to describe Hebrew slaves who, as argued above, have probably been enslaved in order to pay off debts. Francis Brown, Samuel Rolles Diver, and Charles Augustus Briggs, *Enhanced Brown-Driver-Briggs Hebrew and English Lexicon* (Oxford: Clarendon, 1977), 344; and William Lee Holladay, ed. *A Concise Hebrew and Aramaic Lexicon of the Old Testament* (Grand Rapids, MI: Eerdmans, 1988), 113.

27. Ezekiel 34:27 looks forward to the eschatological shepherd breaking the yoke of foreign oppressors: "They shall be secure on their soil; and they shall know that I am the Lord, when I break the bars of their yoke, and save them from the hands of those who enslaved them."

28. Claus Westermann, *Isaiah 40–66: A Commentary*, Old Testament Library (Philadelphia: Westminster, 1969), 337.

29. John H. Walton, Victor H. Matthews, and Mark W. Chavalas, *The IVP Bible Background Commentary: Old Testament* (Downers Grove, IL: InterVarsity, 2000), 639; and Westermann, *Isaiah 40–66*, 366.

30. This text is evoked in Luke 4:18–19 as Luke depicts Jesus as the one fulfilling the role of the Isaianic servant anointed by the Spirit of the Lord.

31. The Hebrew construction here is an infinitive absolute with an imperfect verb. The imperfect verb has a permissive force in this use, and the infinitive absolute serves to emphasize the force of the imperfect verb. For this reason—emphasizing the permission to eat of nearly every tree in the garden—the translation "you may freely eat" is quite appropriate. (See *Gesenius' Hebrew Grammar* (*GKC*), ed. E. Kautzsch, trans. A. E. Cowley, 2nd ed. (Oxford: Oxford University Press, 1910), §107s; and Paul Joüon and T. Muraoka, *A Grammar*

of Biblical Hebrew, Subsidia biblica (Rome: Pontificio Istituto Biblico, 2000), 14/II:§§113l, 23h. Nonetheless, the use of *freely* should not be considered evidence of a pointed emphasis on free will; it is a gloss intended to communicate the emphasized permissive force.

32. In this case, the infinitive absolute + imperfect verb construct has a different force, insofar as the imperfect verb has a future affirmative force. Accordingly, the infinitive absolute intensifies the affirmative force, meaning that a translation "surely die" or "doomed to die" would be more appropriate (see *GKC* §113n; and Joüon and Muraoka, *Grammar of Biblical Hebrew*, §123e).

33. Gordon Wenham, *Word Biblical Commentary: Genesis 1–15* (Dallas: Word, 1998), 87.

34. Stek, "Salvation, Justice," 137–38; cf. Bader-Saye, "Freedom of Faithfulness," 449.

35. There are provocative parallels between the threats of Deuteronomy 28 and the consequences of the fall in Genesis 3. Deuteronomy 28:16–18 warns against difficulty with harvest and food, in parallel to Genesis 3:17–19. Deuteronomy 28:18, 32, 41, 53–57 warn of difficulty with children, in parallel to Genesis 3:16. Deuteronomy 28:48–68 warns of being conquered and exiled, in parallel to Genesis 3:23–24. Intriguingly, the coup de grâce of the curses of Deuteronomy 28 comes in verse 68, which warns that the exodus will be reversed and the Israelites will be sold back into slavery in Egypt: "The Lord will bring you back in ships to Egypt, by a route that I promised you would never see again; and there you shall offer yourselves for sale to your enemies as male and female slaves, but there will be no buyer."

36. Karl Barth, *Church Dogmatics*, vol. IV, part 1 (Peabody, MA: Hendrickson, 2010), 449–50.

37. This text communicates the role of the individual human moral choice in relation to punishment or blessing. While not denying the collective aspects of Israel's sin and fate, it balances those components with the reality that the collective fate of the nation is not reducible only to the actions of their leaders but is also the aggregate of many actions of infidelity committed by the individual members of the community. It is more precise, from a historical perspective, to speak of the nation of Judah, but Ezekiel casts Judah as Israel. Thus, to avoid confusion (outside the present footnote), the present essay will continue to use the term *Israel* even in relation to the book of Ezekiel—with apologies to proper Old Testament scholars.

38. This is similar to the view of the exile presented by 2 Kings 20:17–18; 21:11–15, which blames the kings Hezekiah and Manasseh for the Babylonian exile. J. Galambush, "Ezekiel," in *The Oxford Bible Commentary*, ed. John Barton and John Muddiman (Oxford: Oxford University Press, 2001), 547.

39. Christopher J. H. Wright, *Ezequiel: Un nuevo corazón y un nuevo espíritu*, Comentario Antiguo Testamento Andamio, trans. Dámaris Stunt, 2nd ed. (Barcelona: Andamio, 2011), 215–16; cf. the earlier affirmation that all the world belongs to God, in Exodus 19:5; so also Psalm 24:1.

40. The point is not to deny the historical reality that one generation is marked by the actions of the previous generation but to communicate that each generation nonetheless has responsibility before God and posterity to decide how they will live in whatever situation they find themselves. See also Robert W. Jenson, *Brazos Theological Commentary on the Bible: Ezekiel* (Grand Rapids, MI: Brazos, 2009), 148.

41. Jenson, 147.

42. So also God miraculously executed Achan and his entire family for Achan's sin (Josh. 7:10–26, especially v. 24).

43. H. L. Ellison, *Ezekiel: The Man and His Message* (Grand Rapids, MI: Eerdmans, 1956), 71.

44. Steven Tuell, *Ezekiel*, Understanding the Bible Commentary Series (Grand Rapids, MI: Baker, 2009), 108.

45. Wright, *Ezequiel*, 219–20.

46. Notice the way that this text links death and human free will, much as Genesis 3 does.

47. Alfred Bloom, "Human Rights in Israel's Thought: A Study of Old Testament Doctrine," *Interpretation* 8, no. 4 (1954): 430; and Ronald E. Clements, *Ezekiel*, Westminster Bible Companion (Louisville, KY: Westminster John Knox, 1996), 80.

48. Tuell, *Ezekiel*, 120; cf. Bloom, "Human Rights," 429.

49. Wright, *Ezequiel*, 339; cf. Deuteronomy 6:14–15, which says that God would wipe out the Israelites for worshipping other deities.

50. Clements, *Ezekiel*, 162; and Tuell, *Ezekiel*, 245.

51. Tuell, *Ezekiel*, 246. This is what Moses feared in Numbers 14:16; see Wright, *Ezequiel*, 341.

52. Christopher J. H. Wright, *The Bible Speaks Today: The Message of Ezekiel: A New Heart and a New Spirit* (Leicester, Engl.: InterVarsity, 2001), 290.

53. God makes it clear that he is doing it for his own sake and not for their sake. This is probably not intended to depict God as hardhearted or vindictive but may be evidence that Israel had still not repented of the sins for which they were exiled.

54. Similar new exodus imagery is used in Ezekiel 11:17–20; 20:34–38, 41–42; 28:25–26; 34:12; 37:12–14, 21; 39:27–38 to describe the end of the exile. Wright, *Ezequiel*, 345. So also in Isaiah 43:14–21; 49:8–13, 22–23; 51:9–11. *NIDOTTE* 2:499; and Goldingay, "Man of War," 98.

55. Jenson, *Ezekiel*, 278–79.

56. Jenson, 280.

57. For detail, see *NIDOTTE* 2:749–54; Holladay, *Hebrew and Aramaic Lexicon*, 171; and "Heart," in *Dictionary of Biblical Imagery*, ed. Leland Ryken, James C. Wilhoit, and Tremper Longman III (Downers Grove, IL: InterVarsity, 1998), 368–69.

58. The "heart of stone" is a motif developed earlier in the book: Ezekiel 2:4; 3:7; similarly, Isaiah 6:9–10 says that God hardened Israel's heart in response to their prior rebellion.

59. Galambush, "Ezekiel," 557; and Wright, *Ezequiel*, 348.

60. Similar sentiments occurred earlier in Ezekiel 11:19 and Jeremiah 31:33. This motif, under the influence of Jeremiah 31 and Ezekiel 11, 18, and 36, appears in John 6:45; Romans 2:5, 15; 2 Corinthians 3:3; and Hebrews 8:8–16; 10:16.

61. The transformation of the hearts of the people of God, just like the restoration of God's name on earth, are not prerequisites for God's decision to restore Israel from exile; rather, they are entailments of God's plan of restoration for his people; cf. Wright, *Ezequiel*, 344. For an exegetically savvy treatment of how to square the role of human repentance in

Ezekiel 18 and divine transformation of the human heart in Ezekiel 36, see Casey A. Strine, "The Role of Repentance in the Book of Ezekiel: A Second Chance for a Second Generation," *Journal of Theological Studies* 63, no. 2 (2012): 467–91.

62. Clements, *Ezekiel*, 163; and Wright, *Ezequiel*, 349. Similarly, in Deuteronomy 30:6, God circumcises Israel's heart *so that* they will love (*lĕʾahăbāh*) God with all their hearts and souls, as required in Deuteronomy 6, and therefore live. Wright, *Ezequiel*, 349.

63. The exact same dynamic occurs in Deuteronomy 30:2 and 10, which tell Israel to turn their hearts to God, and verse 6 avers that God will circumcise Israel's heart. Wright, *Ezequiel*, 240.

64. Cf. Tuell, *Ezekiel*, 119.

65. So Clements, *Ezekiel*, 81–82: "What Ezekiel and Jeremiah were concerned to bring to the fore, in setting the foundations of the New Israel, was the freedom of choice that lies open to each individual. Each can make the decision to repent and find life—a new dimension of life—in which God will remain real and present, even though the familiar landmarks of the old nation of Israel have fallen down."

66. Gerard Manley Hopkins, "Patience, hard thing! the hard thing but to pray," in *The Gospel in Gerard Manley Hopkins: Selections from His Poems, Letters, Journals, and Spiritual Writings*, ed. Margaret R. Ellsbeg (Elsmore, Australia: Plough, 2017).

67. Leslie C. Allen, *Psalms 101–150*, Word Biblical Commentary (Waco, TX: Word, 1983), 141; and John E. Goldingay, *Psalms*, vol. 3, *Psalms 90–150*, Baker Commentary on the Old Testament Wisdom and Psalms (Grand Rapids, MI: Baker Academic, 2008), 381.

68. "The deuteronomic concept of loving God is . . . applied to the Torah." Allen, *Psalms 101–150*, 136.

69. Robert Alter, *The Book of Psalms: A Translation with Commentary* (New York: Nelson, 2007), 424. So also Psalm 118:5: "Out of my distress I called on the Lord; the Lord answered me and set me in a broad place [*bamerĕḥāb*]." Allen suggests, "The idea of spaciousness is spiritualized and here refers to a life free from restrictions of distress and so free to develop its full potential." Allen, *Psalms 101–150*, 136. This is possible, although I do wonder whether, against the background of the exile and forced displacement, simply having the liberty to perambulate where one wills is a sufficient explanation of this verse. In personal correspondence, Casey Strine also pointed out to me that this text includes an echo of Genesis 26:22, in which Isaac and Rebekah find a new place to live and call it *Rehoboth* (from the same root).

70. Compare with Psalm 19:13; Genesis 4:7. Allen, *Psalms 101–150*, 138.

71. "The Psalmist's delight and dedication issue not merely from a selfless affirming of whatever Yhwh approves, but from an awareness that such affirming is in our interests." Goldingay, *Psalms*, 3:401.

72. This text was drawn to my attention by Bader-Saye, "Freedom of Faithfulness," 447.

73. Barth, *Church Dogmatics*, vol. III, part 2, 196–97.

Old Testament Texts about Freedom

Selections for Dialogue

The Exodus: The Paradigm for Liberation from Oppression and Belonging to God

Exodus 6:2–9

[2]God also spoke to Moses and said to him: "I am the LORD. [3]I appeared to
Abraham, Isaac, and Jacob as God Almighty, but by my name 'The LORD' I
did not make myself known to them. [4]I also established my covenant with
them, to give them the land of Canaan, the land in which they resided as
aliens. [5]I have also heard the groaning of the Israelites whom the Egyptians
are holding as slaves, and I have remembered my covenant. [6]Say therefore
to the Israelites, 'I am the LORD, and I will free you from the burdens of the
Egyptians and deliver you from slavery to them. I will redeem you with an
outstretched arm and with mighty acts of judgment. [7]I will take you as my
people, and I will be your God. You shall know that I am the LORD your
God, who has freed you from the burdens of the Egyptians. [8]I will bring you
into the land that I swore to give to Abraham, Isaac, and Jacob; I will give it
to you for a possession. I am the LORD.'" [9]Moses told this to the Israelites;
but they would not listen to Moses, because of their broken spirit and their
cruel slavery.

Exodus 19:3–6

[3]Then Moses went up to God; the LORD called to him from the mountain,
saying, "Thus you shall say to the house of Jacob, and tell the Israelites:
[4]You have seen what I did to the Egyptians, and how I bore you on eagles'
wings and brought you to myself. [5]Now therefore, if you obey my voice
and keep my covenant, you shall be my treasured possession out of all the
peoples. Indeed, the whole earth is mine, [6]but you shall be for me a priestly

kingdom and a holy nation. These are the words that you shall speak to the Israelites."

Submission to the Law of God Rooted in the Exodus Liberation

Deuteronomy 6:4–9, 12–19

[4]Hear, O Israel: The Lord is our God, the Lord alone. [5]You shall love the Lord your God with all your heart, and with all your soul, and with all your might. [6]Keep these words that I am commanding you today in your heart. [7]Recite them to your children and talk about them when you are at home and when you are away, when you lie down and when you rise. [8]Bind them as a sign on your hand, fix them as an emblem on your forehead, [9]and write them on the doorposts of your house and on your gates. . . . [12]Take care that you do not forget the Lord, who brought you out of the land of Egypt, out of the house of slavery. [13]The Lord your God you shall fear; him you shall serve, and by his name alone you shall swear. [14]Do not follow other gods, any of the gods of the peoples who are all around you, [15]because the Lord your God, who is present with you, is a jealous God. The anger of the Lord your God would be kindled against you and he would destroy you from the face of the earth. [16]Do not put the Lord your God to the test, as you tested him at Massah. [17]You must diligently keep the commandments of the Lord your God, and his decrees, and his statutes that he has commanded you. [18]Do what is right and good in the sight of the Lord, so that it may go well with you, and so that you may go in and occupy the good land that the Lord swore to your ancestors to give you, [19]thrusting out all your enemies from before you, as the Lord has promised."

Legislating and Systematizing the Exodus Liberation: Slavery and the Jubilee

Leviticus 25:8, 10–13, 39–42, 55

[8]You shall count off seven weeks of years, seven times seven years, so that the period of seven weeks of years gives forty-nine years. . . .[10]And you shall hallow the fiftieth year and you shall proclaim liberty throughout the land to all its inhabitants. It shall be a jubilee for you: you shall return, every one of you, to your property and every one of you to your family. [11]That fiftieth year shall be a jubilee for you: you shall not sow, or reap the aftergrowth, or harvest the unpruned vines. [12]For it is a jubilee; it shall be holy to you: you shall eat only what the field itself produces. [13]In this year of jubilee you shall return, every one of you, to your property. . . .

39If any who are dependent on you become so impoverished that they sell themselves to you, you shall not make them serve as slaves. 40They shall remain with you as hired or bound laborers. They shall serve with you until the year of the jubilee. 41Then they and their children with them shall be free from your authority; they shall go back to their own family and return to their ancestral property. 42For they are my servants, whom I brought out of the land of Egypt; they shall not be sold as slaves are sold. . . .

55For to me the people of Israel are servants; they are my servants whom I brought out from the land of Egypt: I am the Lord your God.

Free Will and Personal Responsibility

Genesis 2:15–17; 3:1–7, 22–24

15The Lord God took the man and put him in the garden of Eden to till it and keep it. 16And the Lord God commanded the man, "You may freely eat of every tree of the garden; 17but of the tree of the knowledge of good and evil you shall not eat, for in the day that you eat of it you shall die." . . .

3 1Now the serpent was more crafty than any other wild animal that the Lord God had made. He said to the woman, "Did God say, 'You shall not eat from any tree in the garden'?" 2The woman said to the serpent, "We may eat of the fruit of the trees in the garden; 3but God said, 'You shall not eat of the fruit of the tree that is in the middle of the garden, nor shall you touch it, or you shall die.'" 4But the serpent said to the woman, "You will not die; 5for God knows that when you eat of it your eyes will be opened, and you will be like God, knowing good and evil." 6So when the woman saw that the tree was good for food, and that it was a delight to the eyes, and that the tree was to be desired to make one wise, she took of its fruit and ate; and she also gave some to her husband, who was with her, and he ate. 7Then the eyes of both were opened, and they knew that they were naked; and they sewed fig leaves together and made loincloths for themselves. . . .

22Then the Lord God said, "See, the man has become like one of us, knowing good and evil; and now, he might reach out his hand and take also from the tree of life, and eat, and live forever"—23therefore the Lord God sent him forth from the garden of Eden, to till the ground from which he was taken. 24He drove out the man; and at the east of the garden of Eden he placed the cherubim, and a sword flaming and turning to guard the way to the tree of life.

Ezekiel 18:1–4, 19–20, 30–32

1The word of the Lord came to me: 2What do you mean by repeating this proverb concerning the land of Israel, "The parents have eaten sour grapes,

and the children's teeth are set on edge"? [3]As I live, says the Lord GOD, this
proverb shall no more be used by you in Israel. [4]Know that all lives are mine;
the life of the parent as well as the life of the child is mine: it is only the
person who sins that shall die. . . .

[19]Yet you say, "Why should not the son suffer for the iniquity of the father?" When the son has done what is lawful and right, and has been careful
to observe all my statutes, he shall surely live. [20]The person who sins shall die.
A child shall not suffer for the iniquity of a parent, nor a parent suffer for the
iniquity of a child; the righteousness of the righteous shall be his own, and
the wickedness of the wicked shall be his own. . . .

[30]Therefore I will judge you, O house of Israel, all of you according to
your ways, says the Lord GOD. Repent and turn from all your transgressions;
otherwise iniquity will be your ruin. [31]Cast away from you all the transgressions that you have committed against me, and get yourselves a new heart
and a new spirit! Why will you die, O house of Israel? [32]For I have no pleasure
in the death of anyone, says the Lord GOD. Turn, then, and live.

Moral Transformation to Make Possible the Free Submission to God

EZEKIEL 36:16–28

[16]The word of the LORD came to me: [17]Mortal, when the house of Israel lived
on their own soil, they defiled it with their ways and their deeds; their conduct in my sight was like the uncleanness of a woman in her menstrual period. [18]So I poured out my wrath upon them for the blood that they had shed
upon the land, and for the idols with which they had defiled it. [19]I scattered
them among the nations, and they were dispersed through the countries; in
accordance with their conduct and their deeds I judged them. [20]But when
they came to the nations, wherever they came, they profaned my holy name,
in that it was said of them, "These are the people of the LORD, and yet they
had to go out of his land." [21]But I had concern for my holy name, which
the house of Israel had profaned among the nations to which they came.
[22]Therefore say to the house of Israel, Thus says the Lord GOD: It is not for
your sake, O house of Israel, that I am about to act, but for the sake of my
holy name, which you have profaned among the nations to which you came.
[23]I will sanctify my great name, which has been profaned among the nations,
and which you have profaned among them; and the nations shall know that
I am the LORD, says the Lord GOD, when through you I display my holiness
before their eyes. [24]I will take you from the nations, and gather you from all
the countries, and bring you into your own land. [25]I will sprinkle clean water

upon you, and you shall be clean from all your uncleannesses, and from all
your idols I will cleanse you. [26]A new heart I will give you, and a new spirit
I will put within you; and I will remove from your body the heart of stone
and give you a heart of flesh. [27]I will put my spirit within you, and make you
follow my statutes and be careful to observe my ordinances. [28]Then you shall
live in the land that I gave to your ancestors; and you shall be my people,
and I will be your God.

The Law as the Guide for Personal Freedom, Ensuring Liberty from Oppressors

Psalms 119:43–48, 133–134

[43]Do not take the word of truth utterly out of my mouth,
for my hope is in your ordinances.
[44]I will keep your law continually,
forever and ever.
[45]I shall walk at liberty,
for I have sought your precepts.
[46]I will also speak of your decrees before kings,
and shall not be put to shame;
[47]I find my delight in your commandments,
because I love them.
[48]I revere your commandments, which I love,
and I will meditate on your statutes. . . .
[133]Keep my steps steady according to your promise,
and never let iniquity have dominion over me.
[134]Redeem me from human oppression,
that I may keep your precepts.

Freedom from Oppression in the Moral Vision of the Prophets

Isaiah 58:6–7

[6]Is not this the fast that I choose:
to loose the bonds of injustice,
to undo the thongs of the yoke,
to let the oppressed go free,
and to break every yoke?
[7]Is it not to share your bread with the hungry,

and bring the homeless poor into your house;
when you see the naked, to cover them,
and not to hide yourself from your own kin?

ISAIAH 61:1–3

1The spirit of the Lord GOD is upon me,
because the LORD has anointed me;
he has sent me to bring good news to the oppressed,
to bind up the brokenhearted,
to proclaim liberty to the captives,
and release to the prisoners;
2to proclaim the year of the LORD's favor,
and the day of vengeance of our God;
to comfort all who mourn;
3to provide for those who mourn in Zion—
to give them a garland instead of ashes,
the oil of gladness instead of mourning,
the mantle of praise instead of a faint spirit.

The Motif of Freedom in New Testament Texts

An Introduction

Susan Eastman

The motif of freedom is a consistent—indeed, dominant—theme through the varied writings of the New Testament. In this essay, I provide discussion of freedom as found in some key texts quoted in the following chapter, ranging from the gospels to Paul's letters, to the letter to the Hebrews, and James. It is tempting to set the discussion in conversation with other first-century views of freedom, such as those found in Stoicism and Hellenistic Judaism; but for the sake of brevity, I will keep the focus only on the New Testament.[1] Before looking more closely at a few key texts, I will highlight some consistent themes and the assumptions implicit in them, particularly in comparison with modernist understandings of freedom.

First, we might tend to think of freedom in terms of the autonomy of the individual; across the board, the New Testament authors never think in this way.[2] Rather, *freedom* is a relational term. Whether the issue at hand is "freedom from sin," "freedom from death," or social forms of freedom and slavery, the term always concerns persons in relationship and the characteristics of the relational matrices in which human beings "live and move and have their being." There is a self, but there is never a purely self-determining self. There are human agents, but they are always both constrained and constituted in connection with other agencies and environmental factors.[3]

Second, these constraining and liberating factors include matters of social status and location but, more importantly, from the perspective of the New Testament writings, external agencies that are spiritual realities. On the enslaving side is the power of evil. Sometimes this power or force is named as demons (*daimonia*), or the devil (*ho diabolos*), or satan (*satanas*). Sometimes it is named as sin (*hamartia*) and death (*thanatos*). The relationship between these entities is complex and debated, but overall, sin, death, and evil are greater than human individuals and social institutions, and they are not ultimately intrinsic to human personhood, which is created in the image of God.

Hence, liberation always comes from God because ultimately only God has the power to free human beings from the powers of evil and death. From the perspective of Christian faith, God has done this through entering the fray, so to speak, in the incarnation, death, and resurrection of Jesus Christ. Human liberation, that is, depends on divine initiative, action, and power. But just as enslavement is enacted socially and interpersonally, so also freedom is worked out socially and interpersonally in the human sphere.

Third, freedom concerns human agency in relationship to divine action; to act in concert with God's will, which is always ultimately for human flourishing, is to act in freedom. In this the New Testament authors surely draw on their grounding in the teachings of the Torah and the Prophets. Conversely, to act contrary to God's will is not to act as a free agent but rather to exhibit a kind of slavery to sin, which is depicted as a slavemaster that drives human beings to act contrary to their deepest desires.

In what follows I offer some orienting comments for interpreting the New Testament texts on freedom that are found in the following chapter, along with more in-depth discussion of selected passages. I focus first on the themes of freedom *from* sin and death, and freedom *for* human flourishing, which in practice means freedom to love and to serve other human beings. Then I comment on texts that portray Jesus as the one who liberates human beings *from* bondage and isolation and *for* community and mutual love. The final section concerns social slavery and freedom in practical terms, in the nascent Christian communities located in the slave economy of the Roman Empire. I close with some observations regarding the relational metaphors the New Testament authors deploy to depict freedom.

Freedom from Sin and Death

In John 8:34, Jesus says, "everyone who does sin is a slave to sin." Romans 6:14–23 concerns liberation from sin as a slavemaster, into the realm of God's gracious gift of life. Romans 8:2 further elucidates the meaning of freedom from sin as freedom from "the law of sin and death," which means the law in the grip of sin and death. Hebrews 2:14–15 depicts liberation from lifelong bondage to the fear of death. In what follows, our focus is on John 8:31–36, with a few comments on Romans 6:14–23.

John 8:31–36

Speaking to "the Jews who had believed in him" Jesus challenges them to "remain [Greek, *menō*] in my word" if they want to be his disciples and thereby to "know the truth" that will make them "free." The conditional clause, "If you remain in my word" is in a form in Greek that implies a probable positive outcome: "If you remain in my word (and you probably will!)." Nonetheless, Jesus's listeners do not take kindly to his promise, "the truth *will* make you free," because it so clearly implies that at present they are *not* free—they are slaves! They protest by referring to their lineage as children and heirs of Abraham: they are not children of a slave; therefore, they are not slaves.

The kinship language and social power dynamics in this interchange are crucial to understanding what is going on: slaves are low status, they have no rights of kinship, and they have no future, including no right of inheritance. All of this comes into play in the conversation between Jesus and his would-be followers, when Jesus depicts sin as a form of slavery and puts his listeners in the category of "slaves" and "sinners." They immediately interpret his depiction in terms of belonging, lineage, kinship, and future inheritance, and Jesus agrees with their way of framing the issue. For both Jesus and his conversation partners, the dispute is not about individual freedom of choice; rather, it is about who their "father" truly is. Thus, Jesus's opponents do not claim individual autonomy; they claim Abraham as their father. Jesus in turn frames freedom as a matter of being a child in the household of God, where the son makes one free and guarantees one's future. Jesus emphasizes this sense of destiny through the repetition of the word *remain* (*menō*) in v. 35: "The slave does not remain forever; the son remains forever."

Hence, freedom is a matter of identity, status, and belonging. Jesus reframes this kinship language in terms of belonging to the son in the household, which in John's gospel means Jesus as the Son of God. Freedom is a matter of a relational bond and social matrix that liberates, over against a relational bond with sin, which enslaves. Verses 32 and 36 drive home the point: "the truth will set you free" (v. 32) parallels "if the Son sets you free, you are free indeed" (v. 36). Therefore, the identity of the truth cannot be separated from the identity of the Son as united to God the Father and as witness to the reality of God. For this reason, the truth that liberates is not a "what" but a "who," not a concept or set of facts or beliefs but the living God. Soon after this Jesus says, "I speak of what I have seen with my Father" (8:38). Later in John, Jesus makes the startling claim, "I am the way, the truth, and the life" (14:6). Consequently, truth—and, with it, freedom—is bound up with the identity and origin of Jesus as the one who both witnesses to the truth of God and incarnates it, making it present with liberating power.

Romans 6:14–23

Something similar happens in Romans 6:14–23. The entire passage is bracketed by the language of divine grace, or gift. The word translated *grace* in verse 14 is *charis*, which also means "gift." In the final verse (23), the word translated *free gift* is *charisma*, again bringing home the connection between *grace* and *gift*. This divine gift of life is contrasted with death as "the wages of sin"; in the context of the intervening paragraph on slavery to sin and liberation from sin, "the wages of sin is death" (v. 23) does not mean that God punishes sin with death. Rather, it means that sin, like a slave owner (or a colonial power) repays its minions with death; God, on the other hand, graciously gives life. Contained in that gift is the power to resist sin's dominion and thereby to be free, precisely through union with God as one's Lord and master.

Freedom to Love: The Social Outworking of Freedom

The goal of freedom *from* sin and death is freedom *for* others. The following two passages illustrating such freedom come from authors who often are contrasted with one another: Paul and James. In regard to the social outworking of freedom, however, they are in agreement. I comment briefly on each.

Galatians 5:13–15

Galatians 5:13 translates literally, "You were called to freedom, brothers and sisters, but do not let your freedom become an opportunity [*aphormē*] for the flesh [Greek, *sarx*], but through love serve one another as slaves [*douleuete*]." The word *aphormē* has the sense of "staging area" or "base of operations" in a military sense, clarifying that Paul sees "the flesh" (*sarx*) not simply as self-indulgence, although it includes that meaning, and not simply as passions, including sexual passions, but as something bigger than the individual—a hostile force that takes on a life of its own and drives humanity toward evil and lethal ends. Therefore, *sarx* does not simply signify the body, although it involves bodily actions, nor is it primarily a quality of individuals, although it involves individuals. Rather, it has a corporate force and expression. For examples of "the flesh" we might think of the kinds of groupthink that lead to genocide, or hatred toward one group, or racism, as well as the fires of jealousy and resentment that destroy relationships. Such behavior is never an exercise of "freedom" but an expression of corporate as well as individual bondage to sin. To speak of "freedom to sin" is nonsensical from the perspective of Paul. One might think one is "choosing" to do wrong, but such choice is in fact an expression of bondage, whether or not it is recognized as such. It is rather like an alcoholic "choosing" to have a drink, and then another drink, and then another.

In the context of Galatians, here "freedom" signifies freedom from both sin and the condemnation and judgment that the law pronounces on sin. Paul wants the Galatians to know that such freedom can be exercised only in mutual love and service. He is concerned with the quality of life together in the community, so that the terminology of slavery, here used in a positive sense, implies a kind of mutual belonging in love, issuing in communal life characterized by the "fruit" of the Spirit of God: "love, joy, peace, patience, kindness, goodness, faithfulness, gentleness, self-control" (5:22–23), over against the communally destructive "works of the flesh": sexual sins, idolatry, sorcery, enmity, strife, jealousy, anger, selfishness, dissension, and so forth (5:20–21). It is as slaves of Christ, living together in the household of God, that believers are to exercise such love for one another.[4]

Such love is also the fulfillment of the Mosaic law; in Galatians 5:14 Paul cites Leviticus 19:18, "You shall love your neighbor as yourself," as the fulfillment of the whole law. In this he follows in the footsteps of Jesus (Matt. 22:39) and anticipates James 2:8, which also cites Leviticus 19:18.

James 1:22–25

Like Paul, James is concerned with the social outworking of freedom, although he phrases this in terms of "the law of liberty." This law of liberty is the same as "the implanted word" to which James refers in the immediately preceding verse (James 1:21); thus, James has in mind the law working internally in the hearts of believers, perhaps echoing the promise of Jeremiah 31:33: "I will put my law within them, and I will write it upon their hearts; and I will be their God, and they shall be my people." As doers of this "word," James's listeners will be like those who see themselves in a mirror and act on what they see. That is, their identity and their actions will be in harmony with one another; such harmony is a form of freedom. This "law of liberty" is "perfect" or "complete" (*teleios*). James uses similar terminology in James 2:8–12: "If you complete or perfect [*teleion*] the royal law, according to the scripture, 'You shall love your neighbor as yourself,' you do well." Then he gives an example of what such love looks like: it is the refusal to show partiality to the wealthy, paying attention to the rich and neglecting the poor. James concludes, "If you fail at one point in keeping the law, you are guilty of the whole law." The conclusion restates James 1:22: "So speak and so act as those who are to be judged by the law of liberty." Hence, "the law of liberty" appears to be the law both as it empowers believers and also as it is an enactment of the law that grants liberty to others.

Jesus as Liberator

As we saw in John 8:31–36, Jesus incarnates and enacts freedom. One key passage demonstrating Jesus as the liberator is Luke 4:16–21, where Jesus begins his public ministry by quoting Isaiah 61:1–2 and 58:6: "The Spirit of the Lord is upon me, because he has anointed me to proclaim the good news to the poor; he has sent me to proclaim release [*aphesis*] to the captives and recovery of sight to the blind, to set at liberty [*aphesin*] those who are shattered and broken; to proclaim the acceptable year of the Lord."

I will draw our attention briefly to three matters in this verse. First is the repetition of the Greek word *aphesis*, which translates as "deliverance," "release," or "cancellation of a debt." The same word is used elsewhere in the New Testament to signify forgiveness of sins (Luke 3:3; 24:47; Mark 1:4; 3:29; Matt. 26:28; Acts 2:38; 5:31; 10:43; 26:18). *Aphesis* also translates "the year of Jubilee" in the Septuagint Greek version of Leviticus 25:50; the *year of Jubilee* is "the year of *aphesis*"—the year of release from debt slavery, to be precise. According to Leviticus 25, every fifty years was to be a year of release, when debts were forgiven and those indentured for debt were released and sent back to their homes.[5] The year of Jubilee was intended to push a reset button on society by releasing people from debt and freeing them from backbreaking economic burdens that they could never shake off by themselves. Such release is the meaning of Jesus's quotation from Isaiah 61:2 proclaiming "the acceptable year of the Lord." Jesus proclaims at the very outset of his public ministry that the promised liberation from debt bondage and resulting social inequality is present now, in his own actions and words.

Second, the word translated *oppressed* (*tethrausmenous*) means "shattered." Translations vary from *oppressed* (NRSV) to *bruised* (KJV), to *downtrodden* (NAS). The word vividly illustrates the social reality from which Jesus intends to free people. Freedom here means release from physical and psychological destruction due to economic and social circumstances, which are the social outworking of corporate sin. Jesus is quoting Isaiah 58:6: "Is not this the fast that I choose: to loose the bonds of wickedness, to undo the thongs of the yoke, to let the oppressed go free, and to break every yoke?" With this as the headline for his first public sermon, Jesus announces his message and ministry as "good news to the poor."

Third, the sequel to that proclamation is equally radical, and it pushes beyond the boundaries set in Leviticus 25. According to Leviticus, freedom from debt slavery applied only to members of the people of Israel. The Israelites were not to enslave their own people but were rather to buy slaves from the foreigners among them; furthermore, such slavery was generational (Lev. 25:44–46). Jesus undoes this ethnic limitation on freedom. In a way reminiscent of the passage from John 8:31–36, he refuses to accept the shallow affirmation of his listeners. Rather, he reminds them of two stories from their own tradition, in which Gentile outsiders received succor and healing, while Jewish insiders went hungry and unhealed. The stories make clear that his good news of liberation from economic and social bonds extends to the stranger, the outsider, and the socially ostracized; this is one of the main themes of Luke's gospel, but it is to be found in all the other gospels as well.

Two pictures of liberation, one from Luke and one from Mark, illustrate the point. I offer a few comments on the passage from Luke and discuss Mark 5:1–20 in more depth. Luke 13:10–17 tells the story of Jesus healing a woman who was crippled for eighteen years. Luke narrates this condition as the effect of a crippling spirit that has imprisoned the woman; indeed, Jesus ascribes her crippled condition to Satan's bondage. Here we see Jesus setting a prisoner free physically and socially, just as he promised in his sermon in Nazareth. And as in Nazareth, he performs this liberating activity in contravention of existing norms by healing the woman on the Sabbath day and thereby (according to some interpretations of the law of the Sabbath) going against the divine commandment. In his rebuke of the leader of the synagogue, Jesus elevates the marginalized woman to a place of worth and importance, shaming the religious leaders who appear to care more about their livestock than another human being. The practical, physical, and social components of this freedom are striking, in marked contrast to ancient Stoic ideas of freedom as primarily an inner disposition detached from outward circumstances.[6]

Mark 5:1–20

Mark 5:1–20 tells the story of Jesus healing a man possessed by unclean spirits. It is instructive to note the social situation of this man, who is constrained by concentric circles of bondage and isolation. He is inwardly overrun, an occupied territory taken over by hostile and inimical forces in the form of demons who call themselves "Legion, because there are so many of us" (Mark 5:9). In the Roman army that occupied Palestine, a "legion" was a military unit of four to six thousand soldiers. The name thus calls up an image of Roman oppression, even as it emphasizes the overwhelming power of the inward forces enslaving the demoniac. Socially, the man is outwardly ostracized by the town and routinely chained and tied up, although the chains are ineffective. He lives among the tombs, in an unclean place of the dead, in the Decapolis, a Gentile region far beyond the bounds of respectability for a Jewish rabbi. Like his healing of the crippled woman, Jesus's encounter with this tormented man transgresses social boundaries.

Jesus begins by asking the demoniac his name. That is, he distinguishes between the man and the demons, even though the man himself cannot make such a distinction and has lost his capacity to speak for himself. Jesus thus forms an alliance with the man, over against the unclean spirits, and after he casts out the demons, he sends the man back to his community: "Go and tell what the Lord has done for you." We see here a restoration of agency, voice, and community, even in the face of real potential social conflict. For this is not a private matter. Jesus's action results in economic loss through the drowning of the pigs that form the primary economic base of this Gentile region. The casting out of the demons results in social reversals, as the townspeople see the demoniac clothed and in his right mind. No wonder they beg Jesus to leave. Such practical freedom has social and economic consequences that are not always welcome in the status quo.

And that observation leads to the final set of passages, on social slavery and freedom.

Social Slavery and Freedom

In discussing the texts on social slavery, I focus on the topic of freedom despite the temptation to focus on issues of equality. And that proves to be rather illuminating because it is clear that, from the viewpoint of the early Christians, freedom is distinct from matters of equality or social status, which neither guarantee *nor* inhibit freedom "in Christ." Such a disjunction between "freedom" and "equality" can be seen to have both positive and negative effects, certainly from the standpoint of the history of interpretation over the past two millennia. None of the texts cited in the next chapter explicitly challenges the institution of slavery, which was ubiquitous in the Roman Empire; rather, Colossians 3:22 and Ephesians 6:5–8 enjoin Christian slaves to obey their masters as they obey Christ. It is true that both letters also command Christian slave owners to treat their slaves fairly, keeping in mind that they themselves have a "master in heaven" (Col. 4:1; Eph. 6:9). But they do not tell slave owners to free their slaves, nor do they tell slaves to rebel against their bondage. Thus, while there are seeds here of a pressure or influence for social change within the community of faith, over against the dominant values of the empire, that influence is subtle; there is no call for revolution. There is, rather, a utilization of the extremely familiar trope of slavery to describe all believers as slaves of God, in a mutual belonging that has the potential to reorient their social relations.

In distinctive ways, 1 Corinthians 7:21–23 and Philemon illustrate such potential social transformation. In 1 Corinthians 7, Paul advises converts to remain in the state in which they were when "called"—that is, when they became followers of Christ. The larger passage is headed by this principle (v. 17): "Let each of you lead the life that the Lord has assigned, to which God called you." Paul first applies this advice to circumcision and uncircumcision (v. 19), and then, repeating the principle in verse 20, to the condition of slavery and freedom. Here, however, he makes an exception for slaves: "If you have the opportunity to gain your freedom, make use of it" (v. 21).[7] Such an understanding of the text is undergirded by verse 23: "You were bought with a price [that is, you were freed from slavery by Christ]. Do not be enslaved to anyone!" But insofar as it was not always feasible for a slave to gain freedom, the intervening verse 22 destabilizes the categories of freedom and slavery "in Christ": a slave has the status of a free person through belonging to Christ; the free believer has the status of a slave through belonging to Christ. Thus, in the community of believers, dignity, status, worth, and agency derive from belonging to God above all other masters, in distinction from social markers of status and power.

Obviously, such a destabilizing of societal categories is going to set up a tension between the status of persons in the community of faith and in the larger society. This tension is illustrated in Paul's letter to Philemon, in which he asks Philemon to receive back the slave Onesimus, "no longer as a slave but more than a slave, a beloved brother—especially to me but how much more to you, both in the flesh and in the Lord" (Philem. 16). Here we see a relativizing of social status and social capital in relationship to the status and dignity given by God, with the implication that this God-given status also should create new patterns of relationship between believers. The phrase "both in the flesh and in the Lord" pushes against a purely inward, disembodied interpretation of Paul's exhortation to Philemon to receive Onesimus as a "brother in Christ." He is to receive him thus in ways that are concrete, practical, and socially visible.

Once again, freedom is a relational term: it is a matter of the relationships that constitute human beings and give them dignity and worth, in which human agency is strengthened, over against relationships in which the self is swallowed up, devalued, denied, and absorbed. Thus, there is an inevitable conflict between the status of believers in the context of the community and their status outside the community in the social hierarchies of the time. I suspect such a status conflict must have happened with Onesimus, who is also mentioned in the letter to the Colossians as "the faithful and beloved brother, who is one of yourselves" (Col. 4:9). The implication is that Onesimus was indeed freed and became a leader in the early Christian mission.[8]

Many of the texts studied here under the rubric of "freedom" became deployed in later Christian arguments against slavery in Great Britain and America. A relatively early example comes from an influential tract by the eighteenth-century British abolitionist Granville Sharpe. Published in 1776, the tract is titled "The Law of Liberty: or, royal law, by which all mankind will be judged."[9] Drawing connections between James 1:25, 2:8–12, Galatians 5:14, Matthew 22:37–40, and 1 Corinthians 7:21–23, Sharpe argued against the presumed legality of Christians owning slaves:

> The propriety of citing this glorious and comprehensive law of liberty, in vindication of the natural liberty of mankind *against the Tyranny of Slave-holders*, cannot be doubted or called in question; for though this supreme law virtually prohibits every other kind of *Oppression*, yet its very title leads us to a more particular and express application of it against the toleration of slavery among Christians: because it seems to be thus eminently distinguished by the appointment of God himself in his Holy Word, as *the peculiar Antidote* against that *baneful Evil* (slavery) which is most opposite and repugnant to its glorious title—"the law of liberty." This "law of liberty," this supreme, this "royal law," must therefore be our guide in the interpretation and examination of all Laws which relate *to the Rights of Persons*, because it excludes *Partiality*, or *Respect of Persons*, and consequently removes all ground for the pretence [*sic*] of any *absolute Right of Dominion inherent in the Masters* over their Slaves: for as all Ranks of Men are equal *in the Sight of God* (the Christian *Slave*, or Servant, being *the Freeman* of the Lord, and the Christian *Master* the *Servant* of Christ, 1 Cor. 7:22) there is no doubt but that the same *Christian* Qualities are necessary to be maintained by the *Christian* master, that are required of the *Christian* servant; as *Humility, Forgiveness of Trespasses* or *Debts, and* (though not *Submission,* yet certainly) *Brotherly Love towards Inferiors,* with *unfeigned Charity* and *universal Benevolence,* founded on the glorious Maxim, or *Royal Law,* "Thou shalt love thy neighbor as thyself." All which are as indispensably

> necessary to form the disposition of a *true Christian Master*, as they are absolutely incompatible with the oppressive and tyrannical Claims of our American Slaveholders![10]

Concluding Remarks: Freedom, Slavery, Kinship, and Friendship

As we have seen, in the New Testament *freedom* is relationally mediated and expressed. It is not a matter of individual independence and autonomy but rather of belonging to relational matrices that strengthen and liberate human agency, over against those that do not. Ultimately, such freedom comes from belonging to God, who is known through Jesus Christ and present and active in the community of faith. Thus, in a way that may be shocking to modern interpreters, freedom is not expressed through individual autonomy but rather through belonging to God alone as one's master, over all other potential masters. New Testament authors do not hesitate to use the language of slavery to depict such belonging, in contrast to the debilitating and ultimately lethal slavery of being controlled by sin. In the human relationship to God, the language of slave and master signifies God's absolute authority and power; in mutual human interactions, it signifies mutual belonging to Christ, leading to mutual love and service (Gal. 5:13). Paradoxically, one can be both a slave and free; Augustine captured this paradox when he addressed God as the one "whom to serve is to reign as a king."

Nonetheless, it would be misleading to end with slavery as the dominant social metaphor for freedom in the New Testament. Rather, the language of slavery is modified by two other common tropes in ancient Greco-Roman culture: kinship and friendship. As we see in John 8:31–36, Jesus contrasts the status of slavery with that of sonship: "The slave does not have a permanent place in the household; the son has a place there forever. So if the son makes you free, you will be free indeed" (John 8:35–36). The point is that sons, unlike slaves, have the right of inheritance and therefore have a secure future.[11] Paul makes a similar point in Galatians 4:1–7, where he contrasts the effective state of slavery with adoption as sons. Adoption was a common practice in the Roman Empire, by which wealthy Roman citizens ensured that their property went to the person of their own choosing. Paul describes his converts as those adopted by God and bound to God in a filial relationship mediated by the divine Spirit sent into their hearts: "And because you are sons, God has sent the Spirit of his Son into our hearts, crying, 'Abba, Father!' So through God you are no longer a slave but a son, and if a son, then an heir" (Gal. 4:6–7). This relational metaphor of kinship extends to interpersonal connections between members of the community and is far more common than the language of slavery for depicting the bonds between believers. As demonstrated in Philemon, the shift from the relationship of master and slave to the bond between brothers and sisters in the Lord potentially destabilizes the hierarchy of social slavery. To be a "brother in the Lord" is ipso facto to be a "beloved brother" with a claim on one's respect and love (Philem. 16).

Alongside the motif of sibling relationship is the motif of friendship. In John 15:15, in the midst of his final discourse to his disciples, Jesus says, "No longer do I call you slaves, for the slave does not know what his master is doing; but I have called you friends, for all that I have heard from my Father I have made known to you." In other words, friends share knowledge with one another; here Jesus invites his disciples into a shared understanding of God's will. Crucially, that mutual knowledge is to bear a very particular fruit, the fruit of mutual love between believers (John 15:16). In the larger context, the entire shift from slavery to friendship is bracketed by the love commandment: "This is my commandment, that you love one another as I have loved you. Greater love has no one than this, that a person lay down his life for his friends. You are my friends if you do what I command you" (John 15:12–14). Almost immediately Jesus repeats himself: "This I command you, to love one another" (John 15:17). By implication, friendship means one is willing to die for another person; such love is simply the outworking of Jesus's friendship and solidarity with human beings—to the point of, in fact, dying for them. The friendship and love Jesus commands from his disciples grows out of this divine solidarity, enacted among the believers through the Spirit of truth dwelling among them (John 14:15–17). This is the social enactment of Jesus's earlier promise, "You will know the truth, and the truth will make you free" (John 8:32).

In conclusion, freedom is supremely enacted and experienced in love for one's fellow human beings. It has nothing to do with a presumed freedom to have one's own way or act in destructive ways. Rather, freedom arises out of bonds of mutual love and service, grounded in divine grace, which is gifted freely out of divine abundance.

Notes

1. The Stoic philosopher Epictetus argued, "no bad man is free" (*Disc.* 4.1.5). To the boastful young man who thinks he does whatever he wants, Epictetus says mockingly, "Were you never commanded by your sweetheart to do something you didn't wish to do?

Did you never cozen your pet slave? Did you never kiss his feet?" (*Disc.* 4.1.17). Philo, the first-century Jewish philosopher, expounds on the same Stoic idea in "Every Good Man is Free": "For in very truth he who has God alone for his leader, he alone is free, though to my thinking he is also the leader of all others, having received the charge of earthly things from the great, the immortal King, whom he, the mortal, serves as viceroy" (*Prob.* 3.20). Both Philo and Epictetus envision freedom in terms of an inner process of detachment from external influences and an individual decision to act in accordance with the divine will.

2. It is debatable whether the notion of autonomy existed in the first-century Mediterranean world. A. A. Long, for example, argues that the Stoics were the forerunners of modern notions of the autonomous individual. See his "Representation and the Self in Stoicism," in *Stoic Studies* (Cambridge: Cambridge University Press, 1996), 264–85. For an opposing view, see Christopher Gill, *The Structured Self in Hellenistic and Roman Thought* (Oxford: Oxford University Press, 2006), 328–44, 359–70.

3. For discussion of this notion of the relational self in contemporary and Stoic thought and in the letters of Paul, see S. G. Eastman, *Paul and the Person: Reframing Pauline Anthropology* (Grand Rapids, MI: Eerdmans, 2017).

4. Paul speaks of himself and his fellow missionaries as "slaves of Christ" or "slaves of God" (Rom. 1:1; Gal. 1:10; Phil. 1:1).

5. "And if your brother becomes poor beside you, and sells himself to you, you shall not make him serve as a slave: he shall be with you as a hired servant and as a sojourner. He shall serve with you until the year of the jubilee; then he shall go out from you, he and his children with him, and go back to his own family, and return to the possession of his fathers. For they are my servants, whom I brought forth out of the land of Egypt; they shall not be sold as slaves. You shall not rule over him with harshness, but shall fear your God" (Lev. 25:39–43).

6. As we shall see, such a dispositional understanding of freedom is also present in Christian thought, with one striking difference: inward freedom amid outward social bondage comes not through one's inner "acropolis," to use a Stoic term, but through belonging to Christ. See further below.

7. The Greek translated here as "make use of it" is *mallon chrēsai*. Because the referent for *it* is not clear, some translations prefer to interpret Paul's meaning as "make use of your present condition of slavery." For example, the NRSV reads, "Even if you can gain your freedom, make use of your present condition now more than ever." But nothing in the Greek demands such a translation, and in view of verse 23, the RSV translation used here is more persuasive. For extensive discussion of the translation issues, see Anthony Thiselton, *The First Epistle to the Corinthians*, The New International Greek Testament Commentary (Grand Rapids, MI: Eerdmans, 2000), 553–65.

8. The name Onesimus appears again in the early second-century Epistle of Ignatius to the Ephesians (Ign. Eph. 1–6), in which the early martyr Ignatius encourages the Ephesian Christians to respect Onesimus their bishop. Whether this is the same Onesimus is difficult to determine. For discussion, see John W. Martens, "Ignatius and Onesimus: John Knox Reconsidered," *Second Century* 9, no. 2 (Summer 1992): 73–86.

9. "The law of liberty: or, royal law, by which all mankind will certainly be judged!" Granville Sharpe, *The law of liberty: or, royal law, by which all mankind will certainly be judged!*. . . *By Granville Sharp*, Oxford Text Archive, 2011, http://ota.ox.ac.uk/id/5214.

10. Sharpe, 30–32.

11. I choose to keep the male pronoun here because it maintains the link between filial status and inheritance in the ancient Mediterranean. At the same time, insofar as the language of sonship is sometimes used interchangeably with the word for "children" (*tekna*) and "human being" (*anthropos*), the terminology is inclusive of women as well as men. The same may be said for "brothers" (*adelphoi*), which the NRSV now translates inclusively as "brothers and sisters."

New Testament Text about Freedom

Selections for Dialogue

Freedom from Sin and Death

John 8:31–36

31 Then Jesus said to the Jews who had believed in him, "If you continue in
my word, you are truly my disciples; 32 and you will know the truth, and
the truth will make you free." 33 They answered him, "We are descendants
of Abraham and have never been slaves to anyone. What do you mean by
saying, 'You will be made free'?"

34 Jesus answered them, "Very truly, I tell you, everyone who commits sin
is a slave to sin. 35 The slave does not have a permanent place in the household; the son has a place there forever. 36 So if the Son makes you free, you
will be free indeed."

Romans 6:14–23

14 For sin will have no dominion over you, since you are not under law but
under grace.

15 What then? Should we sin because we are not under law but under grace?
By no means! 16 Do you not know that if you present yourselves to anyone as
obedient slaves, you are slaves of the one whom you obey, either of sin, which
leads to death, or of obedience, which leads to righteousness? 17 But thanks
be to God that you, having once been slaves of sin, have become obedient
from the heart to the form of teaching to which you were entrusted, 18 and
that you, having been set free from sin, have become slaves of righteousness.
19 I am speaking in human terms because of your natural limitations. For just
as you once presented your members as slaves to impurity and to greater and
greater iniquity, so now present your members as slaves to righteousness for
sanctification.

[20]When you were slaves of sin, you were free in regard to righteousness.
[21]So what advantage did you then get from the things of which you now are
ashamed? The end of those things is death. [22]But now that you have been
freed from sin and enslaved to God, the advantage you get is sanctification.
The end is eternal life. [23]For the wages of sin is death, but the free gift of God
is eternal life in Christ Jesus our Lord.

Romans 8:1–4

There is therefore now no condemnation for those who are in Christ Jesus.
[2]For the law of the Spirit of life in Christ Jesus has set you free from the law
of sin and of death. [3]For God has done what the law, weakened by the flesh,
could not do: by sending his own Son in the likeness of sinful flesh, and to
deal with sin, he condemned sin in the flesh, [4]so that the just requirement
of the law might be fulfilled in us, who walk not according to the flesh but
according to the Spirit.

Hebrews 2:11–18

[11]For the one who sanctifies and those who are sanctified all have one Father.
For this reason Jesus is not ashamed to call them brothers and sisters, [12]saying,

"I will proclaim your name to my brothers and sisters,
in the midst of the congregation I will praise you."
[13]And again,
"I will put my trust in him."
And again,
"Here am I and the children whom God has given me."

[14]Since, therefore, the children share flesh and blood, he himself likewise
shared the same things, so that through death he might destroy the one
who has the power of death, that is, the devil, [15]and free those who all their
lives were held in slavery by the fear of death. [16]For it is clear that he did not
come to help angels, but the descendants of Abraham. [17]Therefore he had to
become like his brothers and sisters in every respect, so that he might be a
merciful and faithful high priest in the service of God, to make a sacrifice of
atonement for the sins of the people. [18]Because he himself was tested by what
he suffered, he is able to help those who are being tested.

Freedom to Love: The Social Outworking of Freedom

Galatians 5:1, 13–15

For freedom Christ has set us free. Stand firm, therefore, and do not submit
again to a yoke of slavery. . . .

[13]For you were called to freedom, brothers and sisters; only do not use
your freedom as an opportunity for self-indulgence, but through love become slaves to one another. [14]For the whole law is summed up in a single
commandment, "You shall love your neighbor as yourself." [15]If, however,
you bite and devour one another, take care that you are not consumed by
one another.

James 1:22–25

[22]But be doers of the word, and not merely hearers who deceive themselves.
[23]For if any are hearers of the word and not doers, they are like those who
look at themselves in a mirror; [24]for they look at themselves and, on going
away, immediately forget what they were like. [25]But those who look into the
perfect law, the law of liberty, and persevere, being not hearers who forget
but doers who act—they will be blessed in their doing.

Jesus as Liberator

Luke 4:16–30

[16]When he came to Nazareth, where he had been brought up, he went to the
synagogue on the sabbath day, as was his custom. He stood up to read, [17]and
the scroll of the prophet Isaiah was given to him. He unrolled the scroll and
found the place where it was written:

[18]"The Spirit of the Lord is upon me,
because he has anointed me
to bring good news to the poor.
He has sent me to proclaim release to the captives
and recovery of sight to the blind,
to let the oppressed go free,
[19]to proclaim the year of the Lord's favor."

[20]And he rolled up the scroll, gave it back to the attendant, and sat down.
The eyes of all in the synagogue were fixed on him. [21]Then he began to
say to them, "Today this scripture has been fulfilled in your hearing." [22]All
spoke well of him and were amazed at the gracious words that came from his
mouth. They said, "Is not this Joseph's son?" [23]He said to them, "Doubtless
you will quote to me this proverb, 'Doctor, cure yourself!' And you will say,
'Do here also in your home town the things that we have heard you did at
Capernaum.'" [24]And he said, "Truly I tell you, no prophet is accepted in the
prophet's home town. [25]But the truth is, there were many widows in Israel
in the time of Elijah, when the heaven was shut up for three years and six

months, and there was a severe famine over all the land; [26]yet Elijah was sent
to none of them except to a widow at Zarephath in Sidon. [27]There were also
many lepers in Israel in the time of the prophet Elisha, and none of them
was cleansed except Naaman the Syrian." [28]When they heard this, all in the
synagogue were filled with rage. [29]They got up, drove him out of the town,
and led him to the brow of the hill on which their town was built, so that
they might hurl him off the cliff. [30]But he passed through the midst of them
and went on his way.

Two Pictures of Liberation

Luke 13:10–17

[10]Now he was teaching in one of the synagogues on the sabbath. [11]And just
then there appeared a woman with a spirit that had crippled her for eighteen
years. She was bent over and was quite unable to stand up straight. [12]When
Jesus saw her, he called her over and said, "Woman, you are set free from
your ailment." [13]When he laid his hands on her, immediately she stood up
straight and began praising God. [14]But the leader of the synagogue, indig-
nant because Jesus had cured on the sabbath, kept saying to the crowd,
"There are six days on which work ought to be done; come on those days
and be cured, and not on the sabbath day." [15]But the Lord answered him and
said, "You hypocrites! Does not each of you on the sabbath untie his ox or
his donkey from the manger, and lead it away to give it water? [16]And ought
not this woman, a daughter of Abraham whom Satan bound for eighteen
long years, be set free from this bondage on the sabbath day?" [17]When he said
this, all his opponents were put to shame; and the entire crowd was rejoicing
at all the wonderful things that he was doing.

Mark 5:1–20

They came to the other side of the sea, to the country of the Gerasenes.
[2]And when he had stepped out of the boat, immediately a man out of the
tombs with an unclean spirit met him. [3]He lived among the tombs; and no
one could restrain him any more, even with a chain; [4]for he had often been
restrained with shackles and chains, but the chains he wrenched apart, and
the shackles he broke in pieces; and no one had the strength to subdue him.
[5]Night and day among the tombs and on the mountains he was always howl-
ing and bruising himself with stones. [6]When he saw Jesus from a distance,
he ran and bowed down before him; [7]and he shouted at the top of his voice,
"What have you to do with me, Jesus, Son of the Most High God? I adjure
you by God, do not torment me." [8]For he had said to him, "Come out of the

man, you unclean spirit!" [9]Then Jesus asked him, "What is your name?" He replied, "My name is Legion; for we are many." [10]He begged him earnestly not to send them out of the country. [11]Now there on the hillside a great herd of swine was feeding; [12]and the unclean spirits begged him, "Send us into the swine; let us enter them." [13]So he gave them permission. And the unclean spirits came out and entered the swine; and the herd, numbering about two thousand, rushed down the steep bank into the sea, and were drowned in the sea. [14]The swineherds ran off and told it in the city and in the country. Then people came to see what it was that had happened. [15]They came to Jesus and saw the demoniac sitting there, clothed and in his right mind, the very man who had had the legion; and they were afraid. [16]Those who had seen what had happened to the demoniac and to the swine reported it. [17]Then they began to beg Jesus to leave their neighborhood. [18]As he was getting into the boat, the man who had been possessed by demons begged him that he might be with him. [19]But Jesus refused, and said to him, "Go home to your friends, and tell them how much the Lord has done for you, and what mercy he has shown you." [20]And he went away and began to proclaim in the Decapolis how much Jesus had done for him; and everyone was amazed.

Concerning Social Slavery and Freedom

1 Corinthians 7:21–23

[21]Were you a slave when called? Never mind. But if you can gain your freedom, avail yourself of the opportunity. [22]For he who was called in the Lord as a slave is a freedman of the Lord. Likewise he who was free when called is a slave of Christ. [23]You were bought with a price; do not become slaves of men.

Colossians 3:22

Slaves, obey your earthly masters in everything, not only while being watched and in order to please them, but wholeheartedly, fearing the Lord.

Ephesians 6:5–9

[5]Slaves, obey your earthly masters with fear and trembling, in singleness of heart, as you obey Christ; [6]not only while being watched, and in order to please them, but as slaves of Christ, doing the will of God from the heart. [7]Render service with enthusiasm, as to the Lord and not to men and women, [8]knowing that whatever good we do, we will receive the same again from the Lord, whether we are slaves or free. [9]And, masters, do the same to them. Stop threatening them, for you know that both of you have the same Master in heaven, and with him there is no partiality.

The Letter of Paul to Philemon

Paul, a prisoner of Christ Jesus, and Timothy our brother,

To Philemon our dear friend and co-worker, 2to Apphia our sister, to Archippus our fellow soldier, and to the church in your house:

3Grace to you and peace from God our Father and the Lord Jesus Christ.

4When I remember you in my prayers, I always thank my God 5because I hear of your love for all the saints and your faith toward the Lord Jesus. 6I pray that the sharing of your faith may become effective when you perceive all the good that we may do for Christ. 7I have indeed received much joy and encouragement from your love, because the hearts of the saints have been refreshed through you, my brother.

8For this reason, though I am bold enough in Christ to command you to do your duty, 9yet I would rather appeal to you on the basis of love—and I, Paul, do this as an old man, and now also as a prisoner of Christ Jesus. 10I am appealing to you for my child, Onesimus, whose father I have become during my imprisonment. 11Formerly he was useless to you, but now he is indeed useful both to you and to me. 12I am sending him, that is, my own heart, back to you. 13I wanted to keep him with me, so that he might be of service to me in your place during my imprisonment for the gospel; 14but I preferred to do nothing without your consent, in order that your good deed might be voluntary and not something forced. 15Perhaps this is the reason he was separated from you for a while, so that you might have him back forever, 16no longer as a slave but more than a slave, a beloved brother—especially to me but how much more to you, both in the flesh and in the Lord.

17So if you consider me your partner, welcome him as you would welcome me. 18If he has wronged you in any way, or owes you anything, charge that to my account. 19I, Paul, am writing this with my own hand: I will repay it. I say nothing about your owing me even your own self. 20Yes, brother, let me have this benefit from you in the Lord! Refresh my heart in Christ. 21Confident of your obedience, I am writing to you, knowing that you will do even more than I say.

22One thing more—prepare a guest room for me, for I am hoping through your prayers to be restored to you.

23Epaphras, my fellow prisoner in Christ Jesus, sends greetings to you, 24and so do Mark, Aristarchus, Demas, and Luke, my fellow workers.

25The grace of the Lord Jesus Christ be with your spirit.

Thematic Dimensions of Freedom

Christian Texts from the Classical Period

Jonathan Chaplin

As conceived by the 2019 Building Bridges Seminar, the classical Christian period runs all the way from the first to the seventeenth centuries (CE). A single chapter cannot provide a comprehensive overview of the range and diversity of textual sources on freedom produced during an era that begins prior to the conversion of Constantine and ends at the birth of modernity. Rather, we focus on passages from selected works, chosen because they seem to convey recurring and representative thematic dimensions of freedom across much of the period. Upon perusal of these selections—which can be found in the chapter following this one—it is quickly evident that these texts rearticulate many of the central meanings of freedom in the Hebrew and Christian scriptures summarized so lucidly in the chapters herein by Christopher Hays and Susan Eastman. Rather than commenting on each passage individually, I highlight six thematic dimensions that are either evident on the surface of these texts or at least might shed some broader light on them. Others might well explain them in different terms. Indeed, given the vast diversity within the tradition over such an extended period, others might well have highlighted different themes entirely.[1]

Freedom and Creation

It is true that, as Christopher Hays points out, the first and definitive ancient Hebrew experience of God is of exodus, of liberation from imperial oppression—the overturning and repair of a violated order of justice and freedom. This experiential priority, however, presupposes a prior ontological constitution of human freedom in the very structure of the created (natural) order—as is attested in numerous ways in the Hebrew and Christian scriptures, albeit usually indirectly. Such order is not understood as a constraint on freedom but rather as its primordial, constitutive condition—as what makes possible any kind of being, action, agency or relationship across the whole created order. Freedom is not essentially over against givenness; it is itself a "given" of created being—a divine "gift," as Augustine puts it.[2] Admittedly, this ontology of freedom is rarely on the surface of the biblical text. It comes to be articulated much more explicitly in the work of patristic and medieval Christian theologians and philosophers like Ambrose, Augustine, and Aquinas, as a result of an extended critical engagement with Greco-Roman ideas of cosmic order, nature, reason, and natural law.

Freedom and Humanity

Assuming such a generic ontology of freedom, Christian thinkers gave special attention to human freedom. We might sum up the emerging notion thus: freedom is the embodied, volitional, and intellectual ("rational") capacity for, and the spiritual, moral, and social vocation to, the exercise of responsible human agency. Let me add here that by *responsible* I mean respons*iveness* to the givenness of created order. For human freedom is always only responsive, in that it is exclusively an interaction with such givenness. It is not that human freedom starts where created order (or divine will) leaves off: humans have nothing to act on (or with) apart from created givens. Human freedom is thus radically other than divine creation, which brings something out of nothing and designs it from scratch.

But equally, human freedom is always an undetermined response: thus, Aquinas asserts that the "rational creature" is "not compelled by natural necessity to do what he ought to do, but has the free choice of proceeding according to 'his own counsel.'"[3] Human freedom is natural but never determined by material or biological conditions. It consists in exercising one's will according to reason, which means (inter alia) in conformity with natural order and directed toward natural ends—toward created human "goods." The notion of reason it assumes is thus profoundly different to modern Enlightenment notions, such as "Reason" as supreme arbiter of truth, or instrumental rationality as a calculative technique for achieving human objectives or desires.

Freedom and Salvation

As the chapters by Hays and Eastman convey, in Christian Scripture, to be "saved" is to be transferred from an oppressive form of "slavery" (whether to imperial rule, distorted desire, or demonic possession) to a liberating form of "slavery" in which alone true freedom is to be found. Thus, Augustine's text sets out how, if humans had exercised their freedom in alignment with their "sovereign Lord," they would have enjoyed a blessed (felicitous) existence, enjoying all created gifts in proper measure and experiencing harmonious fellowship with their Creator. "Rational creation has been so made that it is to man's advantage to be in subjection to God." But he goes on: "It is calamitous for him to act according to his own will, and not to obey the will of his Creator." Humanity has indeed so acted—"fallen away from the works of God to its own works." This is its "first evil act of will," producing multiple evil deeds with all their dehumanizing and death-dealing consequences.[4] Choosing evil has plunged humans into a debilitating slavery to misdirected and self-defeating desires, and their freedom "can only be restored by him who had the power to give it at the beginning," through his chosen instrument, the "saviour and liberator" Jesus Christ.[5]

Most classical writers assumed that such salvation begins with the conversion of the individual to Christ, which brings about their radical liberation from the powers of sin, evil, "the desires of the flesh," and, ultimately, death (I discuss the social dimension in the next section). It effects a restoration of true personal agency. Ambrose expresses a widely held view that such "freedom" is, first of all, a spiritual freedom from the internal tyranny of sin, which can be obtained and enjoyed in spite of adverse external social circumstances, such as even human slavery.[6] Equally, while Ambrose recognizes here that the freedom offered by social liberations such as manumission is of some value, he insists that lacking them does not detract from authentic spiritual freedom. The truly free person is the wise person who has acquired the learning (that is, the necessary spiritual transformation and moral formation) to live virtuously in accordance with the divine will, as expressed in nature and in scripture, irrespective of external circumstances.

Fast-forwarding a millennium for a moment, the theme of internal spiritual freedom is radically and forcefully reasserted in the Protestant Reformation, represented here first by one of Luther's earliest writings. It is sometimes said that in Luther we find a far-reaching (and, for some, regressive) turn toward interiority. This is true in the sense that Luther's overriding mission was to liberate believers from the stifling legalistic imperatives of a corrupt Roman Catholic hierarchy that was heaping excessive, enslaving obligations on believers as a necessary means to salvation (and generating substantial revenues in the process). His mission was to retrieve St. Paul's notion of the freedom of the Christian from such works of the law and to insist that the only spiritually worthwhile works are those done freely—out of love of Christ and neighbor—and not out of compulsion or in expectation of tangible reward. Mere law conformity has no salvific value in itself. Thus, a Christian can be a "perfectly free lord of all, subject to none" because he has been liberated from sin by the gospel of grace (the "Word"). Calvin closely echoes this notion.

Yet in both Luther and Calvin, such "interior" freedom was coupled with a robust insistence that it be wholly deployed in service of God and neighbor. The believer was not only to be redeemed from sin but also made "holy" or "sanctified"—conformed progressively to the will of God. This might involve the kind of intense spiritual wrestling depicted in the John Donne poem ("o'erthow me" to "make me new"—for my "Reason . . . is captiv'd").[7] Thus, for Luther a Christian is simultaneously "a perfectly dutiful servant of all, subject to all." While a Christian is not bound "in conscience" either to Mosaic law or to ecclesiastical law, he stands under "the royal law" (the "law of Christ"), which enjoins him, as "the outer man," to live righteously—to practice "good works" of all kinds.[8] To fail to do so would be "wicked." Calvin equally warns believers not to confuse the proper "abolition of human constitutions" (= laws) with the overthrowing of all obedience—to God, and, as we'll see, to legitimate human authorities.

Freedom and Sociality

Hays and Eastman amply display how freedom in Christian Scripture is never thought of as an individual power or possession but is always understood relationally. Humans are freed from the slavery of sin in order to experience restored participation in just and peaceable community. Humans were designed to form and enjoy such community already from the beginning. Biblical relationality (the egalitarian polity of Israel, the inclusive fellowship of the church) presupposes an original created capacity for and inclination toward sociality, in which freedom is unthinkable for an individual abstracted from a web of empowering human relations. This is intimated already in the Genesis account of the creation of man and women for each other, which the tradition often took to be the exemplar of the constitutive sociality of humankind as a whole. Thus, Augustine: "God created man as one individual; but that did not mean that he was to remain alone, bereft of human society. God's intention was that in this way the unity of human society and the bonds of human sympathy be more emphatically brought home to man, if men were bound together not merely by likeness in nature but also by the feeling of kinship."[9]

Later thinkers (e.g., Aquinas, Calvin) observed that such "kinship" might come to expression in a variety of social forms, each embodying diverse natural (creation-based) norms and, in some cases, also redemptive norms. These various forms might be said to express the evolving human responsiveness to created human social needs, inclinations, and capacities. And in contrast to the dominant paradigm in Greco-Roman thought, the political community is merely one such form, accorded no morally or spiritually privileged place in human society. Aquinas, while he cites Aristotle favorably in our passage, elsewhere asserts that man is not only a political but also a social animal.[10]

Freedom and Law

The notion of freedom as constituted through sociality allows the proper sense in which humans are obliged to obey various kinds of law or authority to come into view. Here again there are threads of commonality amid a wide diversity of conceptions. For Aquinas, freedom is not inherently opposed to conformity to social norms nor to obedience to human authorities or laws. Rather, because humans, both rulers and ruled, are rational, they can and must both deliberate about whether a particular human law or authority is *in fact* rational and thus whether it rightly obliges its subjects.[11] It is true that Aquinas does defend the notion of a natural hierarchy in created order. His own applications of that notion to the human realm at times offend against modern (and modern Christian) sensibilities (for example, in gender relations). But this idea should be read in light of two of his more plausible claims in the passage. One is that authority relations of some kind are necessary for any ordered human society. The other is that the authority to command is conditional on the rationality of the commandment (not just the office of the one who commands): "in order that what [the will of a superior] commands may have the character of law, the will must itself be in accord with some rule of reason";[12] which is to say that it must be just.[13] In the same vein, Ambrose denies the Aristotelian presumption that there could be "natural slaves"; slavery is a human artifact and a product of foolishness, not a rational created given.[14] Aquinas agrees.

Aquinas insists that law, like any act of will, "is something belonging to reason."[15] Human law, itself a constraint on others' wills, must be ruled by reason as the criterion of its validity. If law is rational in this sense, it is not inimical to freedom but a condition of its social exercise. Indeed, the primary end toward which rational human law must be directed is "the common happiness"—the shared good of the whole and not just the cumulative separate goods of its parts.[16] The very *telos* of law itself expresses the intrinsic sociality of all human action.

Of course, the classical authors knew full well that human will and human law are frequently not rational but often arbitrary, unjust, and oppressive—though it is fair to say that vigorous protests against oppression are rarely to the fore in their writings, and neither are the prophetic, disruptive, and liberative thrusts of the New Testament texts brought out in Susan Eastman's paper. Francisco de Vitoria's highly circumspect and qualified analysis of the Conquistadores' brutal treatment of the American Indians lacks the moral urgency of his contemporary Bartolomé de las Casas but is instructive precisely because it deploys formal Thomistic categories for a critical political purpose.[17] Vitoria echoes the traditional Christian view that "slavery is a civil and legal condition, to which no man can belong by nature."[18] Because all rational human beings possess the natural right (freedom) to govern themselves, the legitimacy of the Spanish conquest is itself placed in question. Even though Indians are unbelievers, they prove their rationality—a condition of true dominion—in their manifest ability to maintain an ordered society. Vitoria thus defends the Indians' right to "natural dominion"—that is, freedom of self-governance, prior to conquest—and (at much greater length elsewhere in the text) defines the criteria by which alone such dominion could be curtailed.[19]

In very different circumstances, and with little reliance on typically Thomistic language, Luther and Calvin both offered robust defenses of the office of temporal or civil government as a divinely authorized institution.[20] They did not construe political authority as arising naturally but upheld the earlier patristic view, shared by Augustine, that political authority was a "providentially" ordained instrument for the maintenance of order and (a measure of) justice in fallen human society. They could certainly level pointed critiques at particular rulers, but they had little patience with talk of disobedience or rebellion.[21] Subjection to the external rules of civil government was a Christian obligation, even though its remit was, as Calvin put it, confined to "matters of the present life, not only to food and clothing, but to the enacting of laws which require a man to live among his fellows purely, honourably, and modestly."[22] While the Reformers' remarks on civil government can seem quiescent, even conducive to authoritarianism, Calvin, for example, was nevertheless able to propose a wide range of reforms in Geneva pursuant to economic and social justice, reflecting his high estimation of government as an "honourable calling" under God and of law as performing a positive pedagogical function (and not merely a negative, restraining function, as for Luther).

Freedom and Religion

Calvin's account of the limited remit of the jurisdiction of civil government presents a natural segue into the John Locke passage. For in spite of Calvin's restriction of that remit to "matters of this present life," he equally insists that civil government has a divinely given duty to protect "true religion" and to extirpate dangerous religious falsehoods from the public realm. Thus, in defining the scope of government power, he warns (in another passage) against "the folly of those who would neglect the care of divine things and devote themselves merely to the administration of justice among men; as if God had appointed rulers in his own name to decide the earthly controversies, and omitted what was of far greater moment, his own pure worship as prescribed by his law."[23] The rationale was not that civil rulers were equipped to exercise "spiritual jurisdiction" (that was the exclusive preserve of duly appointed ministers of the Reformed churches) but that it fell within their public order remit to enforce a high degree of religious uniformity—in the interests of social trust and civic stability. Calvin's specific account of the complementary jurisdictions of "spiritual" and "civil" government differed in important ways from Thomistic and other medieval accounts. But in affirming the broad duty of civil government to enforce true religion within their territory, he was merely reiterating the predominant tradition of Christendom since the time of Theodosius, who imposed Christianity by law across the Roman Empire.

When we turn to Locke's *Letter concerning Toleration*, we are reminded just how far Protestant political theology traveled in a little over a century—one dominated by religious wars. Locke's *Letter* draws on a developing tradition of Protestant dissent originating with the sixteenth-century Swiss Anabaptists and extended by seventeenth-century Baptists such as Roger Williams, by Quakers, and by assorted others such as Sebastian Castellio (an adversary of Calvin) and John Milton. This tradition eventually breaks fundamentally with the Christendom model. Locke marshals a number of biblical, historical, philosophical, and political arguments (of variable cogency[24]) against this model and in favor of religious toleration of dissenting individuals and churches, and he denies outright that there could be such a thing as "a Christian commonwealth." His definition of the scope of civil authority sounds at first blush rather like Calvin's "matters of this present life": "Civil interests I call life, liberty, health, and indolency of body; and the possession of outward things, such as money, lands, houses, furniture, and the like." But Locke is emphatic that this scope "neither can nor ought in any manner to be extended to the salvation of souls."[25] It cannot include any regulatory authority over, or public privileging of, any spiritual matters at all, whether liturgies, doctrines, or appointments. Such toleration is far from unqualified, however: excluded are those who are bound by higher loyalty to a foreign power (Catholics and Muslims) or those whose oaths cannot be trusted (atheists). Much debate has ensued over Locke's account of the "just bounds" between the jurisdictions of the church and civil government. My own view is that, for all the *Letter*'s momentous and abiding insights, Vatican II's *Declaration on Religious Freedom* offers a substantially superior account of those bounds.

Notes

1. One of the themes omitted is the long-standing debate over free will versus predestination (the prior election of some individuals to salvation, implying also, for the more logically stringent, the prior election of some individuals to damnation). Augustine, Aquinas, Martin Luther, and John Calvin all supported versions of predestination, without necessarily denying the subjective human experience of free choice. A good rule of thumb is that when an intellectual problem turns out to be so tortuously complex as to be persistently insoluble, it has probably been wrongly construed at the outset. I favor a reading that sees election not as individual but corporate, referring to the "People of God" collectively. If pressed to take a position on the historical debate, it would be a version of the compatibilism Christopher Hays endorses (see Hays's chapter in the present volume).

2. See Augustine of Hippo, *City of God*, Book XII, chapter 21 (also presented in the next chapter of the present volume). One might also claim that there are nonhuman agents, fitted with specific possibilities of action according to their created natures. This claim was not always acknowledged in the tradition, insofar as irrational creatures were not thought to possess freedom at all. The idea tries to capture the biblical suggestion that nonhuman creatures nevertheless fulfill their allotted purpose(s) in creation (consciously or not) and, indeed, render their own kind of praise to the Creator. See Pope Francis, *Laudato Si'* (2015), http://www.vatican.va/content/francesco/en/encyclicals/documents/papa-francesco_20150524_enciclica-laudato-si.html.

3. Thomas Aquinas, *Summa theologiae*, in R. W. Dyson, ed. and trans., *St Thomas Aquinas: Political Writings* (Cambridge: Cambridge University Press, 2002), 58.

4. Augustin, *City of God*, Book 14, chap. 11. See Philip Schaff, trans. *St Augustin's City of God and Christian Doctrine* (New York: Christian Literature Publishing, 1890), 272.

5. Augustine, 272.

6. Ambrose, Letter No. 7 to Justus, Corpus Scriptorum Ecclesiasticorum Latinorum (CSEL), http://csel.sbg.ac.at/en/.

7. See John Donne, "Batter my heart," included in the next chapter of this volume.

8. See excerpts from Martin Luther, "The Freedom of the Christian," included in the next chapter of the present volume.

9. Augustine, *City of God*, 241.

10. Aquinas, *Summa theologiae*, 5–6.

11. Or, as contemporary moral philosophers would put it, whether it is obligation-generating. Where it is not, because irrational or unjust, classical thinkers usually thought it a distinct question whether or not one should nevertheless obey it, even if one was not

bound in conscience. For a variety of more or less plausible reasons, most counselled obedience to even irrational or unjust laws (sometimes with the exception of sustained tyranny).

12. Aquinas, *Summa theologiae*, 78.

13. In our passage, Aquinas raises the long-standing debate over whether "the will of the prince has the force of law." Roman imperial apologists asserted that the mere "will of the prince" was sufficient to render a law valid. Along with many Christian thinkers, Aquinas (subtly) challenges this by saying, in effect, "but only if it is rational" (= just).

14. Ambrose, Letter No. 7 to Justus.

15. Aquinas, *Summa theologiae*, 77.

16. Aquinas, 79. "Common happiness" means "common good," which is the term he uses later in this same passage (80).

17. Vitoria was long associated with the Spanish court, functioning (he hoped) as a kind of critical insider.

18. From "On the American Indians" | *De Indis* in Anthony Pagden and Jeremy Lawrence, eds., *Vitoria: Political Writings* (Cambridge: Cambridge University Press, 1991), 231 and following.

19. See "On the American Indians."

20. Calvin himself also devised a detailed and highly prescriptive polity for the Reformed churches themselves and was zealous to see it enforced in Geneva and elsewhere, albeit with only partial success. It is often remarked that while Luther had a passion for liberty, Calvin had a passion for order.

21. In the face of sustained persecution, however, their successors were forced to change tack radically on the point.

22. John Calvin, *Institutes of the Christian Religion*, trans. Henry Beveridge (Edinburgh: Calvin Translation Society, 1845).

23. Calvin, 3: XX ("On Civil Government").

24. For example, his claim that toleration is "*the* chief characteristic mark of the true Church" cannot be right.

25. John Locke, *A Letter concerning Toleration* (1689), edited and introduced by James H. Tully (Indianapolis: Hackett, 1983), 26.

Christian Thought on Freedom in the Classical Period

Selections for Dialogue

Ambrose
(Aurelius Ambrosius, Bishop of Milan; d. 397)

Letter 7: To Justus

True freedom originates in grace, consists in wisdom, is ordered to virtue, and is unaffected by external circumstances.

9. It is not nature, then, that makes a man a slave, but folly; and it is not emancipation which makes him free, but learning. Esau, after all, was born a free man and made a slave. Joseph was sold into slavery and was appointed to a position of power, ruler of those who had purchased him. . . .

15. The free man, therefore, is the wise man, "bought with a price," . . . "redeemed by the precious blood" (1 Pet. 1:18f)—for it is important to recognize our Purchaser—"bought with the coin" of grace. . . .

17. Yes, he is free who has not suffered the highest bidder as his master, nor seen the finger raised to bid at auction; but freer still is he who is free within himself, free by the laws of nature. He knows that the rule of nature governs morals, not status, and that the measure of all what a man contributes does not correspond to human *fiat* but to natural principles. . . .

18. Or is he free, do you think, who buys votes and cares more for popular acclaim than for the prudent judgment of the wise? Is he free, who is swayed by the winds of popular opinion, who dreads the whispers of the masses? It is not freedom which the slave receives on manumission, and acquires from the hand of the magistrate. For freedom consists, I believe, in virtue—not the virtue of expansive liberality, but a virtue which is demanded and possessed by a sense of [one's] proper pride, unswayed by others' opinions. For the wise man is always a free man, always highly regarded, always presiding

over the laws. "The law," after all, "has not been ordained for the just man, but for the unjust" (1 Tim. 1:9). The just man "is the law to himself." He has no further need to call the image of virtue to mind, since he carries it locked within his heart, "having the work of the law written on the tablets of his heart" (cf. Rom. 2:14f). . . .

19. The wise man, then, is free, since whoever does what he wills is free; but not every volition is good, and it is the sign of the wise man that he wills whatever is good; he hates evil, because he has chosen the good. So if he has chosen what is good, in determining his own choice and making choices of his own activity, he is free. . . .[1]

Augustine of Hippo (350–430)

City of God
De civitate Dei (426)

Freedom is living according to the Creator's design: humans are created for felicity through obedience, and for fellowship not solitude; free will is lost through disobedience and can only be restored by divine salvation.

Book XII, chapter 21: Man, on the other hand, whose nature was to be a mean between the angelic and bestial, He created in such sort, that if he remained in subjection to His Creator as his rightful Lord and piously kept His commandments, he should pass into the company of the angels, and obtain, without the intervention of death, a blessed and endless immortality; but if he offended the Lord his God by a proud and disobedient use of his free will, he should become subject to death, and live as the beasts do—the slave of appetite, and doomed to eternal punishment after death. And therefore God created only one single man, not, certainly, that he might be a solitary, bereft of all society, but that by this means the unity of society and the bond of concord might be more effectually commended to him, men being bound together not only by similarity of nature, but by family affection. And indeed He did not even create the woman that was to be given him as his wife, as he created the man, but created her out of the man, that the whole human race might derive from one man.[2]

Book XIV, chapter 11: But the first evil will, which preceded all man's evil acts, was rather a kind of falling away from the work of God to its own works than any positive work. And therefore the acts resulting were evil, not having God, but the will itself for their end; so that the will or the man himself, so far as his will is bad, was as it were the evil tree bringing forth evil fruit. Moreover, the bad will, though it be not in harmony with, but opposed to nature, inasmuch as it is a vice or blemish, yet it is true of it as of all vice, that it cannot exist except in a nature, and only in a nature created out of nothing, and not in that which the Creator has begotten of Himself, as He begot the Word, by whom all things were made. For though God formed man of the dust of the earth, yet the earth itself, and every earthly material, is absolutely created out of nothing; and man's soul, too, God created out of nothing, and joined to the body, when He made man. But evils are so thoroughly overcome by good, that though they are permitted to exist, for the sake of demonstrating how the most righteous foresight of God can make a good use even of them, yet good can exist without evil, as in the true and supreme God Himself, and as in every invisible and visible celestial creature that exists above this murky atmosphere; but evil cannot exist without good, because the natures in which evil exists, in so far as they are natures, are good. . . . The will, therefore, is then truly free, when it is not the slave of vices and sins. Such was it given us by God; and this being lost by its own fault, can only be restored by Him who was able at first to give it. And therefore the truth says, "If the Son shall make you free, ye shall be free indeed"; which is equivalent to saying, If the Son shall save you, ye shall be saved indeed. For He is our Liberator, inasmuch as He is our Saviour.[3]

Book XIV, chapter 12: But by the precept He gave, God commended obedience, which is, in a sort, the mother and guardian of all the virtues in the reasonable creature, which was so created that submission is advantageous to it, while the fulfillment of its own will in preference to the Creator's is destruction.[4]

Thomas Aquinas (1225–1274)

Summa theologiae (1265–1274)

For Thomas, human freedom consists in exercising will according to reason and in conformity with natural order and toward natural ends. Human law, a constraint on will, must be ruled by reason and ordered to the common good if law is rational. It is not inimical to freedom but a condition of its social exercise.

Second Part of the Second Part, Question 104: On obedience

Article 1: Whether one man is bound to obey another

Reply: As the actions of natural things proceed from natural powers, so do human actions proceed from the human will. In the natural order, it happens of necessity that higher things move lower things by the excellence of the natural powers divinely given to them. Hence in human affairs also superiors must move inferiors by their will, by virtue of a divinely-established authority. But to move by reason and will is to command. And so just as in the divinely instituted natural order lower natural things are necessarily subject to higher things and are moved by them, so too in human affairs inferiors are bound to obey their superiors by virtue of the order of natural and Divine law.

Reply to Objection 1: God has left man "in the hand of his own counsel," not as though it were lawful for him to do everything that he might wish, but because, unlike non-rational creatures, he is not compelled by natural necessity to do what he ought to do, but has the free choice of proceeding according to "his own counsel." And just as he must proceed according to his own counsel in doing other things, so also must he do so in the matter of obeying his superiors. For as Gregory says: "When we humbly yield ourselves up to the voice of another, we overcome ourselves in our own hearts."[5]

Reply to Objection 2: The Divine will is the first rule by which all rational wills are regulated; but it is according to the divinely instituted order that one will should stand closer to this will than another. And so the will of the one man who commands can be as it were a second rule to the will of the other who obeys.

First Part of the Second Part, Question 90: The essence of law

Article 1: Whether law is something belonging to reason

Reply: Law is a kind of rule and measure of acts, by which someone is induced to act or restrained from acting. . . . Now the rule and measure of human acts is reason . . . for it pertains to reason to direct to an end, which . . . is the guiding principle in all matters of action. . . . [Thus] law is something belonging to reason.

Reply to Objection 3: Reason receives its power of moving from the will. . . . For it is because someone first wills an end that his reason then proceeds to issue commands concerning the things which are directed to that end. But in order that what it commands may have the character of law, the will must itself be in accord with some rule of reason. And it is in this way that we are to understand that the will of the prince has the force of law: otherwise . . . the will of the prince would have more the character of iniquity than of law.

Article 2: Whether law is always directed to the common good

Reply: Now, just as reason is the first principle of human acts, so reason itself must be guided by something which is the first principle of everything it does; and it is to this guiding principle that law must chiefly and mainly be directed. Now, the first principle in practical matters, which are the object of practical reasoning, is the final end: and the final end of human life is happiness or blessedness. . . . Law must therefore attend especially to the ordering of things towards blessedness. Moreover, since every part of something is ordered in relation to the whole as imperfect to perfect, and since one man is part of a perfect [i.e., a complete or self-sufficient] community, law must attend to the ordering of individual things in such a way as to secure the common happiness. Hence the Philosopher[6] . . . says at Ethics V that we call those lawful acts "just which tend to produce and preserve happiness and its components for the political community" [i.e., the State].[7]

Francisco de Vitoria (c.1483–1546)

On the American Indians Lately Discovered (1539)

De Indis

Rational human beings possess the natural right (freedom) to govern themselves. Aquinas's theory of natural law is here invoked by Vitoria to assess the legitimacy of the Spanish conquest of the native Indians. He defends the Indians' natural right to "natural dominion" (i.e., freedom of self-governance) prior to conquest and defines the criteria by which one such dominion could be curtailed by the Conquistadores.

q.1 a.3: Whether unbelievers can be true masters.

We must now discuss of *whether a man can be deprived of dominion by reason of being an unbeliever*. On the one hand it seems that he can. Heretics can have no dominion (*dominium*) . . . so unbelievers, who are not better than heretics, can have no dominion either. . . .
I reply with the following propositions:

It is no impediment for a man to be a true master, that he is an unbeliever. This is the conclusion of St. Thomas Aquinas, *ST* II–II.10.10. This can be proved first by authority, from Holy Scripture, which often calls unbelievers . . . "kings"; Paul (Rom. 13:1–5) and Peter (1 Pet. 2:13–14, 18) gave orders to obey the rulers who in their day were all unbelievers. . . .

We also have a proof based on reason. Aquinas shows that unbelief does not cancel either natural or human law, but all forms of dominion derive from natural or human law; therefore they cannot be annulled by lack of faith. . . .

q.1 a.6: Whether madmen can be true masters. . . .

3. *These madmen too may be true masters*. For a madman too can be the victim of injustice; therefore he can have legal rights. . . .

4. *The barbarians are not prevented by this, or by the argument of the previous article, from being true masters.* The proof of this is they are not in point of fact madmen, but have judgment like other men. This is self-evident, because they have some order in their affairs: they have properly organized cities, proper marriages, magistrates and overlords, laws, industries, and commerce, all of which require the use of reason. They likewise have a form of religion, and they correctly apprehend things which are evident to other men, which indicates the use of reason. . . .

q.1 Conclusion: The conclusion . . . is that the barbarians undoubtedly possessed as true dominion, both public and private, as any Christians. . . . They could not be robbed of their property, either as private citizens or as princes, on the ground that they were not true masters. It would be harsh to deny to them, who have never done us any wrong, the rights we concede to Saracens and Jews, who have been continual enemies of the Christian religion. . . .

Aristotle certainly did not mean to say that ["natural slaves"] thereby belong by nature to others and have no rights of ownership over their own bodies and possessions. Such slavery is a civil and legal condition, to which no man can belong by nature. . . . [Nor did he mean that those who are "natural masters"] had a legal right to arrogate power to themselves over others on the grounds of their superior intelligence, but merely that they are fitted by nature to be princes and guides. . . . It may be . . . that these arguments can provide legal grounds for subjecting the Indians, but that is a different matter. . . .[8]

Martin Luther (1483–1546)

On the Freedom of the Christian (1520)
De Libertate Christiana
Von der Freiheit eines Christenmenschen

For the Protestant reformers, Christian freedom and thus freedom in the church is primarily an interior, spiritual freedom from supposedly salvific, but in fact oppressive, "works of the law," and spiritually worthwhile "works" should be done freely not out of compulsion. Freedom in society is, by contrast, secured by "civil" government that is exterior, "temporal," and coercive.

A Christian is a perfectly free lord of all, subject to none. A Christian is a perfectly dutiful servant of all, subject to all. . . .

Man has a twofold nature, a spiritual and a bodily one. According to the spiritual nature, which men refer to as the soul, he is called a spiritual, inner, or new man. According to the bodily nature, which men refer to as flesh, he is called a carnal, outward, or old man, of whom the Apostle writes in II Cor. 4[:16], "Though our outer nature is wasting away, our inner nature is being renewed every day."

First, let us consider the inner man to see how a righteous, free, and pious Christian, that is, a spiritual, new, and inner man, becomes what he is. It is evident that no external thing has any influence in producing Christian righteousness or freedom, or in producing unrighteousness or servitude. . . . None of these things touch either the freedom or the servitude of the soul. . . . One thing, and only one thing, is necessary for Christian life, righteousness, and freedom. That one thing is the most holy Word of God, the gospel of Christ. . . . It is clear, then, that a Christian has all that he needs in faith and needs no works to justify him; and if he has no need of works, he has no need of the law; and if he has no need of the law, surely he is free from the law. It is true that "the law is not laid down for the just" [I Tim. 1:9]. This is that Christian liberty, our faith, which does not induce us to live in idleness or wickedness but makes the law and works unnecessary for any man's righteousness and salvation. . . . Yes, since faith alone suffices for salvation, I need nothing except faith exercising the power and dominion of its own liberty. Lo, this is the inestimable power and liberty of Christians. . . .

[Now regarding] the outer man. Here we shall answer all those who, offended by the word "faith" and by all that has been said, now ask, "If faith does all things and is alone sufficient unto righteousness, why then are good works commanded? We will take our ease and do no works and be content with faith." I answer: not so, you wicked men, not so.[9]

John Calvin (1509–1564)

Institutes of the Christian Religion

Institutio Christianae Religiones (1536)

14. Since by means of this privilege of liberty which we have described, believers have derived authority from Christ not to entangle themselves by the observance of things in which he wished them to be free, we conclude that their consciences are exempted from all human authority. . . . Paul hesitates not to say that Christ has died in vain, if we place our souls under subjection to men (Gal. v. 1, 4; 1 Cor. vii. 23). . . . Christ is obscured, or rather extinguished to us, unless our consciences maintain their liberty. . . . [But] the moment the abolition of human constitutions is mentioned, the greatest disturbances are excited, partly by the seditious,

and partly by calumniators, as if obedience of every kind were at the same time abolished and overthrown.

15. Therefore, lest this prove a stumbling-block to any, let us observe that in man government is twofold: the one spiritual, by which the conscience is trained to piety and divine worship; the other civil, by which the individual is instructed in those duties which, as men and citizens, we are bound to perform. . . . To these two forms are commonly given the not inappropriate names of spiritual and temporal jurisdiction, intimating that the former species has reference to the life of the soul, while the latter relates to matters of the present life, not only to food and clothing, but to the enacting of laws which require a man to live among his fellows purely, honorably, and modestly. The former has its seat within the soul, the latter only regulates the external conduct. We may call the one the spiritual, the other the civil kingdom. Now, these two, as we have divided them, are always to be viewed apart from each other. . . . By attending to this distinction, we will not erroneously transfer the doctrine of the gospel concerning spiritual liberty to civil order, as if in regard to external government Christians were less subject to human laws, because their consciences are unbound before God, as if they were exempted from all carnal service, because in regard to the Spirit they are free. . . .[10]

John Donne (1572–1631)

Holy Sonnet No. 14

Batter my heart, three-person'd God, for you
As yet but knocke, breathe, shine, and seeke to mend;
That I may rise and stand, o'erthrow mee, and bend
Your force to break, blow, burn, and make me new.
I, like an usurp'd town to another due,
Labor to admit you, but oh, to no end;
Reason, your viceroy in mee, mee should defend,
But is captiv'd, and proves weak or untrue.
Yet dearely I love you, and would be lov'd fain,
But am betroth'd unto your enemy;
Divorce mee, untie or break that knot again,
Take mee to you, imprison mee, for I,
Except you enthrall me, never shall be free,
Nor ever chast, except you ravish mee.

John Locke (1632–1704)

Letter Concerning Toleration (1689)

I esteem . . . toleration to be the chief characteristic mark of the true Church. . . . "The kings of the Gentiles exercise leadership over them," said our Savior to his disciples, "but ye shall not be so." The business of true religion is . . . not instituted in order to the erecting of an external pomp, nor to the obtaining of ecclesiastical dominion, nor to the exercising of compulsive force, but to the regulating of men's lives, according to the rules of virtue and piety. . . . If, like the Captain of our salvation, [those who seek to convert others] sincerely desired the good of souls, they would tread in the steps and follow the perfect example of that Prince of Peace, who sent out His soldiers to the subduing of nations, and gathering them into His Church, not armed with the sword, or other instruments of force, but prepared with the Gospel of peace and with the exemplary holiness of their conversation. This was His method. . . .

I esteem it above all things necessary to distinguish exactly the business of civil government from that of religion and to settle the just bounds that lie between the one and the other. . . . The commonwealth seems to me to be a society of men constituted only for the procuring, preserving, and advancing their own civil interests. Civil interests I call life, liberty, health, and indolency of body; and the possession of outward things, such as money, lands, houses, furniture, and the like. It is the duty of the civil magistrate, by the impartial execution of equal laws, to secure unto all the people in general and to every one of his subjects in particular the just possession of these things belonging to this life. . . . Now that the whole jurisdiction of the magistrate reaches only to these civil concernments. . . and that it neither can nor ought in any manner to be extended to the salvation of souls, these following considerations seem unto me abundantly to demonstrate. First, because the care of souls is not committed to the civil magistrate, any more than to other men. It is not committed unto him, I say, by God; because it appears not that God has ever given any such authority to one man over another as to compel anyone to his religion. . . . In the second place, the care of souls cannot belong to the civil magistrate, because his power consists only in outward force; but true and saving religion consists in the inward persuasion of the mind, without which nothing can be acceptable to God. . . .

A church . . . I take to be a voluntary society of men, joining themselves together of their own accord in order to the public worshipping of God in such manner as they judge acceptable to Him, and effectual to the salvation of their souls. I say it is a free and voluntary society. Nobody is born a member of any church; otherwise the religion of parents would descend unto children by the same right of inheritance as their temporal estates. . . . But since the joining together of several members into this church-society . . is absolutely free and spontaneous, it necessarily follows that the right of making its laws can belong to none but the society itself; or, at least (which is the same thing), to those whom the society by common consent has authorized thereunto. . . . In this manner ecclesiastical liberty will be preserved on all sides, and no man will have a legislator imposed upon him but whom himself has chosen. . . .

As the magistrate has no power to impose by his laws the use of any rites and ceremonies in any Church, so neither has he any power to forbid the use of such rites and ceremonies as are already received, approved, and practiced by any Church; because, if he did so, he would destroy the Church itself: the end of whose institution is only to worship God with freedom after its own manner. You will say, by this rule, if some congregations should have a mind to sacrifice infants, or (as the primitive Christians were falsely accused) lustfully pollute themselves in promiscuous uncleanness, or practice any other such heinous enormities, is the magistrate obliged to tolerate them, because they are committed in a religious assembly? I answer: No. These things are not lawful in the ordinary course of life, nor in any private house; and therefore neither are they so in the worship of God, or in any religious meeting. . . . The part of the magistrate is only to take care that the commonwealth receive no prejudice, and that there be no injury done to any man, either in life or estate.

But there is absolutely no such thing under the Gospel as a Christian commonwealth. There are, indeed, many cities and kingdoms that have embraced the faith of Christ, but they have retained their ancient form of government, with which the law of Christ hath not at all meddled. He, indeed, hath taught men how, by faith and good works, they may obtain eternal life; but He instituted no commonwealth. . . .

[But there are limits to what civil government can tolerate]. I say, first, no opinions contrary to human society, or to those moral rules which are necessary to the preservation of civil society, are to be tolerated by the magistrate. . . . [Second], these, therefore, and the like, who attribute unto the faithful, religious, and orthodox, that is, in plain terms, unto themselves, any peculiar privilege or power above other mortals, in civil concernments; or who upon pretense of religion do challenge any manner of authority over such as are not associated with them in their ecclesiastical communion, I say these have no right to be tolerated by the magistrate; as neither [third] those that will not own and teach the duty of tolerating all men in matters of mere religion. . . . [Fourth], that Church can have no right to be tolerated by the magistrate which is constituted upon such a bottom that all those who enter into it do thereby ipso facto deliver themselves up to the protection and service of another prince. . . . It is ridiculous for anyone to profess himself to be a Mahometan only in his religion, but in everything else a faithful subject to a Christian magistrate, whilst at the same time he acknowledges himself bound to yield blind obedience to the Mufti of Constantinople, who himself is entirely obedient to the Ottoman Emperor. . . . Lastly, those are not at all to be tolerated who deny the being of a God. Promises, covenants, and oaths, which are the bonds of human society, can have no hold upon an atheist. . . .

Notes

1. Ambrose composed the letter sometime before 381 CE. Ambrose, *Letter No. 7: To Justus*, trans. Paul Arnold, O. Faller and M. Zelzer, eds., in *Corpus Scriptorum Ecclesiasticorum Latinorum*, vol. 82 (Salzburg: Austrian Academy of Sciences), para. 9, 15, 17, 18, 19. By kind permission of Austrian Academy of Sciences.

2. Philip Schaff, trans. *St Augustin's City of God and Christian Doctrine* (New York: Christian Literature Publishing, 1890), 241.

3. Schaff, 272.

4. Schaff, 273.

5. Thomas is citing Gregory of Nyssa (ca. 335–ca. 395).

6. By "the Philosopher," Thomas means Aristotle.

7. Excerpts from *Summa theologiae* are taken from R. W. Dyson, ed. and trans., *St. Thomas Aquinas: Political Writings* (Cambridge: Cambridge University Press, 2002), 57, 58, 76, 77, 78, 79. Reprinted by permission of Cambridge University Press.

8. From "On the American Indians" | *De Indis* in Anthony Pagden and Jeremy Lawrence, eds., *Vitoria: Political Writings* (Cambridge: Cambridge University Press, 1991), 231 and following. Reprinted by permission of Cambridge University Press.

9. *De Libertate Christiana* | *Von der Freiheit eines Christenmenschen*. Martin Luther, "The Freedom of the Christian," trans. W. A. Lambert, rev. by Harold J. Grimm in *Three Treatises* (Philadelphia: Fortress, 1970), 277, 278, 279, 284, 290. Used by permission.

10. John Calvin, *Institutes of the Christian Religion*, trans. Henry Beveridge (Edinburgh: Calvin Translation Society, 1845).

Freedom in Modern Christian Thought

Introduction to Selected Texts

Peniel Jesudason Rufus Rajkumar

To survey notions of freedom embraced during a vast and polysemic period that included among its milestones (and tombstones) a new world order of political democracies birthed through the French and the American revolutions; the scourge of two world wars and the gradual rise of new imperial powers; the aftermath of Western colonialisms; the "unholy alliance of the missionary, the military, and the merchant" that altered not just geographical landscapes but landscapes of the mind;[1] the rapid and pervasive rise of corporate and global capitalism; the Kantian thrust of the individual as the locus of moral attention and responsibility; and the almost "Cinderella-ish narrative" of the emergence of experience as the chosen bride of philosophy (and, to some extent, theology)—indeed, even to scratch the surface would be complex at its best.

"Where shall my wondering soul begin?"

During the modern period Christian thought has taken many literary forms. The poetry, sermons, classroom materials, and scholarly treatises chosen for study at the 2019 Building Bridges Seminar demonstrate this. Rather than attempting to synthesize the disparate array of modern Christian writings on freedom, here we simply examine some fragments. What, however, shall be our starting place? "Where shall my wondering soul begin?" Charles Wesley captures, in the first line of one of his well-loved hymns, the dilemma. My reply? Having indicated the challenge of defining the modern period, I will proceed to contextualize several Christian texts that are characteristic of it; and when I take that step, I begin with Wesley.

The Narrative Nature of Freedom in the Modern Period

In her public lecture on the opening day, Rosalee Velloso Ewell reminded us rightly of our identity as *homo narratus*.[2] We are story-formed storytellers. One thing that characterizes most of the examples of Christian thought from the modern period is their embeddedness in, as well as their embodiment of, specific contexts and questions—both personal and political—that characterized the zeitgeist of the modern period. They offer diverse "thick descriptions" of freedom as they emerge in the dialectical interface of faith/experience and context. Two texts, more than the rest, are ideal examples of such thick descriptions of freedom. With these two individual and personal accounts of freedom—the first by Charles Wesley, the second by Dietrich Bonhoeffer—let us begin.

"And Can It Be That I Should Gain" by Charles Wesley (1707–88)

Believed to have been composed on Whitsunday (Pentecost), May 21, 1738, the hymn "And Can It Be That I Should Gain" offers a picture of freedom that captures what is often referred to in evangelicalism as Charles Wesley's conversion experience—the moment wherein he embraced a new life with God.

While his brother John described his own conversion experience in terms of a strange warming of the heart, Charles describes his new life through two metaphors. The first, which he employs toward the end of the hymn's fourth stanza, describes freedom from imprisonment of the spirit as he walked out of the dungeon he was in: "My chains fell off; my heart was free." The second metaphor, used in the same stanza, is one of waking of his spirit: his spirit, which lay "bound in sin and nature's night," is awakened by the "quick'ning ray" that is diffused by divine eyes, freeing his spirit with darkness. The language of "quick'ning" has resonances with the parable of the lost son, who, midway through his saga, comes to his senses.

This experience of spiritual freedom/conversion/rebirth almost invariably leads to a life of discipleship—of following Jesus free from the fear of condemnation. This model of freedom continues to provide an influential understanding of spiritual freedom with a soteriological core. It is captured in the other stanzas of Wesley's hymn and is, in many ways, a rehearsal of the Augustinian tradition. The other stanzas speak of the blood of Jesus, who left his father's throne, bled for Adam's helpless race, and died for Wesley, so that he could boldly approach the eternal throne and claim his crown.

It is worth noting that Charles Wesley, an exemplar of eighteenth-century Evangelical Protestantism, was also a representative of the European Age of Enlightenment; he was, for example, a contemporary of Voltaire. While Charles and his brother John would have differed sharply with Voltaire on matters of theology, they would have concurred with him on knowledge's transformative potential. And whereas the Anglican stream of Christianity that had formed them talked in terms of the equal authority of scripture, tradition, and reason, the Wesleys added a fourth leg—experience—to that stool. On the role of experience in verifying knowledge, Voltaire would have agreed.

"Stations on the Road to Freedom" by Dietrich Bonhoeffer (1906–45)

Alongside Wesley's model of freedom that God provides through Christ, we find a different model of freedom that emerges in the German theologian Dietrich Bonhoeffer's poem, "Stations on the Road to Freedom"—the stations being discipline, action, suffering, and death.

Disillusioned by the church's silence in the face of the rise of the Nazi party as well as the appointment of Hitler as the chancellor of Germany in 1933, Bonhoeffer became part of the resistance movement and latter plotted to assassinate Hitler, for which he was sentenced to death. According to Bonhoeffer's sister Susanne Bonhoeffer, "Stations on the Road to Freedom" is an autobiographical poem written on the eve of July 21, 1944, a day after the failed plot to assassinate Hitler—which would ultimately lead to his hanging by the Gestapo in April 1945.

What stands out for me in this poem is the way in which Bonhoeffer interprets freedom in relation to action, suffering, and death. "Freedom comes only through deeds," he writes; "Faint not nor fear, but go out to the storm and the action trusting in God whose commandment you faithfully follow." Such a call to embrace agency needs to be understood in the light of his words on civil courage, which, he says "depends on a God who demands responsible action in a bold venture of faith, and who promises forgiveness and consolation to the (person) who becomes a sinner in that venture."[3]

Another uniqueness of Bonhoeffer's character is his understanding of death as a station on the way to freedom. Although Bonhoeffer was writing this poem in a context of the looming possibility of death, this was not the first time that he talks about death as freedom. On August 3, 1944, he noted, "On the way to freedom death is the greatest of feasts."[4] In a sermon preached in London in 1934, he said, "Death is grace, the greatest gift of grace that God gives to people who believe in him . . . it beckons to us with heavenly power, if only we realise that it is the gateway to our homeland, the tabernacle of joy, the everlasting kingdom of peace."[5]

Such viewing of action, suffering, and death as stations on the road to freedom emerges from an understanding of discipleship that is "bound to the suffering of Christ" and a view of the cross as God's way of freedom: freedom of "being-for-others." We gain this freedom not by virtue of God's omnipotence but of God's vulnerability and suffering. The theme of freedom and God's vulnerability invariably leads us to another influential theologian of the twentieth century.

The Humanity of God by Karl Barth (1886–1968)

Given that this essay was prepared for a meeting in Switzerland, I must necessarily reach out for that fruit at the center of the garden of Protestant theology: Karl Barth. From the vast corpus of Barth's writings, we have chosen a portion of his *Die Menschlichkeit Gottes* (The Humanity of God)—a lecture he gave on September 25, 1956, at a meeting of the Swiss Reformed Ministers Association. It leads us to the theme of freedom through what many have considered the basis of Barth's theology: the incarnation.[6]

Some think that what Barth is trying to do in his lecture on God's humanity—and particularly in the excerpt we are considering—is to offer a corrective of an idea he expressed in his earlier volumes of *Church Dogmatics*. As Barth explains in his own words, "however well it may have been meant and however much it may have mattered, was nevertheless said, somewhat severely and brutally, and moreover . . . in part heretically."[7] In a way that resonates with Philippians 2: 7, which speaks of Jesus Christ's self-emptying love, Barth writes of God's divinity (the exact word used is *deity*) as not being a prison where God can exist only in and for Godself, but rather as also God's freedom to be with and for us. It is, to put it mildly, using Barth's own words, "richly dynamic, endlessly surprising, and deeply mysterious."[8] We cannot but agree with Daniel W. Hardy that, "not only does Barth—like his beloved Mozart—love thematic interplay, he also concentrates on particular themes, bringing them into new combinations and contrapositions, within an ever forward spiralling theological whole."[9] Although, as you will see, there is only one entrance point, it is (in fact) a point that allows us to be led into everything.[10] The point being made is that the sovereignty of God's freedom, in its infinite outpouring, remains undiminished and inexhaustible.

At this point, it may be a good idea to juxtapose Barth's text about God's freedom with Stanley Hauerwas's reflections on human freedom.

"Freedom as the Presence of the Other," from *The Peaceable Kingdom: A Primer in Christian Ethics* (1991) by Stanley Hauerwas (b. 1940)

Ethicist Stanley Hauerwas writes about the freedom and agency of the human being as the "presence of the other." According to Hauerwas, the freedom designed for human beings is to respond to the story of God and be part of the fulfillment of God's desire for us to serve in God's kingdom. However, we discover and live our freedom only in the presence of and our response to the other. The other is God's key for us to enter into God's story because it is "through the need of the other that the greatest hindrance to my freedom, namely my own self-absorption, is rendered irrelevant."[11]

The "other" contains a didactic as well as a salvific relevance for our freedom, helping us to recognize the limits of our freedom, which also opens new horizons for our maturity into the freedom to be part of God's story. For Hauerwas, freedom in this context is the capacity to be called from oneself by another. In his *The Peaceable Kingdom*, Hauerwas argues that "the church as a community called to be a sign of the Kingdom of God cannot shield itself from the other . . . because the community itself was formed by the presence of the ultimate stranger, Jesus Christ"—the one who came to his own but whose own received him not, as we read in the gospel of John.[12]

Declaration on Religious Freedom (*Dignitatis humanae*) promulgated by His Holiness Pope Paul VI (December 7, 1965)

The modern period was a time characterized by the recurrence of the question of the place and power of religion within political democracies. *The Declaration on Religious Freedom (Dignitatis humanae): On the Right of the Person and of Communities to Social and Civil Freedom in Matters Religious*, promulgated by His Holiness Pope Paul VI, December 7, 1965, during the Second Vatican Council, is one document that addresses this question. The document, as its Latin name implies, explores the personal and political implications of human dignity in relation to the vexed question of religious freedom. The declaration affirms that "the right to religious freedom has its foundation in the very dignity of the human person." It is an understanding of dignity that is closely linked to a Kantian notion of autonomy and respect for person. Therefore, there is stress on human beings acting on their own judgment, enjoying and making sense of a responsible freedom, not driven by coercion but motivated by a sense of duty.

In political terms, this declaration advocates for the protection of religious communities from encroachment by the state in the free exercise of religious freedom—which extends beyond mere freedom to worship without coercion. Rather, it includes the right of religious communities not to be hindered in their public teaching and witness to their faith as well as their right to establish educational, cultural, charitable, and social organizations. However, this protectionism is also extended to society, which has the "right to defend itself against possible abuses committed on the pretext of freedom of religion."

What is further interesting about this document is that any appeal for the restriction of freedom is based on juridical norms that "arise out of the concern for effective safeguarding of rights of all citizens, care for genuine public peace and protection of public morality." In their assessment of this document, Stanley Hauerwas and Jana Bennett note with interest that, while this document claims that the doctrine of freedom it asserts is rooted in divine revelation, and that revelation does indeed disclose the dignity of the human person, revelation does not, however, provide unambiguous affirmation of the right to immunity from coercion regarding religion. Nevertheless, Hauerwas and Bennett highlight this Vatican II document's implication of Catholicism's compatibility and convergence with certain forms of democracy.[13] It thereby provides a useful example of how religion and politics may interanimate each other in response to specific questions. The Second Vatican Council's social teachings on human dignity were an important factor in the development of liberation theology, to which we now turn.

Theologies of Liberation: Faith Seeking Freedom?

If theology be defined as "faith seeking understanding," liberation theology is "faith seeking liberation." Premised on an epistemological preference for the marginalized, liberation theologians take up disparate questions, always striving to overcome the false dichotomy between the spiritual and the political. When studying liberation theology, we do well to draw correlations between important theological concepts and each author's respective contemporary context. Christian feminist theology also has a liberative bent; therefore, we consider it here as well. With this in mind, we shall prepare for close reading of three exemplars: Peruvian theologian Gustavo Gutiérrez (b. 1928), V. Devasahayam, and Elisabeth Schüssler Fiorenza (b. 1938), each of whom develops identity-specific and holistic ideas of liberation.

In his influential book *A Theology of Liberation* (1973), Gutiérrez introduces us to three levels of liberation—each of which influences the other: political liberation, liberation in the course of history, and liberation from sin.

In working out his theology, he emphasizes how incomplete each form of liberation would be without the others. The idea of liberation is worked out in relation to the biblical concept of the Kingdom of God, which holds in itself political, historical, and cosmic/eschatological dimensions. The aim is to restore relationships not just between human beings but also relationships between human beings and God. There is a historic as well as eschatological dimension to liberation, which is completed by a combination of the two.

The concept of the Kingdom of God also provides a strong spiritual–theological link between the many different Asian Christian projects—among them, Taiwanese homeland theology, Indian *dalit* theology, Korean *minjung* theology, Philippine theology of struggle, and Asian feminist theology (such as that of Kwok Pui-Lan). As Peter Phan explains, conceiving spirituality as service to the Kingdom of God "allows Asians to overcome the pronounced individualism of their religions and ethics and to view the spiritual quest as necessarily comprising the quest for social justice."[14] Spirituality as service to the Kingdom of God occupies a central place in Asian theologies of liberation. By way of example, Phan points to the work of such theologians as Michael Amaladoss, R. S. Sugirtharajah, Tissa Balasuriya, Aloysius Pieris, and Chung Hyun Kyung, among others.

Whereas our example of Gutiérrez's thought comes from a widely read monograph, from Bishop V. Devasahayam we have an excerpt from one of his Bible studies—the tenth of ten composed by him that compose *Dalits and Women: Quest for Humanity*—a volume that emerged out of the Gurukul Summer Institute, 1992.[15] Hence, his text on the Eucharist developed in a particular context in which Christian Dalits face discrimination within the Christian community, even at the most egalitarian of tables: the Lord's Supper—which, for many, serves as a microcosm of God's kingdom of justice and equality. Devasahayam, himself a Dalit, seeks to subvert this discrimination by pointing out the theological ironies of corrupting the ritual practice of Eucharist. He thereby lifts up notions of liberation, just sharing, and equality, which are implicit in New Testament passages related to the Eucharist.

Devasahayam's piece challenges Indian Christians to become a bit more like the one they meet and receive at the Eucharistic table—Jesus Christ, our Lord (the one who came to his own, but his own received him not). In a context of discrimination and division, Devasahayam lifts up the importance of rediscovering the Eucharistic table both as a table that feeds us in our faith imagination and as a table that teaches us the right way to stay hungry—hungry for justice.[16] He counsels Christians to ask themselves, How do the wounds of the broken and bleeding Christ enable them to let the stranger in?

Groundbreaking when first published, *In Memory of Her: A Feminist Theological Reconstruction of Christian Origins* (1983) is one of the earliest works by Elisabeth Schüssler Fiorenza, currently a professor at Harvard Divinity School. It remains one of her best known. In it she speaks of spirituality that calls women to form an *ekklesia* of women for the liberation of women. Such a spirituality, Schüssler Fiorenza asserts, will set women free from the structural sin of sexism so that they may rediscover their identity as children of God. She contends that, after it deconstructs patriarchal myths that have perpetuated oppression, this spirituality will foster a calling characterized by commitment, accountability, and solidarity. This *ekklesia* of women begins with the solidarity of common experience of discrimination, she says; it then comes to be marked by an integrative and inclusive solidarity that transcends division.[17]

Reflections

Rooted in human experience, as all of them are, these diverse texts on freedom lift up for us what it means for Christians to live into the fullness of God's freedom—to live into the freedom of being and becoming God's children. This freedom impinges on human beings at both the individual and communitarian levels, urging them to overcome all "unfreedoms" that bind them internally and externally, such that they become part of God's "kin-dom," which is characterized by justice and peace and joy in the Holy Spirit (Rom. 14:17b). It is a freedom shaped by God's self-revelation in Jesus Christ—who both promises life in all its fullness but also bids us to resist, even unto death (as did Bonhoeffer) the powers and principalities of modern-day xenophobias exacerbated and expressed by the supremacist, caste-ist, and patriarchal ideologies that shaped the contexts of Bonhoeffer, Devasahayam, and Schüssler Fiorenza. The challenge posed to Christians by freedom founded in Christ is its demand that they be reshaped such that they become a sign of the one in which they live, move, and have their being (Acts 17:28): Jesus Christ, for freedom, has set us free—not for self-indulgence but for service to one another in love (Gal. 5:1, 13).

Notes

1. Aloysius Pieris, "Asia's Non-Semitic Religions and the Mission of Local Churches," in *An Asian Theology of Liberation*, 35–50 (Quezon City, Philippines: Claretian, 1988), 50.

2. See, in this volume, C. Rosalee Velloso Ewell, "Who Gets to Decide What Freedom Is?"

3. Dietrich Bonhoeffer, "Stations on the Way to Freedom," in *Letters and Papers from Prison*, trans. Reginald Fuller, 512–14 (Minneapolis: Augsburg Fortress, 2009), 513.

4. Dietrich Bonhoeffer, "Miscellaneous Notes," in *Letters and Papers from Prison*, 495.

5. Bonhoeffer preached this sermon in London in 1934. For the full text, see "As a Mother Comforts Her Child (Wisdom 3:3)," in *The Collected Sermons of Dietrich Bonhoeffer*, ed. Isabel Best, 101–8 (Minneapolis: Fortress Press, 2012), 106.

6. For elaboration, see Daniel W. Hardy, "Karl Barth," in *The Modern Theologians*, 3rd ed., ed. David Ford with Rachel Muers, 21–42 (Oxford: Blackwell, 2005).

7. Karl Barth, "The Humanity of God," trans. John Newton Thomas, in *The Humanity of God*, 37–68 (Richmond, VA: John Knox Press, 1960), 38, 43.

8. Karl Barth, *Church Dogmatics* (Edinburgh: T&T Clark, 1936–77, English translation of *Kirchliche Dogmatik*, 1932–1970, I/1), xii, 29.

9. George Hunsinger, *How to Read Karl Barth: The Shape of His Theology* (New York: Oxford University Press, 1991), 28.

10. Hardy, "Karl Barth," 27.

11. Stanley Hauerwas, *The Peaceable Kingdom: A Primer in Christian Ethics* (Notre Dame, IN: University of Notre Dame Press, 1991), 44.

12. Hauerwas, 85.

13. Stanley Hauerwas and Jana Bennett, "Catholic Social Teaching," in *The Oxford Handbook of Theological Ethics*, ed. Gilbert Meilaender and William Werpehowski, 520–37 (Oxford: Oxford University Press, 2005), 521.

14. Peter C. Phan, "Christian Social Spirituality: A Global Perspective," in *Catholic Social Justice*, ed. Philomena Cullen, 18–40 (New York: T & T Clark, 2007), 33.

15. See V. Devasahayam, *Dalits and Women: Quest for Humanity* (Madras, India: Gurukul Summer Institute, 1992), 260, 261, 263. When he composed these teaching tools, Devasahayam was associate professor of theology at Gurukul Lutheran Theological College, Madras (Chennai).

16. Gerard W. Schlabach, "Breaking Bread: Peace and War," in *The Blackwell Companion to Christian Ethics*, ed. Stanley Hauerwas and Samuel Wells, 360–74 (Oxford: Wiley, 2008).

17. See Elisabeth Schüssler Fiorenza, *In Memory of Her: A Feminist Theological Reconstruction of Christian Origins* (New York: The Crossroad Publishing Company, 1987), 346, 349.

Christian Writings from the Modern Period

Selections for Dialogue

Charles Wesley (1707–1788)

Hymn: "And Can It Be That I Should Gain"

1 And can it be that I should gain
An int'rest in the Savior's blood?
Died He for me, who caused His pain?
For me, who Him to death pursued?
Amazing love! how can it be
That Thou, my God, should die for me?

Refrain:
Amazing love! how can it be
That Thou, my God, should die for me!

2 'Tis mystery all! Th'Immortal dies!
Who can explore His strange design?
In vain the firstborn seraph tries
To sound the depths of love divine!
'Tis mercy all! let earth adore,
Let angel minds inquire no more. [Refrain]

3 He left His Father's throne above,
So free, so infinite His grace;
Emptied Himself of all but love,
And bled for Adam's helpless race;
'Tis mercy all, immense and free;
For, O my God, it found out me. [Refrain]

4 Long my imprisoned spirit lay
Fast bound in sin and nature's night;
Thine eye diffused a quick'ning ray,
I woke, the dungeon flamed with light;
My chains fell off, my heart was free;
I rose, went forth and followed Thee. [Refrain]

5 No condemnation now I dread;
Jesus, and all in Him is mine!
Alive in Him, my living Head,
And clothed in righteousness divine,
Bold I approach th'eternal throne,
And claim the crown, through Christ my own. [Refrain][1]

Dietrich Bonhoeffer (1906–1945)

"Stations on the Road to Freedom: A Poem" (1944)
Letters & Papers from Prison

Discipline
If you would find freedom, learn above all to discipline your senses and your soul. Be not led hither and thither by your desires and your members. Keep your spirit and your body chaste, wholly subject to you, and obediently seeking the goal that is set before you. None can learn the secret of freedom, save by discipline.

Action
To do and dare—not what you would, but what is right. Never to hesitate over what is in your power, but boldly to grasp what lies before you. Not in the flight of fancy, but only in the deed there is freedom. Away with timidity and also reluctance! Out into the storm of event, sustained only by the commandment of God and your faith, and freedom will accept you with exultation.

Suffering
O wondrous change! Those hands, once so strong and active, have now been bound. Helpless and forlorn, you see the end of your deed. Yet with a sigh of relief you resign your cause to a stronger hand, and are content to do so. For one brief moment you enjoyed the bliss of freedom, only to give it back to God, that he might perfect it in glory

Death
Come now, Queen of the feasts on the road to eternal freedom! O death, cast off the grievous chains and lay low the thick walls of our mortal body and our blinded soul, that at last we may behold what we have failed to see. O freedom, long have we sought thee in discipline and in action and in suffering. Dying we behold thee now, and see thee in the face of God.[2]

Karl Barth (1886–1968)

The Humanity of God (1963)

God's high freedom in Jesus Christ is His freedom for *love*. The divine capacity which operates and exhibits itself in that superiority and subordination is manifestly also God's capacity to bend downwards, to attach Himself to another and this other to Himself, to be together with him. This takes place in that irreversible sequence, but in it is completely real. In that sequence there arises and continues in Jesus Christ the highest communion of God with man. God's deity is thus no prison in which He can exist only in and for Himself. It is rather His freedom to be in and for Himself but also with and for us, to assert but also to sacrifice Himself, to be wholly exalted but also completely humble, not only almighty but also almighty mercy, not only Lord but also servant, not only judge but also Himself the judged, not only man's eternal king but also his brother in time. And all that without in the slightest forfeiting His deity! All that, rather, in the highest proof and proclamation of His deity! He who *does* and manifestly *can* do all that, He and no other is the living God. . . .[3]

Pope Paul VI (1897–1978)

Dignitatis humanae
(Declaration on Religious Freedom)

On the right of the person and of communities to social and civil freedom in matters religious, promulgated by His Holiness Pope Paul VI on December 7, 1965.

1. People nowadays are becoming increasingly conscious of the dignity of the human person;[4] a growing number demand that people should exercise fully their own judgment and a responsible freedom in their actions and should not be subject to external pressure or coercion but inspired by a sense of duty. At the same time, to prevent excessive restriction of the rightful freedom of individuals and associations, they demand constitutional limitation of the

powers of government. This demand for freedom in human society is concerned chiefly with the affairs of the human spirit, and especially with what concerns the free practice of religion in society. This Vatican council pays careful attention to these spiritual aspirations and, with a view to declaring to what extent they are in accord with truth and justice, searches the sacred tradition and teaching of the church, from which it draws forth new insights in harmony with the old.

The sacred council begins by proclaiming that God himself has made known to the human race how people by serving him can be saved and reach happiness in Christ. We believe that this one true religion exists in the Catholic and Apostolic church, to which the Lord Jesus entrusted the task of spreading it among all peoples when he said to the apostles: "Go therefore and make disciples of all nations baptizing them in the name of the Father and of the Son and of the Holy Spirit, teaching them to observe all that I have commanded you" (Mt 28:19–20). All are bound to seek the truth, especially in what concerns God and the church, and to embrace it and hold on to it as they come to know it.

The sacred council likewise proclaims that these obligations bind people's consciences. Truth can impose itself on the human mind by the force of its own truth, which wins over the mind with both gentleness and power. So, while the religious freedom which human beings demand in fulfilling their obligation to worship God has to do with freedom from coercion in civil society, it leaves intact the traditional catholic teaching on the moral obligation of individuals and societies towards the true religion and the one church of Christ. Furthermore, in dealing with the question of liberty the sacred council intends to develop the teaching of recent popes on the inviolable rights of the human person and on the constitutional order of society.

2. The Vatican council declares that the human person has a right to religious freedom. Freedom of this kind means that everyone should be immune from coercion by individuals, social groups and every human power so that, within due limits, no men or women are forced to act against their convictions nor are any persons to be restrained from acting in accordance with their convictions in religious matters in private or in public, alone or in association with others. . . .

It is in accordance with their dignity that all human beings, because they are persons, that is, beings endowed with reason and free will and therefore bearing personal responsibility, are both impelled by their nature and bound by a moral obligation to seek the truth, especially religious truth. They are also bound to adhere to the truth once they come to know it and to direct their whole lives in accordance with the demands of truth. But human beings cannot satisfy this obligation in a way that is in keeping with their own nature unless they enjoy both psychological freedom and immunity from external coercion. Therefore, the right to religious freedom is based not on subjective attitude but on the very nature of the individual person. For this reason, the right to such immunity continues to exist even in those who do not live up to their obligation of seeking the truth and adhering to it. The exercise of this right cannot be interfered with as long as the just requirements of public order are observed. . . .

4. . . . Religious communities also have the right not to be hindered by legislation or administrative action by the civil authority in the selection, training, appointment and transfer of their own ministers, in communicating with religious authorities and communities in other parts of the world, in erecting buildings for religious purposes, and in the acquisition and use of the property they need. . . .

Also included in the right to religious freedom is the right of religious groups not to be prevented from freely demonstrating the special value of their teaching for the organization of society and the inspiration of human activity in general. Finally, the right of people, prompted by their own religious sense, to be free to hold meetings or establish educational, cultural, charitable and social organizations is based on their nature as social beings and on the nature of religion. . . .

7. . . . Furthermore, since civil society has the right to protect itself against possible abuses committed in the name of religious freedom, the responsibility of providing such protection rests especially with the civil authority. However, this must not be done in an arbitrary manner or by the unfair practice of favoritism but in accordance with legal principles which are in conformity with the objective moral order. These principles are necessary for the effective protection of the rights of all citizens and for the peaceful settlement of conflicts of rights. They are also necessary for an adequate protection of that just public peace which is to be found where people live together in good order and true justice. They are required too for the necessary protection of public morality. . . .

9. . . . What this Vatican council has to say about the individual's right to religious freedom is based on the dignity of the person, the demands of which have become more fully known to human reason through centuries of experience. Furthermore, this teaching on freedom is rooted in divine revelation, and for this reason, Christians are bound to respect it all the more conscientiously. Although revelation does not affirm, in so many words, the

right to immunity from external coercion in religious matters, it nevertheless makes known the dignity of the human person in all its fullness. It shows us Christ's respect for the freedom with which people are to fulfill their duty of believing the word of God, and it teaches us the spirit which disciples of such a Master must acknowledge and follow in all things.

11. God calls people to serve him in spirit and in truth. Consequently, they are bound to him in conscience, but not coerced. God has regard for the dignity of the human person which he himself created; human persons are to be guided by their own judgment and to enjoy freedom. This fact received its fullest manifestation in Christ Jesus in whom God perfectly revealed himself and his ways. For Christ, who is our master and Lord[5] and at the same time is meek and humble of heart,[6] acted patiently in attracting and inviting his disciples.[7] He supported and confirmed his preaching by miracles to invite the faith of his hearers and give them assurance, but not to coerce them.[8] He did indeed denounce the unbelief of his listeners but he left vengeance in God's hands until the day of judgement.[9] When he sent his apostles into the world he said to them: "The one who believes and is baptized will be saved; the one who does not believe will be condemned" (Mk 16:16). He himself recognized that weeds had been sown through the wheat but ordered that both be allowed to grow until the harvest, which will come at the end of the world.[10]

He did not wish to be a political Messiah who would dominate by force[11] but preferred to call himself the Son of Man who came to serve, and "to give his life as a ransom for many" (Mk 10:45). . . . He recognized civil authority and its rights when he ordered tribute to be paid to Caesar, but he gave dear warning that the greater rights of God must be respected: "Render therefore to Caesar the things that are Caesar's, and to God, the things that are God's" (Mt 22:21). Finally, he brought his revelation to perfection when he accomplished on the cross the work of redemption by which he achieved salvation and true freedom for the human race. For he bore witness to the truth[12] but refused to use force to impose it on those who spoke out against it. His kingdom does not establish its claims by force,[13] but is established by bearing witness to and hearing the truth and it grows by the love with which Christ, lifted up on the cross, draws people to himself.[14]

Gustavo Gutiérrez (b. 1928)

A Theology of Liberation (1973)

This radical liberation is the gift which Christ offers us. By his death and resurrection he redeems us from sin and all its consequences, as [the Medellín

Conference says very well]: "It is the same God who, in the fullness of time, sends his Son so that, in the flesh, he might come to liberate all men from all forms of slavery to which sin has subjected them: hunger, misery, oppression, and ignorance, in a word, that injustice and hatred which have their origin in human selfishness." This is why the Christian life is a passover, a transition from sin to grace, from death to life, from injustice to justice, from the subhuman to the human. Christ introduces us by the gift of his Spirit into communion with God and with all human beings. More precisely, it is because he introduces us into this communion, into a continuous search for its fullness, that he conquers sin—which is the negation of love—and all its consequences.

In dealing with the notion of liberation in Chapter 2, we distinguished three levels of meaning: political liberation, human liberation throughout history, liberation from sin and admission to communion with God. In the light of the present chapter, we can now study this question again. These three levels mutually affect each other, but they are not the same. One is not present without the others, but they are distinct: they are all part of a single, all-encompassing salvific process, but they are to be found at different levels. Not only is the growth of the Kingdom not reduced to temporal progress; because of the Word accepted in faith, we see that the fundamental obstacle to the Kingdom, which is sin, is also the root of all misery and injustice; we see that the very meaning of the growth of the kingdom is also the ultimate precondition for a just society and a new humanity. One reaches this root and this ultimate precondition only through the acceptance of the liberating gift of Christ, which surpasses all expectations. But, inversely, all struggle against exploitation and alienation, in a history which is fundamentally one, is an attempt to vanquish selfishness, the negation of love. This is the reason why any effort to build a just society is liberating. And it has an indirect but effective impact on the fundamental alienation. It is a salvific work, although it is not all of salvation. As a human work it is not exempt from ambiguities, any more than what is considered to be strictly "religious" work. But this does not weaken its basic orientation or its objective results.

Temporal progress—or, to avoid this aseptic term, let us say, human liberation—and the growth of the Kingdom both are directed toward complete communion of human beings with God and among themselves. They have the same goal, but they do not follow parallel roads, not even convergent ones. The growth of the Kingdom is a process which occurs historically *in* liberation, insofar as liberation means a greater human fulfillment. Liberation is a precondition for the new society, but this is not all it is. While the liberation is implemented in liberating historical events, it also denounces their limitations and ambiguities, proclaims their fulfillment, and impels them effectively toward total communion. This is not an identification. Without liberating historical events, there would be no growth of the Kingdom. But the process of liberation will not have conquered the very roots of human oppression and exploitation of man by man without the coming of the Kingdom, which is above all a gift. Moreover, we can say that the historical, political liberating event *is* the growth of the Kingdom and *is* a salvific event; but it is not *the* coming of the Kingdom, not *all* of salvation. It is the historical realization of the Kingdom and, therefore, it also proclaims its fullness. This is where the difference lies. It is a distinction made from a dynamic viewpoint, which has nothing to do with the one which holds for the existence of two juxtaposed "orders," closely connected or convergent, but deep down different from each other.

The very radicalness and totality of the salvific process require this relationship. Nothing escapes this process, nothing is outside the pale of the action of Christ and the gift of the Spirit. This gives human history its profound unity. Those who reduce the work of salvation are indeed those who limit it to the strictly "religious" sphere and are not aware of the universality of the process. It is those who think that the work of Christ touches the social order in which we live only indirectly or tangentially, and not in its roots and basic structure. It is those who in order to protect salvation (or to protect their interests) lift salvation from the midst of history, where individuals and social classes struggle to liberate themselves from the slavery and oppression to which other individuals and social classes have subjected them. It is those who refuse to see that the salvation of Christ is a radical liberation from all misery, all despoliation, all alienation. It is those who by trying to "save" the work of Christ will "lose" it.[15]

Stanley Hauerwas (b. 1940)

The Peaceable Kingdom: A Primer in Christian Ethics (1991)

"Freedom as the Presence of the Other"

But it may still be objected that some people's capacity for agency, their ability to respond to a truthful story, is so buried by accidents of their history, so crippled by their past, or so determined by a story that has taught them to despise themselves, that they have lost (or never found) the ability to participate in the forming of their character. More plausibly, their lives are so complex, their responses shaped by so many different stories, that the unity of character which seems necessary to order the multiplicity of loyalties in their lives may well seem unattainable.

No guarantee can be given to insure any one person from being so "determined." Yet it is the Christian claim that no one is so completely determined that he or she lacks all means to respond to the story of God and thus find some means to make his life his own. Such a claim is not based on optimistic assumptions about our goodness or our innate ability. Rather it is an affirmation of God's unrelenting desire to have each of us serve in the kingdom. The call to such service we find only in the presence of another, whose need is often the very occasion of our freedom. For it is through the need of another that the greatest hindrance to my freedom, namely my own self-absorption, is finally not so much overcome as simply rendered irrelevant. It is through the other that I am finally able to make peace with myself and thus have the power to make my life my own.

As Christians we believe that peace is most perfectly realized as we learn to find our role in God's story. That is, the peremptory story of peace as peace, the sense of being at home, comes only as we learn to live true to our nature as God's creatures. Moreover God has charged us with the particular responsibility of being his representatives to attract others to that story of peace by manifesting it in our common life. That is why Christians feel such an urgency to witness, to offer the stranger hospitality, so that God's peace might be possessed by all.

It is the privilege of Christians, as well as their responsibility, to tell God's story to those who know it not. But "to tell God's story" is to put the matter far too simply. For God's story is not merely, told; it must be lived. We do not respond to the story simply in itself, rather the story grasps our attention through the form of another person. The "freedom" provided by that narrative thus comes only in the form of someone external to me; it must come in the presence of another. I am an agent just to the extent I have the capacity to be called from myself by another.

We acquire character through the expectations of others. The "otherness" of another's character not only invites me to an always imperfect imitation, but challenges me to recognize the way my vision is restricted by my own self-preoccupation. Thus the kind of community in which we encounter another does not merely make some difference for our capacity for agency, it makes *all* the difference. From this perspective we are not the creators of our character; rather, our character is a gift from others which we learn to claim as our own by recognizing it as a gift. Our freedom is literally in the hands of others. I am free just to the extent that I can trust others to stand over against me and call my own "achievements" into question. It is from them that I learn the story that gives my life a purpose and direction. . . .

The Christian tradition holds us accountable, not to an abstract story, but to a body of people who have been formed by the life of Jesus. By learning to make his life our life we see we are free just to the extent that we learn to trust others and make ourselves available to be trusted by others. Such trust is possible because the story of his life, by the very way we learn it, requires that we recognize and accept the giftedness of our existence: I did not create myself but what I am has been made possible by others. Our dependence on others, of course, has as much potential for evil as it does good—that is exactly why the gospel is so remarkable, as it requires that we transform our distrust to trust on the basis of our knowledge and experience that God's providence is working in all our trusts and distrusts.

God is not necessary, therefore, to ensure the existence of a transcendental "I," nor is God but it correlate to such and "I." Rather God is the ultimate given whom we can confidently trust as the basis of our freedom. By becoming a part of the people who carry the story of Jesus, we are initiated into an adventure through which we learn the disciplines and virtues necessary to make our lives our own. For to continue that story, the life of Christ, is the source of our freedom. We are finally no self, no agent, until we are the self that God has called us to be.[16]

Vedanayagam Devasahayam (b. 1949)

Dalits and Women: Quest for Humanity (1992)

Fr. Antonyraj, a Jesuit Priest and the President of the Dalit Christian Liberation Movement in Tamilnadu has conducted a sociological study on "Discrimination Against Dalit Christians in Tamilnadu." He points to the prevalence of caste discrimination in the church. He points to the abuse of the sacrament of Eucharist to perpetuate the separation. There are two queues to the altar to receive the sacrament, one for the upper castes and one for Dalit Christians. Dalits are expected to go to receive the sacrament only after the upper caste people have participated in it (due to fear of pollution). In extreme cases, Dalits are administered the sacrament through windows. Dalit boys are not allowed to be altar boys. The Corpus Christ procession on Palm Sunday is taken through the streets only of the upper caste people and not taken through the streets of Dalit Christians. For a Dalit, participation in the Sacrament involves a process of social death since the sacrament is used as a means of domination by upper caste people. Fr. Antonyraj states, "It is not possible for us Dalits to celebrate our human dignity in a church which nurtures and promotes caste values and tolerates the practice of untouchability."

The Eucharist: A Sacrament of Liberation

The passover meal symbolised the liberation of the oppressed in Egypt. The Eucharist also symbolises the liberation of humanity from its bondage to sin and satan. William Temple's observation about Christianity is a telling description of the church, which can also be applied to the eucharist. To him, Christianity, the religion of the Word made flesh, is the most materialistic of all religions. We could say that eucharist is the most materialistic action of the church; it is concerned with matter and society; of sharing of matter and of changing and liberating the society. . . .

Fraternal communion is the basis of breaking the bread. Jesus recognises his disciples as his friends and brothers. Paul says that in Christ there is no distinction of free and slave and pleads that each one must treat the other as a "dear brother" (also dear sister) as in Philemon. Jesus has brought out clearly in the Sermon on the Mount of the relationship between worship and human brother/sisterhood (Mt 5:23–24). He maintains that to be a cause of fracture of brotherhood/sisterhood disqualifies one from worship. The persons condemned in the Corinthian passage are those who have failed to recognise (not the bread as the body of Christ, but) fellow Christians as the Lord's body. He challenges that all Christians must be united in fraternity before they dare approach the sacrament. In several orders for the eucharist there is the element of exchange of peace greetings which is the symbol of our acceptance of each other as our brothers and sisters. . . .

Fr. Antonyraj says, "We were slaves in Hinduism. We came to Christianity in search of equality, liberty and brotherhood. Not only do you fail to give us freedom, but you force us into the same slavery again. Your denial of human dignity and justice is slavery and a social death for us. We thought that through faith in the sacrament of Christ, we will be able to overcome our social death and be resurrected to new life of freedom, but out hopes are betrayed."[17]

The 2019 Building Bridges Seminar also commends the close reading of Elisabeth Schüssler Fiorenza, *In Memory of Her: A Feminist Theological Reconstruction of Christian Origins* (New York: Crossroad Publishing Company, 1987), particularly pages 346 and 349.

Notes

1. Charles Wesley penned a vast number of hymns. This one dates from 1738.

2. From Dietrich Bonhoeffer, *Prisoner for God: Letters and Papers from Prison*, ed. Eberhard Bethge, trans. Reginald H. Fuller (New York: The Macmillan Company, 1953), 170.

Published in Germany as *Widerstand und Ergebung—Briefe und Aufzeichnungen aus der Haft* (Munich: Chr. Kaiser Verlag, 1951). Please be aware that, in his essay for the present volume, Peniel Rajkumar is working with a different translation of Bonhoeffer's poem.

3. Karl Barth, "The Humanity of God," in *The Humanity of God*, trans. John Newton Thomas (Louisville, KY: Westminster John Knox, 1996), 48–49.

4. See John XXIII, Encyclical *Pacem In Terris*, April 11, 1963: *Acta Apostolicae Sedis* 55 (1963), 279; see also, 265. Also, Pius XII, Radio Message, December 24, 1944: *Acta Apostolicae Sedis* 37 (1945), 14.

5. See John 13:13.

6. See Matthew 11:29.

7. See Matthew 11:28–30; John 6:67–68.

8. See Matthew 9:28–29; Mark 9:23–24; 6:5–6; Paul V, Encyclical *Ecclesiam Suam*, August 6, 1964: *Acta Apostolicae Sedis* 56 (1964), 642–43.

9. See Matthew 11:20–24; Romans 12:19–20; 2 Thessalonians 1:8.

10. See Matthew 13:30, 40–42.

11. See Matthew 4:8–10; John 6:15.

12. See John 18:37.

13. See Matthew 26 51–53; John 18:36.

14. See John 12:32. Source: Austin Flannery OP, general editor, Laurence Ryan, trans. *Dignitatis humanae (Declaration on Religious Liberty): A Completely Revised Translation in Inclusive Language* (Collegeville, MN: Liturgical Press, 2014), 551–53, 555–56, 558, 559–61. Originally published by Dominican Publications, Dublin, Ireland, 1996. Reprinted with the kind permission of Liturgical Press.

15. Gustavo Gutiérrrez, *A Theology of Liberation: History, Politics and Salvation*, trans. Caridad Inda and John Eagleson, rev. ed., (Maryknoll, NY: Orbis, 1988), 103–4. Reprinted with the kind permission of Orbis Books.

16. From Stanley Hauerwas, "Freedom as the Presence of the Other," part 3, chap. 3, in *The Peaceable Kingdom: A Primer in Christian Ethics* (Notre Dame, IN: University of Notre Dame Press, 1983), 445–46. Reprinted with the kind permission of University of Notre Dame Press.

17. V. Devasahayam, *Dalits and Women: Quest for Humanity* (Madras, India: Gurukul Summer Institute, 1992), 260, 261, 263. Our excerpt comes from the last of ten Bible studies written by V. Devasahayam that compose *Dalits and Women: Quest for Humanity*—a volume that emerged out of the Gurukul Summer Institute, 1992. At the time, Devasahayam was associate professor of theology, Gurukul Lutheran Theological College, Madras (Chennai).

Part Four

Reflections

Conversations on the Theme of Freedom

Reflections on the Building Bridges Seminar at le Château de Bossey

Lucinda Mosher

"Freedom has, and must have, a shape," remarked a longtime participant as the 2019 Building Bridges Seminar got under way; "its content cannot be formless; nor can it be entirely a matter of subjective hermeneutics of the individual believer (or individual faith community). If the tendency of Islam is toward over-specifying that shape and thus reducing the scope of genuine freedom, the tendency of Christianity is to under-specify it, thus leaving the tradition vulnerable to incoherent diversity, flux and indeterminacy."

Indeed, a comparative theological exploration of freedom is a complex undertaking. "All of us come to the convening with our competencies in our own traditions," one Christian explained. "If, during this week, we find new ways to link our new conception of freedom to our texts and institutions, then it is time well spent." This chapter offers a glimpse inside that process of discovery. Drawing on notes taken during small-group study sessions, reports given during daily wrap-up discussions, and memos to the rapporteur after adjournment, it endeavors to convey the tone and content of the Seminar's exploration of the theme of freedom while in residence at le Château de Bossey, a conference center near Geneva, Switzerland. Continuing a custom maintained by the Seminar since its founding in 2002—embrace of the Chatham House Rule—participants are quoted or paraphrased without attribution.

The Choice of Texts

The Seminar has always given pride of place to the dialogical study of scripture; but other sorts of texts may also be on the agenda—and, indeed, that was the case in 2019. The texts selected for study by the 2019 seminar covered a huge time span. "Although working with non-scriptural material heightens the complexities of our deliberations," said one Christian, "I appreciate the opportunity for dialogical study of theological contributions from a wide variety of periods and contexts, especially when we take note of power dynamics present when each was written."

As small-group work got under way, it quickly became obvious that, in the texts chosen for study during this convening, *freedom* does not resonate with Enlightenment notions of autonomy. As one Muslim put it, "our starting point for each session was in an indelibly modern and Euro-American conception of freedom. The friction that arose in response to our textual encounters with different premodern conceptions, both Christian and Islamic, while arresting at times, proved productive, if not generative, in the end."

For the first three days, the seminar studied scripture in small snippets. On Friday, however, the agenda called for engagement of long passages of modern literature. One participant likened it to "throwing a mental switch." Whereas everyone arrives at the seminar committed to their respective scriptural texts, he explained, these secondary texts are different. "They need not have authority." Some might be tempted to dismiss some of them out of hand.

Included among the secondary texts on the 2019 agenda were the Cairo Declaration on Human Rights in Islam and the Marrakesh Declaration. One group expressed skepticism about the worth of such documents, noting how difficult it is to disentangle whatever enduringly valid insights they may contain from the particular framings and emphases arising from the controversial political contexts in which they were penned. In response, one participant affirmed that it had been time well spent: "Although dialogical studying of modern texts heightens the complexities of our deliberations, those texts offer us a mirror for greater reflexivity and a window into the interpretive process of others; and through both the mirror and the window, we then can draw insights in our own quest for what freedom might mean for us today."

Indeed, as can be seen by leafing through the "texts for dialogue" chapters of this volume, the collection of texts chosen to facilitate our study of freedom during our time at le Château de Bossey was interestingly diverse. The collection, for example, included poetry—for which several participants expressed particular gratitude. It may, however, have been overly ambitious. "We had too many texts to consider," was a common sentiment during the closing plenary. Even still, participants welcomed the invitation to point out what was missing—and having such a discussion is very much a part of the Building Bridges Seminar's method. Muslims offered some suggestions, but most of the recommendations came from Christians. "No collection of texts for the seminar will ever seem complete," one noted. "However, in our collection of texts on *freedom*, Black voices were conspicuously absent." The selection of Christian texts did include a Dalit perspective, but one does wonder in what directions the conversation might have gone had the Seminar studied (for example) the section "Christ, Black Power, and Freedom" from James Cone's *Black Theology and Black Power*. More from the Eastern Christian tradition would have been helpful, someone else noted, particularly from the writings of Gregory of Nyssa and Maximus the Confessor. Finally, the collection of selections from the New Testament could have included key passages teaching that, in Christ, the relationship between humans and God is *not* one of servitude.

Freedom's Subtopics

Texts assembled for study had been chosen with an eye toward stimulating discussion of topics such as God's freedom, human freedom to obey God, autonomy versus self-governance in accordance with God's revealed and rational law, freedom from incapacitating addiction and desire, hermeneutic or discursive freedom vis-à-vis scripture and tradition, freedom to differ on religions and polities, and the relationship between personal conviction and public order. While in their parallel conversations all four groups explored most of these topics (among others), certain themes commanded everyone's attention—notably, freedom as service to God, divine freedom and human agency, freedom and law, and freedom of religion.

Freedom as Service to God

Given that the theme of the 2019 convening was freedom, one participant thought it significant that, quite often, conversations converged around themes of service, submission, and authority. Both Christianity and Islam support the notion that faith in and service to the Creator have the potential to liberate human beings from the oppression of superstition, personal whims, and servitude to other creatures.

Yet another participant reported that, "in fact, as a Muslim, I have a certain uneasiness with the notion that *freedom* is a critical concept in Islamic thought." But, he continued, "the notion of 'slave' or 'servant' does come up a lot in the Islamic tradition." That said, Muslims speak of *ibada* (worship) and "the worshiper" more than "servant/slave." In Arabic, the same trilateral root gives us both *worship* and *servant*. Regarding the assertion that to be a servant of God is to be free, one Muslim called it "a transgressive idea!" As another put it, the repeated sense of "slavery to God" is a strong theme in the texts the Seminar had selected for study, and that goes against the Enlightenment sense of autonomy. One Muslim clarified: the Kantian notion that "I give up freely my freedom" could be a definition of Islam—which provides for self-rule and self-government but no choice regarding who created us.[1]

Discussions of freedom as service to God frequently bent in the direction of freedom found or expressed in serving the poor. In *Epistle on Sufism*—a handbook dating from 1045, the author, al-Qushayrī, declares, "Know that the greatest kind of freedom lies in serving the poor." One Muslim highlighted that passage, suggesting to her group that serving the poor is actually more difficult than serving God. One group explored at length the certainty that freedom is both bondage to God (which is a matter of the heart, thus nebulous) *and* service to the needy (which is concrete). As one noted, al-Qushayrī seems to be saying, "If you aspire to freedom, serve God; if you aspire to serve God, serve the poor and the needy."

A second group found that, in the texts under study, the link between bondage and freedom appeared to be quite strong—and this, in turn, seemed rather countercultural. It also raised the question of whether "being needed" is an attribute of God—which, in turn, provoked complex questions regarding agency and sovereignty. In a third group, someone stressed that human freedom and divine freedom are not in competition. A fourth discussion group concurred, with one member noting that "human agency does not impugn the omnipotence of God." Indeed, reported one Christian, "I was struck by the fact that our study materials included little in the way of biblical passages in which the problem of reconciling divine and human freedom were central." By contrast, the selected Islamic texts gave extended attention to this and were much more concerned with safeguarding the utter transcendent sovereignty of God than were the biblical passages.

Divine Freedom and Human Agency

In their efforts to discern what premodern Muslim texts had to say about freedom, each group inevitably came up against *kasb* (the theory of acquisition) and, thus, the need to deal with the question of how Muslim theologians struggled to understand human freedom in the context of God's overwhelming knowledge and power. *Kasb* figures in the excerpt from Al-Ghazālī's "The Principles of the Creed" (*Kitāb Qawāʿid al-ʿAqāʾid*) that was included in the Seminar materials. *Kasb* "is a difficult and elusive concept," declared one of the Christians.

> I came to see it roughly thus: ultimately, God sovereignly creates all human powers, and ordains/determines all human deeds, choices and what

> is chosen. Yet God has given to humans genuine powers of free agency—a power becomes a "quality" of the human servant, even though humans do not "acquire" their powers. But the deed is indeed "acquired" by the human by being the object of a power. Thus, "deeds are the object of God's power as creation, and the object of a person's power in another kind of relationship which is called acquisition."[2]

Some of the Muslims admitted that *kasb* was just as complex and mysterious a notion for them as it was for their Christian discussion partners. One stressed that, during our time together at Bossey, he was far more interested in interrogating the hermeneutical process by which we question scriptures and impose our own agenda on them. In other words, he said, "when we read and try to understand our scriptures, what are the limits of our freedom? How do we avoid doing violence to the text? I suspect that this fascinating question will be with me for a long time to come."

Upon reflection, one Muslim scholar observed that taking sufficient time to clarify *kasb* had been worthwhile. Yet, he clarified, "We had to emphasize to our Christian colleagues that, while the theory may have been of particular significance and interest for certain scholastics in certain eras, its bearing on the everyday religious lives of Muslims has been marginal to nonexistent, both historically and at present."[3]

The 2019 set of study texts included a dozen excerpts from the *Munājāt* (secret supplications; intimate conversations) of the Persian mystic Khwāja ʿAbdallāh al-Anṣārī (1006–1089). An extended dialogue with God rendered in rhyming prose, this work caught the imagination of several of the Christians and sparked lively discussion of freedom and human agency.[4] Among the questions provoked by the *Munājāt* where these: Where is the place of freedom in human existence? How are human beings to connect to other aspects of creation?

Questions about the connection between freedom and human agency related directly, as one group saw it, to questions of evil. In response to a Christian's question, one Muslim outlined three classical Muslim positions on this matter. According to the Ashʿarī school, both good and evil come from God. God creates the action and allows the individual to do evil but does not approve of it. Thus, God gives the individual freedom to do evil but does not gain pleasure from the individual's evil acts. That God foreknows the individual's action in pre-eternity does not mean God is forcing the individual to do something evil. According to the Muʿtazili school, God creates only goodness; evil comes from the individual. The emphasis of this rationalist school of thought is on human agency and divine justice. The Maturidi school takes a middle position, according to which both good and evil come from God, the creator of all things. However, God creates in accordance with rationally discernable principles. Humans have the capacity to discern on their own that some actions are evil; but revelation is the primary source of knowledge about it. Furthermore, another Muslim pointed out, there is an important notion common to the Christian tradition and the Islamic tradition alike: proper freedom is the freedom to choose good.

Freedom and Law

Discussion of freedom and law was animated by interrogation of the very notion of law: What *is* it? What is freedom from it? During a plenary session, one scholar put the matter quite bluntly, asserting, "I am not the only Muslim who has a difficult time conceiving what prompts the Christian toward acts of sacrifice without a legal tradition to motivate those acts. How do Christians go about living their daily lives without the law? Without law, how do you Christians know what to do?" One of the Christians responded to this gentle yet pointed challenge: "Human beings are not confronted with norms in the abstract. They are to be formed, instructed, molded. We know what to do because we have lived in a community that has striven toward full living of Christian life." Later, he reflected further on that exchange:

> We Christians proclaim "freedom in Christ," insisting that the core norm is "love your neighbor" rather than specific rule-following in the mode of Sharia. But in our small-group conversation about this, we struggled to specify any enduring practices that are required by our faith to live that out—in contrast to the small number of quite specific universal expectations imposed in Islam. Why were we inarticulate on that? Do we know more than we are prepared to say? If so, why the hesitancy? If we know less than we say, is that not a problem? Not everything is compatible with "love your neighbor"!

Another Muslim admitted candidly that he, too, had been plagued for some time by the question of how Christians go about living their daily lives without the law. Hence, he was glad it had received substantial attention, noting that "during our small-group sessions, I heard several times that it is the 'spirit' of the law that matters more than its 'letter' for Christians. Yet this argument never added up for me." So, he explained, when one of the Christian scholars suggested (both in small group and in plenary) that it might be helpful for Muslims to approach this question in the light of *adab* (custom) in the Islamic tradition, which is guided more by the personal example of Prophet Muhammad than by Islamic legal categories, "his comment was nothing short of an illumination! It provided an opening that enabled me to appreciate everyday Christian life much more earnestly."

Freedom of Religion

"'If God had so willed, He would have made you one community' (Q 5:48) raises the issue of diversity," noted one of the Muslim women. "It's always a good interfaith conversation-starter." True enough; but during a seminar on freedom, Q 2:256 ("Let there be no compulsion in religion") served that purpose even better. Several Muslims explained that the meaning of *din*, a key word in that verse, is complex. It can mean either "religion" or "way". In the earlier sense of religion as a virtue, one pointed out, *din* can mean the appropriate attitude one should have toward God. "This cannot be compelled," he stressed; "only externals can be compelled." Indeed, apostasy had been a hot topic of discussion in at least two of the seminar's four small groups. If there be no compulsion, then how much "freedom" of religion does a person have?

Complicating the conversation was the fact that, in the seminar's collection of texts, Q 2:256 was juxtaposed uncomfortably with Hadith Bukhari 6922, which says, "Whosoever changes religion, kill him!" What sense is to be made of that? One group immediately moved to the point that religion is not just a private matter. When conversion puts public order at risk, steps should be (and have been) taken, asserted one member. There is tension between public order and freedom. The Qur᾽an is informing, not forbidding. It was an interesting point, to which someone countered: but what about apostasy that does not disturb the public order? Regarding public order, someone else wondered whether "religious freedom" is a thick or thin concept. What is our definition of public order? What are the minimum conditions for "public order"?

One of the Muslims stressed that "a hadith about killing an apostate should not carry the same weight as what the Qur᾽an says"; nor should hadiths be applied to the modern period, he said. They emerged in particular political and social contexts—in this case, a context in which "changing one's religion" meant leaving a community. The "no compulsion" imperative was a central principle of the early Caliphate, another Muslim noted. Continuing the effort to contextualize, yet another scholar noted what historical observations reveal: that actual punishment for apostasy was extremely rare. When Islam's cultural power was strong, apostasy was of little concern. When in a time of insecurity (during the era of the Crusades, for example), then concern about apostasy was considerable.

One scholar suggested that Hadith Bukhari 6922 might originally have addressed a context not unlike that produced by the religious wars of sixteenth- and seventeenth-century Europe. In a context characterized by the belief that the presence of religious dissention in a community could cause everything else to unravel, the sense prevailed that if shared doctrine evaporates, everything else falls apart. In any case, insisted a fourth scholar, the notion that it is appropriate to kill people for having changed their religion is "a position antithetical to all forms of freedom. This impedes the flourishing of the self." In short, among Muslim participants there was a general tendency to give hermeneutical priority to Q 2:256 here. Finally, to complexify the matter in another way, a member of the seminar cautioned that one may hear it said that Q 2:256 has been abrogated by other Qur'an verses. It is a notion he personally rejects, he stressed.

Freedom to Pursue Tangents

Every convening of the Building Bridges Seminar is driven by a rigorous agenda; yet, always, there is opportunity for tangents and surprises. During the 2019 seminar, one such moment occurred in the conference center library. In an effort to make sense of the various New Testament passages assigned for study by Building Bridges 2019, one of the Muslims checked out a commentary, settled himself at a table, and set to work. When he opened the book he had selected, his eye landed on a quotation of Matthew 28:19–20, in which the risen Jesus directs his followers: "Go therefore and make disciples of all nations, baptizing them in the name of the Father and of the Son and of the Holy Spirit, teaching them to obey everything that I have commanded you." In that moment, he says, his perception changed diametrically: "I had always thought (and I believe most Muslims still do) that Christ had come to the lost sheep of Israel only; that preaching to the gentiles was an exclusively Pauline act and had nothing to do with Christ or his immediate disciples. Reading these few verses from Matthew put Christianity in quite a new perspective for me; one that has allowed me to accord St. Paul a lot more respect."

What this moment illustrates is that, especially during interreligious dialogical study of scripture, an effort to understand a passage and its relevance to the main theme may cause the conversation partners to digress at length. We saw this earlier in the seminar's Christians for an explanation of the Islamic notion of *kasb* (acquisition). In another instance, discussion of a passage from *A Theology of Liberation* led one of the Christians to note that its author, Gustavo Gutiérrez, raises constructive eschatological questions about the Kingdom of God.[5] Yet another case of such fruitful meandering was prompted by Muslim questions about Christian demonology.

Among the Bible passages for consideration by the 2019 seminar were stories of Jesus healing a disabled woman (Luke 13:10–17) and casting out demons (Mark 5:1–20). "When my small group looked at the texts from Luke 13 and Mark 5," a Christian explained, "we discussed how the narratives of Jesus healing and casting out demons functioned in the Gospels as demonstrations of his divinity." However, he wanted to make clear that this was not their only function. "When then narratives are read in their sociopolitical contexts" he explained, "it becomes clear that, when they were written, a major implication of each story would have been that the people Jesus healed/exorcized were marginalized and excluded. Jesus was giving them freedom not only from illness/demon possession but from social/political oppression or marginalization."

Among the Christians in this small group, there was strong disagreement about whether the miraculous proof of Jesus's identity was the more clearly primary function of these narratives. By contrast, in response to Muslim queries about whether Christians currently believe in demon possession, their agreement was considerable: among today's Christians worldwide, the range of views is very broad!

Freedom to Be Heard

A Building Bridges Seminar newcomer reported surprise at the degree of meaningful exchange between participants—of concrete evidence of kinship—despite epistemological differences. Throughout the week, the conversational tone was professional, yet it was also friendly and warm. This is what veterans of the project have come to expect. At its core, the purpose of the Seminar is to improve the quality of our disagreements. Reliance on preassigned, well-moderated study and discussion groups all but ensures each participant the freedom to be heard. Muslims and Christians work together with mutual inquisitiveness and respect, deconstructing mutual prejudices while exploring similarities and differences between the two traditions. The Seminar seeks to be a model of best practices in the respectful exchange of ideas and concepts between Muslims and Christians—even about topics on which they will never see eye to eye.

Freedom to Explore

While no one would contest the notion that the heart of the Seminar's methodology is its commitment to small-group sessions devoted to close reading and discussion of texts, most attendees are also quick to affirm the importance of what happens in what one repeat attendee calls "the times and spaces outside the agenda." Without doubt, environment plays an important role. At le Château de Bossey, "the serenity of our surroundings proved a productive element in our conversations," says a frequent Muslim attendee:

> The freedom to retreat—to reground ourselves in those environ—proved restorative for the theological wrestling that we all undertook throughout that week. Unquestionably, the most memorable moments of our seminar involved our spontaneous ventures down through the fields, trails, and nearby town in our attempt to wend our way down to Lake Geneva. Having taken full advantage of our freedom to explore, the fellowship and companionship we shared in our sometimes harrowing, always rewarding excursions was just as important to our theological exchange as our time poring over the texts.

Concurring, one of the Christians says, "My sense is that the careful planning of what happens on the agenda creates the possibility for truly important moments to occur off the agenda." There is need to rest and recharge, but generous blocks of free time serve a further purpose, he explains. "The great value of extended time for open-ended exchange in a congenial setting is this: you get to know people's real concerns, with people able to be frank about the vulnerabilities as well as the strengths of their own traditions."

The week had begun with a declaration, by one of the Christians, that "freedom has, and must have, a shape." In closing, one of the Muslims called the Building Bridges Seminar "a unique learning experience that is made possible by an unusual format and able leadership." What, in a week of close reading and frank conversation, had that unique learning experience conveyed about Christian and Muslim perspectives on freedom's shape? Quite a lot, no doubt.

Notes

1. For deeper understanding, see Henry E. Allison, *Kant's Conception of Freedom: A Developmental and Critical Analysis* (Cambridge: Cambridge University Press, 2020). see also Ian Almond, *History of Islam in German Thought: From Liebnitz to Nietzsche* (New York: Routledge, 2010).

2. See al-Ghazālī's "The Third Pillar of Faith: Knowledge of the Acts of God," in this volume (in "Premodern Islamic Writings on Freedom: Selections for Dialogue").

3. For another Building Bridges Seminar consideration of *kasb*, see Martin Nguyen, "The Contours of God's Power: An Introduction to Passages from the Qur'an and Hadith,"

in *Power—Divine and Human: Christian and Muslim Perspectives*, ed. Lucinda Mosher and David Marshall, 31–41 (Washington, DC: Georgetown University Press, 2019), 38.

4. Ansari's *Munājāt* can be found in this volume in "Premodern Islamic Writings on Freedom: Selections for Dialogue."

5. Here we are referring to the passage from Gustavo Gutiérrez included among the seminar's study. See "Christian Writings from the Modern Period" in this volume.

Subject Index

Note: A separate index follows for Scriptural Citations.

Scriptural Citation Index

Qurʾan

About the Editor

Dr. Lucinda Allen Mosher, rapporteur of the Building Bridges Seminar, is faculty associate in chaplaincy and interreligious studies at Hartford Seminary, where she is codirector of the Master of Arts in Chaplaincy program, senior scholar for Executive and Professional Education, and an affiliate of the Macdonald Center for the Study of Islam and Christian–Muslim Relations. Concurrently, she is senior editor of the *Journal of Interreligious Studies*, president of NeighborFaith Consultancy LLC, and fellow emerita of the Center for Anglican Communion Studies at Virginia Theological Seminary. She is the author or editor of eighteen books, including eight previous volumes of the Building Bridges Seminar series and *The Georgetown Companion to Interreligious Studies* (forthcoming). She has also contributed numerous essays on multifaith matters to academic journals and edited volumes. She received her doctorate in theology from the General Theological Seminary (New York City).

CPSIA information can be obtained
at www.ICGtesting.com
Printed in the USA
BVHW030811030422
632260BV00031B/39